CULTIVATING MINDS

A LOGO CASEBOOK

Sylvia Weir
The Massachusetts Institute of Technology

1817

HARPER & ROW, PUBLISHERS, New York
Cambridge, Philadelphia, San Francisco, Washington,
London, Mexico City, São Paulo, Singapore, Sydney

A Note to the Reader

Out of consideration for the many students
who have worked with me, I have altered
their names and the names of their schools.

Sylvia Weir

To Michael, David, Philip, and Jane

Sponsoring Editor: Peter Richardson
Project Editor: David Nickol
Cover Design: John Hite
Text Art: Fineline Illustrations, Inc.
Production: Willie Lane
Printer and Binder: The Maple-Vail Book Manufacturing Group

Cultivating Minds: A LOGO Casebook

Library of Congress Cataloging-in-Publication Data

Weir, Sylvia.
　Cultivating minds.

　1. Computer-assisted instruction. 2. Handicapped
children—Education—Data processing. 3. Logo
(Computer program language) I. Title.
LB1028.5.W393 1987　　　371.3′9445　　　85-27229
ISBN 0-06-046991-9

86 87 88 89 9 8 7 6 5 4 3 2 1

Contents

Contents

Foreword

Yesterday Michael Murphy drove his wheel chair into the MIT Media Technology Laboratory. Michael's first appearance in Sylvia Weir's book describes his medical condition -- quadraplegic cerebral palsy -- and the frustrated helplessness expressed by the director of the school for the handicapped where he encountered Logo (back in the days before microcomputers had made Logo commonplace). The staff of the school believed that Michael's intelligence was much higher than average. But this intelligence was trapped in a body that could not manipulate objects and could talk only with the greatest difficulty. The school had not been able to liberate it. Michael Murphy was seen as one of their toughest cases. "If you can do something with him," the director said, "then I'll take you seriously."

Weir movingly describes how Logo became the catalyst in a process that "untrapped" Michael Murphy's intelligence. He is now a successful university student, and his visit to MIT yesterday was on business as a member of a committee concerned with providing access to computers for handicapped people. We are not dealing here with abstract debates about the significance of a change in test scores. This is for real.

But what can one anecdotal case study -- or even a hundred -- prove? Certainly not that Logo has a magical power to educate the handicapped or anyone else. Quite the contrary. The story of Michael Murphy is presented more in the spirit of showing how hard and complex a task it is to create effective learning environments than as a promise of an easy panacea. Ten hours a week working at the computer over a period of years went into producing the turn around in Michael Murphy's academic situation. No quick cure! Moreover, his development was special in many ways. It was shaped by personal relationships with MIT researchers -- with whom he spent as much time as he did with computers -- and by the school's social setting -- which allowed him to become a teacher of his fellow students. These circumstances played a role that cannot be measured in the development of his sense of himself and in the liberation of his trapped intelligence.

ix

No, the story of Michael Murphy does not support any claim that computers or Logo will in themselves change how anyone learns. But such technocentric claims are not serious and have nothing to do with what I, or Sylvia Weir, see as the educational role of Logo. The most serious claims about Logo have to do with how it becomes a thread in the weave of an individual's life. To understand deeply what happened to Michael Murphy, we need to think sensitively about his inner life, to look at his personal relationships, and to take account of his social context. We also need to ask ourselves some hard theoretical questions about the nature of learning.

There is no doubt that a Logo experience can touch the psychic lives of many children who, for one reason or another, have not known the feeling of success in school. There is also no doubt that many factors contribute to this process, and that we are only just beginning to understand a few of them. Cases like Michael Murphy exhibit one of these factors in a very pure and powerful form: empowerment of the most elemental kind. Put yourself, if you can, in the place of someone who has never made any physical thing, someone who has never made a mud pie or a drawing or an arrangement of flowers. Suppose also that your ability to speak is so restricted by severe dysarthria that you have never made a speech or even told a story. Then imagine what this machine can mean to you. You can draw on its screen. You can make texts out of words and keep them in your private space, no longer subjected to the favors and the scrutiny of a scribe. I don't think you can imagine these things. But you can grasp enough to know that an encounter with this machine could be the beginnings of profound change in your sense of who you are and of how you might shape your life.

A severely physically handicapped child shows us the extreme of a phenomenon that can take on more subtle but nevertheless deadly forms. Many children whose fingers have the dexterity to wield a pencil still do not learn to use it to write, to calculate, or to draw in more than the most rudimentary fashion. Why? And how could a computer help?

An important theme of Logo research is the idea that individuals can -- and in some cases must -- follow very different learning paths. I like the analogy with left-handedness. Forcing children to conform did serious damage until educators came to understand that poetry written with the left hand is just as good. I think that forcing intellectual style is possibly much more damaging than forcing handedness, and that many children are crippled by mismatch with the intellectual style of the curriculum. The metaphor of "trapped intelligence" applies here in full force.

Liberation of left-handed learners only needed recognition by teachers. Much of Sylvia Weir's book is a plea for recognition of the wider problem. Her prime example of mismatched learners is the category of spatial thinkers -- children who can achieve a high quality of intellectual work when they are allowed to use more spatial ways of thinking than are permitted either by the curriculum or by the classroom methods of contemporary schools.   Her case studies show Logo as a flexible instrument that can be picked up differently by different people.   They provide persuasive evidence that there is a problem and that we have the elements of a solution.

But in this case, recognition is not enough. Left-handed children come provided with a working hand ready to acquire competence. While children with different intellects also come with brains ready to work in their own way, our culture does not necessarily have the intellectual frames for them to use. This book describes what can happen when Logo is used as a supple medium that can nourish more styles than is possible with pencil and paper. It draws attention to a massive need to reinvent new curricula, new methodologies of teaching, and new kinds of tests so we can support these many and varied intellectual styles.

Seymour Papert

The Media Laboratory,
Massachusetts Institute of Technology

Acknowledgments

Several people read and commented on the manuscript of this book in its earlier stages and I am grateful to all of them for the care they have taken in doing so and for their thoughtful comments. William Higginson and Richard Noss were particularly helpful. I want to express my thanks also to the people and the agencies who have supported the work on which this book is based. Dr. J. Howe provided support in the seventies during my stay in the Artificial Intelligence Department at Edinburgh University. Seymour Papert and the members of the MIT Logo group have provided an excellent research environment, and my debt to them is obvious. Grants have come from the Social Science Research Council (Britain), the Office of Special Education in the Federal Department of Education, from the National Science Foundation, and from several private sources: the Mattel, the Hyams, the Grass, and the Mudge Foundations. My particular thanks go to the many children and their teachers with whom I have interacted over the years, and who have allowed me to observe and record their work with Logo. I would like to think that these pioneering efforts will enhance the quality of life for future generations of schoolchildren.

Sylvia Weir

Introduction

The growing use of computers in the classroom has been compared to the introduction of the printing press 500 years ago, or even to the spread of reading and writing 5000 years ago. A major impact is inevitable. Whether that impact is desirable or not will depend on how we handle the introduction of this new technology into our schools. Many are critical of what they see as the latest technological fix whose main effect is to divert scarce resources (Weizenbaum, 1984). Is the attraction of computer-based activity merely the appeal of the exotic, the new, the prestigious, or is it based on genuine advantages that will outlast the novelty? Can computers be assimilated into educational practice that enhances children's learning? More ambitiously, can computers invite and create such good practice? Will they change what occurs in the classroom of the future? Will they help the slow learner, the child with problems? In this book I suggest some answers to these questions, based on my observations of the computer work of children in regular and in special needs classrooms.

Microcomputers have a way of making public the mental workings of their users. When I watch a child work on a computer, it helps me see the steps in her thinking more clearly than I would otherwise. This potential to act as a *window into the mind of the learner* could turn out to be the most valuable contribution of the computer. Teachers have little time to think about the connection between understanding children's thinking and what goes on in the classroom. Ever since the beginning of the school enterprise, they have been faced with an almost impossible task: how to teach a group of growing minds, whose interests, styles of learning, and levels of knowledge are different, sometimes widely different, yet whose

1

needs must be addressed simultaneously. The brightest students get bored; any classroom geared to the average cannot challenge and excite them. Others get lost, repeatedly experiencing "I don't understand" until they begin to conclude "I can't do this, I'm dumb" and so give up.

My aim is to provide educators with a *framework for thinking about their students' thinking*; to give teachers a feeling for the art of fruitful observation, of taking pieces of behavior and drawing inferences in two directions: what does this tell us about educational practice or theory and what does this tell us about basic cognitive theory? I envisage a future in which the issues discussed in this book will become part of the routine training of student teachers. This is not the case at present. I am told that teachers are not interested in theory, that they want to know only what to do in their classrooms now. I believe this is because the theory they are given during their training at present is too far removed from their needs, too unrelated to their classroom concerns.

With this in mind, I have *interwoven case descriptions with theoretical analysis*. Descriptions of the work of average and above average students mingle with accounts of the computer work of children with problems, to provide a set of models to be used in teacher training colleges, as well as by teachers and administrators in the field. I explore ways of using computers to build computational environments that match individual needs and learning styles, both to carry out old activities more easily and to engage in new ones not possible prior to the arrival of the computer.

Used in appropriate ways, the computer can give the student an unprecedented degree of control over her learning. When she is allowed to take the initiative, to set her own goals, she is likely to reveal her own preferred ways of working, to "do it her way." Some of the more interesting observations we have made over the past several years concern the *wide range of styles of working shown by students in a computer setting* (Papert, 1980; Papert et al., 1979; Turkle, 1984; Weir, 1981a). These individual differences in problem-solving style are not well catered to in the average school, and I will show how different needs can be accommodated more easily using the computer than using regular classroom tools.

For example, the computer can support an exploratory, trying-things-out mode of working, which not only may correspond to an individual's natural style, but is often just what is required to solve a problem. In a similar vein, some people are very able in one modality and weak in another; some may be verbally inclined, while others are visualizers. The enormous emphasis on language skills in the traditional curriculum puts individuals with a preference for visualizing at a disadvantage. *A computer graphics screen can allow them to use their spatial skill to make academic progress.* For example, there is a growing appreciation that spatial reasoning is important in the understanding of mathematics (Bishop, 1980), but until now formal spatial reasoning has had little place in the classroom. How much of the curriculum could be introduced in spatial mode? It will be part of my story to show how academic failure may be induced more by inappropriate arrangements for learning in schools than by lack of ability of the students.

These are some consequences of empowering the student. What about the teacher? The computer will serve education well only to the extent that the *teacher gains control over this powerful tool.* It is often the case that teachers are faced with a curriculum whose content has been decided by others: by school committees or by publishers of school texts, who have come to have an enormous say over what is taught in schools, a role they are reluctant to relinquish as they move into the educational software business. Teachers need to be equipped with models of the radical way in which the computer can generate change within their classrooms. They need appropriate training and long-term support to play their role in making decisions about the use of computers in education, so that the development of computational environments can become a joint activity between educators and computer experts.

In the initial stages of studying the classroom use of the computer, I take an *individual case study* approach to explore the flavor of what is possible, following the well-established clinical interview method (Meehl, 1954) for both research and diagnosis in children's thinking (Ginsburg, 1981). Case descriptions are interesting as texts behind which to probe for the "why" and "how" of phenomena and are a prerequisite for carefully controlled large group studies. In particular, they help to decide what the appropriate controls might be. However, it is fallacious to assume that students' free activity alone can tell us why particular behaviors do or do not occur. Direct interventionist steps, for example, setting particular tasks designed to probe particular possibilities, are crucial. In due course, these probes become incorporated into the learning situation itself, so that the boundary between research and teaching becomes blurred.

Just as we can use the computer to match the preferences of the visualizer and so provide a route into academic progress by revealing hidden strengths, so can it be used to liberate the intellect of individuals with severe physical handicap. There are many ways of using electronic devices with physically disabled students. Most approaches are limited to providing electronic communicators to be used with traditional curricular materials. Instead, we (Papert and Weir, 1978) have exploited the potential of the electronic system itself for creating exciting intellectual activities, for giving persons with severely restricted motor ability something exciting to communicate about. This use of the computer as an *information prosthesis* aids the handicapped person by bringing such a person into an information society.[1] As the computer expands a disabled person's range of activities, it opens up possibilities for personal development hitherto not available.

Extending computer opportunities to the physically handicapped is part of the wider aim of achieving universal computer competence, now considered to be a national priority. There are many ways to be educationally handicapped: physically, economically, and culturally. Will computers be universally available, or will the haves get more, both by acquiring home computers and by ensuring that their relatively affluent schools acquire them in large numbers, thus increasing the existing inequities in access to educational resources. The extent to which minorities have been denied rights and opportunities is compounded in the case of technology by the existence of *internalized* restrictions. Why is it that job searches for computer teachers fail to attract minority candidates? Where will the role models come from to break the cycle of neglect? There is a similar imbalance between the sexes. "Ninety-three percent of home (computer) users are male," states a report in *Science* (July, 1984).

Prior to coming into the computer field I was a practicing physician, and it has seemed natural to concern myself with children who have problems. At a personal level, I have found working with handicapped children extraordinarily moving and rewarding. It is a humbling experience to watch a child reaching forward from her wheelchair to carefully and deliberately poke at the keys of a computer keyboard with whatever implement her disability allows her to grasp, to see the straining for the simplest move and the single-minded purpose evident in every line of the body, to feel chagrin at one's own careless acceptance of "normal" movement.

The question arises: How relevant are descriptions of children with special needs to non-specialist teachers? How will an understanding of the processes that go wrong in these children interest workers who are not specialists in the field. *Looking at the work of children with special educational needs has helped me understand the thinking of children in general.* When I talk about Michael's trapped intelligence (Michael is a quadriplegic described in Chapter Seventeen), I have in mind the often hidden intelligence of the ordinary child, the vast amount of know-how often untapped during traditional classroom activity. An autistic child's difficulty in deciding what aspect of a complicated situation to attend to is the

---

1.   A prosthesis is an artificial device to replace a missing part of the body.

extreme form of the problem of relevance that arises in many learning situations. When a physically handicapped person, who suffers from a lack of the experience of doing things, develops a gross disturbance in procedural knowledge, this tells us something about the learning of ordinary children whose educational setting does not provide sufficient hands-on experience of the concepts they are supposed to be acquiring. When a handicapped person becomes adapted to total passivity, because of the perception of those around her that kindness amounts to doing things for her, we are witnessing an extreme form of learned helplessness: the cultivation of a self-image that says, "You have to do it for me; I am helpless without you."

My working hypothesis is that the same underlying mental mechanisms are at work in many special needs children as in so-called normal children. However, because special needs children often come at the extreme end of a spectrum of variation, their behavior can appear to be qualitatively different. They are more vulnerable to deficiencies in their learning environments. Observing such children perform on the computer can often provide a magnified, slowed-down view of familiar processes. The study of perceptual illusions is interesting largely because it sheds light on the processes of non-illusory perception (see, for example, Gregory, 1970). It was the experience of using a computer with an autistic boy in Edinburgh (see Chapter Six) that brought home to me the large perceptual element in learning, and this has become a theme around which I have structured my account of learning about thinking and thinking about learning. What it is that happens when we "see" something in the literal sense of the word has a great deal to do with what it is to "see" something in the sense of "understand" it. *Both are processes of recognition.* I choose a theoretical framework that allows me to talk about how both perception and learning are dependent on bringing a person's stored previous experience to bear on making sense of current experience.

When attempting to provide a framework for thinking about the mind, philosophers and psychologists suggest analogies and metaphors, casting around for something in their ordinary world with which to make the obscure processes of the mind familiar. Plato describes two sorts of "tablets" in the mind: soft ones that take impressions easily but lose them as rapidly and hard ones that are difficult to scratch but once imprinted are hard to erase. A perusal of the psychology of memory yields some rather homely metaphors.

Short-term memory is like a glowing ember which gradually extinguishes with time. Memory is like a patch of wet concrete, on which the pattern of a footprint can be made but there is a period of lability before the concrete has set, during which time the memory can be erased. Remembering has been likened to storing items in warehouses, bookshelves and filing cabinets; recall compared to searching through the items in such repositories; and forgetting to decay, misplacement, loss of a cloakroom ticket, or censorship of rude material. (Oatley, 1975)

Such simple arrangements of the ordinary furniture of our physical environment are not very enlightening when it comes to understanding the human mind; nor are analogies to telephone exchanges and the like. It is helpful to *use what we are learning about information processing on the computer as a metaphor for human information processing.* The idea is not to say that the brain *is* a computer, but that when thinking about the way the mind works, it helps to use some of the insights gained from running sophisticated computer programs, particularly when the behavior of such programs resembles the functioning of the human mind in interesting ways.[2]

For example, computer models can help understand *what the task is that the mind performs,* even when they do not tell us how the mind does it. With respect to the question of how past experience can influence how we see and learn new things, ideas about how knowledge is represented and manipulated in the computer can help us think about human mental representations and processes. I will use the term "schema" to refer to a network of information that represents stored past experience (concepts, rules, codes). During mental activity, these familiar schemas are activated and used by an individual to understand the new experience, to solve some new problem. Everyday experience provides ample evidence of the important role played by *emotional* factors in learning, and the schema theory of mental processing will need to take account of that. It will also need to handle the already mentioned individual differences in behavior. Clearly, there must be more to thinking than the mobilization of existing knowledge, otherwise there would be no progress. For learning to take place, the stored schemas that are activated must be changed and new ones added to accommodate the new experience. Making the appropriate arrangements for this to happen has been the task of all good educators.

But all these theoretical considerations have to be translated into practical classroom terms. Case studies and the theories of individual conceptual change they support are useful to the extent that they help clarify and predict what arrangements will serve the needs of practicing

---

2.   For a readable account of this issue, see Boden, 1977.

teachers. Experienced teachers may react in one of several ways to the arrival of the computer on the education scene. For some, a chance to get into computers becomes the long awaited opportunity: "I was on the verge of giving up! I was really burnt out. And then I became involved in this whole new fascinating world." For others, it feels like the beginning of the end, yet another demand made upon their already overburdened time and energy: "Do I have to get involved with that stuff?" There can be something really daunting for a professional with status in her field, an expert at her work, to have to face a new area of activity, especially one with such high density of formal, technical content. Much has been written about the problems of making a mid-career change. As one who made that change myself, I remember how tough it was, for instance, the struggle to get to the point where one could even ask the questions. Much of the conceptual structure that your informants assume you have is simply not available to you.

If too many of those in leading positions in education find the whole computer presence too burdensome and overwhelming for serious engagement, the effect could be unfortunate. The last thing the experts in the educational field should want is to leave decisions about this whole new area to non-educators. The risk is that we will continue to get the kind of computer aids to instruction that computer experts want to produce, that the computer industry finds most amenable for their purposes, rather than the materials educators want to have or would want to have if they shared with the computer scientist a vision of what could be invented.

The idea is to connect with what teachers already know, by providing a framework for sharing discovery, to encompass an entire community of users. The message to teachers is: Get into the act. Understand what is going on. Participate in using this new tool. Work in this computer-based learning environment, so that responsibility can remain in your hands. The combination of informed teacher and versatile technology is an opportunity to create entirely new experiences for future generations.

The Logo Turtle

In 1948, a British neurophysiologist, Grey Walter, developed an electromechanical device he called a "tortoise" that rolled around obstacles. The Logo turtle was developed in the late 1960s as a computer-controlled device that moved around the world it lived in. The first turtle was a mechanical robot that moved around the floor. It was followed by a graphics screen version. In both these versions, the turtle's state was defined by its position, its orientation, and the state of its pen. These three parameters were controlled by six simple commands: FORWARD and BACK changed the position of the turtle; LEFT and RIGHT changed its heading; and PENUP and PENDOWN changed the state of the pen. Out of these commands came a multitude of combinations, a multitude of movement patterns. Since the turtle could leave a trace of its movement, it could generate geometric and other shapes.

More recently, a range of colors was added. The color of the pen and the background could be changed. The latest change involved multiple moving turtles, or sprites, that can each be given a velocity, a color, and a shape.

Chapter One

STRUCTURED DISCOVERY

"I like this computing because it gets us away from that math." *"Don't be silly. This is math."*

Overheard in a classroom

It does not make sense to ask whether the computer is good or bad. What matters is the nature of the interaction between computer and child; what matters is the potential of the computer, used in a particular way, for cultivating children's thinking. The computer system I have found most useful for exploring this potential is Logo. The introduction of Logo activities into the classroom should not be thought as restricted to the teaching of computer programming. The intention is to support a kind of structured, coherent "messing about" (Hawkins, 1974) as a source of learning potential; the tool is to be the computational environment.

The Quality of the Computer Experience

Many years ago, Dewey pointed out that it was not enough for the supporters of progressive education to insist on the need for experience as the basis for learning nor even on the virtues of active participation in the learning experience. Everything depends on the *quality* of the experience being advocated (Dewey, 1938). The same is true of the computer. There are criteria for the design of computer-based environments that can determine the quality of learning. We can use the computer to increase the learner's control over the learning process in so far as we provide opportunities for her to take the initiative in the computer activity, to set her own goals, to make decisions about the next thing to try in the problem-solving process. The feedback provided by the computer can support long periods of working alone. A learning tool that can support independent activity for long stretches of time is clearly of interest, since it allows teachers the time they so sorely lack to think about their student's thinking. My tool of choice has been Logo.

The Logo System

A decade and a half ago, working first at BBN[1] and then at MIT, Seymour Papert and his colleagues conceived of a fundamentally new way of using computers in education and produced the Logo system. Logo was designed as "a language for learning" (Papert, 1980), as an accessible way to communicate with the computer. There are two senses in which this is to be understood. Logo is a way of learning to program and becoming proficient in working with a computer. At the same time, the student can gain access to a way of thinking and talking about important ideas in a range of disciplines, both aesthetic and scientific. At first the world of education was slow to recognize the possibilities, not the least because the Logo system was implemented on computers whose cost was prohibitive for schools. A major development in the area of computers in education over the past few years has been the availability of cheap Logo systems on a wide range of microcomputers.

This provides a challenge for the Logo community to identify just what a proper use of Logo would look like. As Logo spreads through the schools, so does the controversy about what it can do. For some Logo has become the miracle worker, the panacea for all our educational ills. For others it has become the focus of a critical outpouring against computers in general (*Teachers College Record*, 1984) and a clamor for "rigorous" evaluation of transferable learning before we know what we are dealing with or what the valid controls might be (Pea and Kurland, 1984). Both the hype and the clamor are misleading and premature. Too hasty and mindless an adoption is bound to produce a critical backlash. In spite of its long gestation period, Logo is best regarded as an evolving possibility that will require a period of growth, differentiation, and maturation. The Logo package that computer companies and computer stores are selling now is only the beginning of a story that has yet to be written. Logo is not to be

---

1.   Bolt, Beranek, and Newman, Cambridge, Mass.

viewed as some patent medicine, good for everything regardless. Nor will its benefits emerge as an automatic consequence of its use. Unfortunately, an impression was gained from the early descriptions of Logo that putting the child together with a computer equipped with the Logo system was all that was required. The let-down for those who tried this has produced a great deal of backlash. One is reminded of McCulloch's remark "Don't bite my finger, look where I am pointing." [2] At this moment, effort and energy would be best spent on the cultivation and nurture of the saplings, rather than pulling them up every now and then to look at the roots.

"Logo is not just for kids," wrote Nelson (1982). "It is likely to become a widely used, general purpose language because of both its power and ease of use." A teacher can get going more quickly, can see results sooner. However, this quick accessibility brings its own problems. It is great that within a minute or two of sitting down at the console, something springs out at you on the graphics screen, giving an immediate sense of achievement. By the same token, the ready graphics response has given rise to a misconception about the range and significance of Logo activity.

Contributing in large measure to the problems encountered by teachers who were attracted by the promise of Logo was the paucity of models for achieving that promise. *What would these Logo learning environments look like*?

Microworlds

The first and for a long time the only well-worked-out example of a microworld was turtle geometry, and that was creating problems. What to do when all the excitement has died down? "O.K. I've made some drawings. Now what?" said some children. Already in 1978 the teachers were troubled. "It's not just frustrating, but also boring when you run out of ideas," they said. "The kids want us to provide more ideas and projects. We want to look it up in a book," they told Brookline project evaluator George Hein. [3] But there was no book at that time. The books that have appeared since tend to regard "doing Logo" as learning to program. But what about acquiring aesthetic and scientific concepts?

---

2.   Referred to in the preface to *Embodiments of Mind* (McCulloch, 1965), written somewhat prophetically by Seymour Papert himself.

3.   A year-long study of a class of sixth-graders was carried out in a public school in the Brookline school system in 1977-1978 by the MIT Logo group (reported in Papert et al., 1978, 1979). Each student had between 18 and 26 hours of hands-on Logo experience. George Hein of Lesley College was the evaluator on the project.

Papert (1980) pays homage to the cross-fertilization of ideas from two apparently disparate enterprises. He describes how in 1964 he arrived at the Artificial Intelligence Laboratory at MIT from Piaget's laboratory in Geneva, and how the Logo approach represents the outcome of this transition. In fact, the attempt to get computers to think, known as artificial intelligence, bears a strong resemblance to the research into the acquisition of understanding in children at Geneva.[4] The influence of Piaget on Logo is pervasive. An obvious example is the connection between the role of the turtle in Logo and Piaget's emphasis on the sensorimotor beginnings of intellectual understanding. The imprint of artificial intelligence research is perhaps less visible. In fact, the term *microworld*, used to describe a Logo learning environment, was first used by artificial intelligence workers to describe a *small, coherent domain of objects and activities implemented in the form of a computer program* and corresponding to an interesting part of the real world. Since the real-world counterparts were typically very complex, the microworlds of those early days were simplified versions of reality, acting as experiments to test out theories of intelligent behavior.

Everyone would agree that getting to know one's way around a city is learning. Similarly, we see solving a problem often as getting to know one's way around a microworld in which the problem exists. Think, for example, of what it is like to work on a chess problem (or on a geometry puzzle or trying to fix something). Here the microworld consists of the network of situations on the chessboard that arise when one moves the pieces. Solving the chess problem consists largely of getting to know the relations between the pieces, and how the moves affect things. (Minsky and Papert, 1971)

Papert then went on to use the same term to describe the computer-based environments he was building, since they function in essentially the same way for the child as those earlier microworlds did for their creators. They are places "to get to know one's way around" a set of concepts, problem situations, activities; places in which the student and teacher can test out ideas in a subject domain of interest. This kind of learning environment sounds quite unlike the traditional classroom, with its set curriculum and

---

4.   Artificial intelligence is the building of intelligent computer models, the science of making machines carry out activities that would require intelligence if done by people (Minsky, 1968). We have already met this idea in the comparison of information processing on the computer with human information processing.

didactic teaching style. Microworlds are clearly in the *discovery-learning* tradition.

Discovery Learning

Attempts to provide a learning environment that can lead to creative dis-covery have fallen into disrepute. Some advocates of discovery-based education suggest that an optimal learning environment would leave children alone to discover what they may. Now this may work well for some children, but for others it may be the road to disaster. Most children discover only how easy it is to get lost. An important motif in the discovery-based learning approach is to cultivate children who are comfortable and happy in their learning. Unfortunately, this has often led to a de facto devaluation of academic rigor in favor of "holistic values" and the like, and hence the criticism that discovery-based learning necessarily leads to sloppiness rather than to clarity of thought. The back-to-basics movement reflects this widely held and influential belief.

Both these approaches are based on a false dichotomy: either we have happy children or we have children who are strong academically. Clearly, it would make more sense to find ways of encouraging the growth of happy children who are at the same time intellectually productive and fulfilled and to achieve this academic flowering without creating the accompanying misery that is so pervasive and without excluding a large proportion of those who are our educational responsibility. Logo is described as a "flexible and open-ended yet structured environment." Some practitioners of discovery methods do appreciate, even stress, the need for structured discovery. The problem is that it is all too easy for the idea of structure to get lost. It would help to have structure *built into the medium*. Children in a Logo class often behave as though they were playing. In some ways Logo activities invite the metaphor of *playing with clay*. Carving wood, on the other hand, introduces some sense of response to the internal organization of the material -- carving with the grain -- but this internal meaning speaks only to the initiated few, those with a gift for creative carving.

There is a collection of unfinished works of Michelangelo in the Academia in Florence. As you walk up the central aisle to the statue of David, you are flanked by these emerging figures, wrestling, struggling to get out of the stone. The whole effect is one of power and strength. For this creative artist the internal structure was there under his chisel. All he needed was a chance to chip away at the stone. If the hidden structure remains hidden until the uniquely gifted person comes along and reveals it, we have no useable *general* tool. For us lesser mortals, a more obvious indication of internal structure is required. And this is precisely what carefully designed computational environments have the potential to provide.

Making Computational Environments: Building Bridges

Computers have been used in the classroom in two sharply contrasting ways. On the one hand, children learn to write computer programs, usually in the language BASIC. In quite a different spirit, various computer systems have been written by computer experts to instruct the child. The intention is to promote the acquisition of content in a particular subject domain. Sometimes these teaching programs embody teaching strategies aimed at particular student behaviors (O'Shea and Self, 1983).

Logo cuts across these two uses. It is both a programming system and a tool for creating situations for learning about particular content and about problem-solving strategies in general. The bridge is a useful metaphor here in two senses: as a link between children's intuitive thinking and the act of programming and as a link between programming and the central ideas in some subject matter -- theories of physics, mathematics, biology. For example, turtle geometry is based on building a bridge between intuitive sensorimotor knowledge about moving around in the world and writing programs that drive a turtle round in space (Papert, 1980).

Implementations of Logo

Logo has been implemented on many microcomputers over the past few years: Texas Instruments 99/4A , Apple II and Macintosh, Atari, IBM PC and PC Junior, Commodore 64, Kaypro, Timex Sinclair, Research Machines, and Acorn's BBC machine, DEC Pro 350, and the series of MSX computers.

In addition, Logo has been translated into many languages: Arabic, Dutch, French, German, Italian, Japanese, Portuguese, Russian, Spanish, Wolof (Senegal).

There are differences among the many implementations of Logo. Each has particular features that could influence the choice of Logo system one would make.

Several full accounts of the Logo system are available, for example, Abelson (1982), Watt (1983), and Harvey (1985).

Here is a frequently observed conversation in a Logo classroom between a newcomer (N) struggling with the Logo RIGHT and LEFT commands, and a more experienced Logo programmer (E).

> N: O.K. now, let's turn right a little. Oh no, not right, it's left I need to turn it.
>
> E: Put yourself in the turtle's place, and try out the instructions with your own body.

This "playing turtle," together with the programming activity it supports, exemplifies the first version of the bridge motif:

intuitive understanding -- -- -- --> programming

When a child is programming in an appropriately constructed Logo computational environment, the activities are not confined to the act of programming. The second bridge motif concerns the linking of learning programming with learning content, both traditional and non-traditional classroom material:

programming -- -- -- --> other subject areas

Again, to use turtle geometry as an example, Logo activity is designed to help the student transform the informal, spontaneously acquired knowledge about moving around in space into formal (mathematical) constructs via the programs she writes and into the formal subject as it is traditionally taught in schools. This gives her a way of understanding a whole range of ideas by giving her an intuitive feel for what is going on.

When the two bridging functions are put together -- from the intuitive knowledge to programming and from programming to the subject areas to be learned -- we arrive at a central principle that is really the nub of the matter: A computational environment should be a place where the *learner's intuitions, her current explanations for phenomena, are evoked during the process of learning about some subject matter via programming activity*. The aim is to forge a link between activities in the school and those outside, so as to avoid what for many children is the relative unreality of much formal instruction, as compared to the meaningful control they display over their activities outside school.

Programming can be thought of as "teaching the computer" (Papert, 1980). In using this metaphor, one can explicitly link the process of working through the steps in solving a problem to the process of getting the computer to carry out those steps. What is *not* being proposed is a staged process whereby first the child would be "trained" to do the task, and then having understood that task, would now teach it to the computer. To take that meaning is to use exactly the model of the learning process that is being challenged in this account. It is precisely the model of "first training and then doing" that has misguided our pedagogy for the past many years. *Teaching the computer is itself the training process*, if you want to use that notion. Neither is it to be assumed that there is one singular sequence of steps that all children will necessarily go through.

The student's engagement with the problem turns into "How can I say this in a way that the computer will understand?" For the classroom teacher, too, there can be a shift of emphasis from "How can I make my explanation clearer?" to "How can I set up situations to enable my students to find their way to an understanding?" Observing children in these computational environments can help *teachers* see more clearly what is going on during the learning processes of their students. It can help *researchers* into children's understanding see more clearly what is going on in the heads of their subjects, whose learning in these "real" classroom environments is likely to be more relevant to educational theory than in experiments under laboratory conditions. For the research worker, "How can I test for the presence of skills A, B, and C?" can broaden to "What must I provide so that what my subjects know already and what they can come to know will surface in a clear way for me to observe and probe?"

It is time to take a closer look at some of the things that have surfaced for our scrutiny during Logo sessions over the past several years.

The Many Faces of Logo

Logo is an interactive graphics system.
Logo is a list-processing programming language.
Logo is a philosophy of education.
Logo is a way of learning mathematics.
Logo is a collection of pedagogical principles.
Logo is a tool for creating and editing stories in pictures, words or both together.
Logo activity can serve as a window into the mind of the student.

Turtle geometry is not only drawings. Programming becomes a tool for learning subject-matter. The traditional curriculum metamorphoses into computational environments -- sets of activities designed to support experiences in a particular subject domain.

Logo is not only turtle geometry. The user can represent and manipulate knowledge as lists of words, numbers, and other lists. In addition to graphics primitives, Logo provides facilities for manipulating lists. The alphabet is a good example of an ordered list.

```
MAKE  "VERBS [RUN JUMP WALK BUMP THROW]
 Sets up a list named "verbs"

PRINT  FIRST  :VERBS
 Prints the first member of the list  "verbs", i.e., prints "run"
```

Logo Is Procedural

An important and elegant feature is the ability to combine commands into procedures, which are named and become available as building blocks for larger procedures. For example: REPEAT, FORWARD, and RIGHT are supplied by the system. These can be combined in the definition of the procedure BOX.

```
TO BOX
REPEAT 4 [FORWARD 50 RIGHT 90]
END
```

During the time you are teaching (defining) the word BOX to the computer, it will not execute the commands you give it. Instead, it will store those commands as the meaning of BOX. You are in DEFINE mode. When you get to the end of the definition, you can get the computer to execute the commands by typing BOX. At that point, FORWARD and RIGHT are executed four times and then the program stops. Now BOX has become a primitive that can be combined in its own right, for example, with REPEAT and RIGHT in the definition of a STAR procedure.

```
TO STAR
REPEAT 8 [BOX RIGHT 45]
END
```

Logo activity is constructive; and the Logo language is user-extendable. For a detailed comparison of the Logo language with other languages, see Harvey (1984).

Chapter Two

THE COMPUTER AS EMPIRICAL WINDOW

The turtle geometry microworld allows us to examine the spontaneous generation of numbers under open-ended and under goal-directed conditions of Logo activity. The computer activity serves to catalyze the surfacing of the learner's intuitions. We can observe how students react to seeing the effect of their actions on the screen and the wide range of responses that they make to these effects. This leads to speculation about how numbers are represented in their minds. The chapter ends with a consideration of the educational implications of these observations.

Spontaneous Choice of Number

During the process of constructing a Logo program, it is necessary to choose numbers as inputs for the commands. Often, a number can come alive when you see it as something that does a given amount of work for you. FORWARD 10 takes the turtle twice the distance that FORWARD 5 does. Typically, a student might say:

> How much do I need to go forward here?
> That was FORWARD 20.
> This space is just a little more than twice that.
> Twice 20 . . . 40.
> Let's try FORWARD 45.

So the meaning emerges from the purpose being served, and the purpose may be supplied by the child as part of her active engagement or by the adult teacher or experimenter. Several studies over the past few years have concerned the choice of numbers students make during their early contact with Logo.[1] Our first study looked at spontaneous, open-ended choice of number in situations where the adult refrained from suggesting a goal. We went on to look at number choice when the goal was set by the teacher-experimenter.

What can be learned from the first few numbers used by a Logo student? How much will these depend on age, on mathematical sophistication, and on personal style? Upon being introduced to the command FORWARD, people frequently choose a *single-digit* input. Sometimes, the user resists choosing and asks: What's the scale here? What do you mean "pick any number"? An invitation to "try anything and see" usually produces a response. Having chosen this single digit, the user often shows surprise at how small a distance the turtle travels in response to, say, FORWARD 9. After all, how is a beginner to know that the scale for the size of turtle steps chosen by the implementers of Logo allows the user to fit about two hundred steps on the screen? Experiencing the arbitrariness of the scale is part of sorting out what the computer knows and how to change that.

Out of a group of fifteen children aged 6 to 10 years, seen by Patricia Kellison, the first choices for inputs to FORWARD were as follows: only three chose numbers greater than 10 (39, 100, and 1000); three chose 1; six chose 9; and one each chose 3, 4, and 8. This suggests that to most of these children, what counts as a number is any digit from 1 to 9. Furthermore, it is interesting to note the high proportion of choices that lie at the extremes of the 1 to 9 range, reminiscent of the privileged place that first and last letters in a word have. As I wrote this I noticed that I, too, selected 9 as the input to FORWARD in the previous paragraph.

Let's propose an ultrasimple theory to account for this. Suppose the basic representation of numbers in the very young child is in a string-like structure, each element connected only to the one in front of it and to the one behind it, except the first and the last elements in the string. The last element is connected only to the one before it. The first connects to the one after it, and itself forms the access point to the whole string, so that *the only way to get at the numbers in the string is by entering the string at its first element*. The process of finding a given number would need to

---

1.   These studies were carried out in the MIT Logo laboratory by S. Weir, S. J. Russell, J. Valente, A. Valente, J. Kelly, P. Kellison, and A. Cullen during the period September 1978 to 1983.

start with the first element, see if it matches the given number, for example, 3; if it does not, then the process moves on, takes the next number and checks for a match. When the 3 is found, the process then simply takes the one that follows for the answer. At this stage, the child would be able to count forwards and not backwards. When asked for, say, the number after 3, the child would say, "One, two, three, four. Four." That is to say, the observed behavior would be that the child needs to start from the beginning each time when counting up.[2]

Later, a second point of access to the string is established, namely, at the tail end of the string. Now going backwards along the string is possible. As the child grows, increasing knowledge about number manipulation is recorded as a set of rules, each rule describing a test to be applied to each number obtained in the search along the list. In open-ended activity of the sort we are dealing with in turtle geometry, no constraints are placed by the adults in the situation on what number is to be used, and so no particular test applies. So our children lapse into the situation of the very young child and simply pick the first number encountered in the string. They can pick either 1 or 9 since the string can be accessed at either of these points, but tend not to move along it.[3]

This suggests a little piece of research that Logo teachers could carry out. Look to see if there is a developmental trend in the first number chosen, that is to say, if the pattern of number choice changes with age. The sample I have above is much too small to decide this, and the youngest children are not young enough. All we can say is that the trend is there: two of the three who began with 1 were at the youngest end of the age range -- 6 years, while five of the ones who began with 9 were 8 years or older. The point I am making here is that we have in the past not had many opportunities to observe spontaneous choice of number in children, and so each Logo classroom is a potential source of empirical data about what happens in these circumstances.

When it comes to choosing the second number, a much more constrained situation can arise, since this reflects the student's reaction to seeing the effect of the first number on the turtle. What did the turtle do? What did the number mean to the turtle? Some children do react to feedback and make appropriate choices, jumping immediately to a

---

2.   See Sloman, 1978, for a discussion.
3.   "Lapse into" could mean that the early representation, with its two access points at the beginning and end of the string 1 to 9, is the same representation that in older children becomes the string 1 to 9 that generates the elements out of which all numbers are constructed.

considerably larger number. Thus, among the twelve in our sample who started with a single digit, four made the jump right away: from 1 to 44, 9 to 99, 9 to 100, 9 to 999. However, a surprisingly large number stayed virtually in the same part of the number string, sticking with a single-digit number. Three even stayed at 9. Subsequent progress varied with the child. Some gradually but spontaneously built up to the recognition of the effect of larger numbers. Still others need considerable prompting before using a two-digit number. Here are the first few numbers of five children beginning Logo, observed by Joyce Kelly, to illustrate the range of response obtained (ages in parentheses).

Paul (9): FD l2 FD l00 FD l00 FD l00 BK l000 RT 1 RT 99 FD 10,000 LT 9
Eliza (14): FD 6 FD 9 FD 22 RT 33 FD 55 LT 90 FD 90
Jean (11): FD 7 FD 9 FD 8 FD 20 FD 50 FD 40 FD 100 FD 120
Leah (8): FD 9 FD 3 FD 6 FD 9 FD 7 FD 8 FD 8 FD 7 FD 6 FD 4567
Manny (9): FD 9 FD 7 RT 9 RT 9 RT 98 FD 99 RT 100 FD 100 RT 60

There was a variation in *how long* a child continued to use single-digit input before realizing that a larger number would produce a more useful effect.

1. Paul required feedback only once and then made the jump spontaneously, first with respect to inputs to FORWARD -- from 12 to 100 -- and then for inputs to RIGHT -- from 1 to 99.
2. Eliza used single digits twice before she jumped to a larger number, again on her own initiative. Her jump was smaller than Paul's -- from 9 to 22 as input to FORWARD; but then she stayed with two-digit numbers for the RIGHT command.

In contrast, some children received prompting from the teacher.

3. Jean chose 7, then 9, followed by a retreat to 8; at each step, she complained about the very short distance the turtle was traveling. This led to an intervention by the teacher, after which she moved to the two-digit number 20.
4. Leah was quick to develop a goal. Her goal was to reach the top of the screen. Yet she used nine single-digit numbers in a row, and then when prompted by the teacher to use larger numbers, she chose FORWARD 4567 -- very inappropriate relative to the feedback she was receiving about the turtle's scale.
5. Manny made four small moves, sticking at the 9 "barrier," at which point, again, the teacher intervened to suggest that higher numbers were allowed. That was all he needed.

Variable Inputs

The program BOX shown on page 18 will always draw the same size figure. Much more powerful is a procedure that generates different sizes of boxes by making use of a variable. The idea is to set up a place into which some value will be put at some future point. A ":" is typed immediately in front of the name of the variable, for example, :SIZE in the following procedure.

```
TO VARIABLE.BOX  :SIZE
REPEAT  4  [FORWARD  :SIZE  RIGHT 90]
END
```

Giving the input 60 to the procedure VARIABLE.BOX, by typing VARIABLE.BOX 60, will give you a bigger box than if the input to the procedure was 30, typed as VARIABLE.BOX 30.

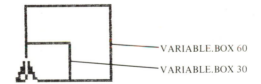

VARIABLE.BOX 60

VARIABLE.BOX 30

Using variables in this way provides a concrete way of approaching the abstract notion of an algebraic variable as it occurs in school mathematics.

In addition to looking at the size of the number chosen, we can distinguish several *kinds* of number chosen. Four out of the above five children moved toward an almost exclusive preference for *multiples of ten*. In contrast, many children use numbers like 45, 67, 23, 12 or 33, 88, 44. They are either pushing the same key twice or pushing adjacent keys -- a choice related to the proximity of the keys, that is, to typing convenience. One-finger typing tends to produce repeated numbers, while typing with several fingers produces runs of consecutive numbers. It is interesting to note that, when these runs of consecutive numbers occur, they more frequently go up rather than down.

The tendency to go in a sequence up the number string in a way that is unrelated to the immediate goal of the activity occurred in an extreme form in a child at the Feltham School.[4] James, a 14-year-old quadriplegic, showed a surprising and idiosyncratic number choice. There were many places in his work with turtle geometry where he started with 14, which was his age, as the input for a turtle command, and then continued along the number sequence regardless of whether he was instructing the turtle to turn right, to go forward, or to go back and regardless of the needs of the problem. James built his Christmas tree out of procedures he had been given. He was required to provide numbers as input to these procedures. Using the BALL procedure with different inputs, he produced Figure 2.1. His program instructions, given alongside the figure, show his peculiar choice of numbers. His solution was to treat the problem as though it were a counting forward problem rather than choosing numbers appropriate to the need.

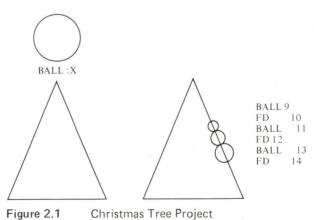

BALL :X

```
BALL 9
FD      10
BALL    11
FD 12
BALL    13
FD      14
```

Figure 2.1   Christmas Tree Project

4.   The name of the school has been changed to preserve the anonymity of the individuals described. James was taught by Jose Valente.

In terms of the theory enunciated earlier, he appeared to have no rules for modifying the number yielded by his basic number-string accessing mechanism.   Incidently, such behavior was not anticipated, and its existence would not have been suspected had Logo not provided the appropriate stage on which he felt free to perform and show us what numbers he would choose *spontaneously*, rather than being asked to work with numbers supplied by his teacher.

Constraining the Choice: Introducing Goals

Situations arising from *student-supplied* goals form the standard Logo fare and are useful to study. During his second lesson, Brian decided to see how much it would need to get the turtle from the top of the screen to the bottom of the screen. An appropriate sequence of moves would be first to get within striking distance of where one is aiming, and then home in on the target by successive approximation. Brian did just that. He went:

BK 75 BK 65 BK 34 BK 6 BK 5 BK 4 BK 5 BK 6 BK 3 BK 3

followed immediately by a series of moves to get back to the top of the screen,

FD 196 FD 2 FD 4 FD 5 FD 3

and then

BK 196 BK 13

to reach the bottom again. The 196 input to FD is interesting. Why didn't he just add up all the numbers (75 + 65 + 34 + 6 + 5 + 4 + 5 + 6 + 3 + 3) and give the exact figure? Did he make a rough computation, or did he attempt a complete addition and perform this inaccurately? Or was it an estimated visual measure? Answers to these kinds of questions require more systematic observation and this creates a dilemma. We are interested in having a structured situation so that we can obtain systematic *group* data while, at the same time, we want to retain the characteristic feature of Logo, namely, that the activities have meaning for the *individual* student who thus retains a strong sense of involvement in solving the problem. Finding the right situation is not easy, since there are rather a large number of variables in any Logo problem-solving setting.

Number Choice as Constrained by Teacher-Experimenter Goals

One setting in which number choice is constrained by a goal external to the student is the *target game* (Figure 2.2), in which the child is asked to move the turtle to the target.

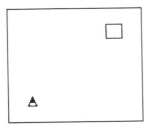

Figure 2.2   Target Game

Since the turtle starts off pointing straight up, and the target is off to one side, this game required inputs to the RIGHT and LEFT turn commands. Refining number inputs to the turn commands so as to change the direction the turtle will move presents problems for most students. In the example quoted above (page 22), we saw a marked contrast between Paul's sure touch in choosing numbers for FORWARD movements and a less than impressive choice in estimating degree of turn. With his first few FORWARD moves he showed an immediate response to feedback by adjusting the size of his input and chose multiples of ten for his inputs. This was not the case for the turn commands. RIGHT 99 is not a particularly "useful" angle for getting a regular figure or for keeping track of where you are in spatial navigating tasks. But how can a beginner know that?

Here is the usual depiction of an angle.

In turtle geometry, the angle between two lines is the amount you would need to turn if you were to do the following: (1) Start off facing in the direction of one of the lines. (2) Turn on your heel until you are facing in the direction of the other line.

Seeing angles as the amount of change in direction gives a good intuitive basis for an understanding of the concept, gives a physical meaning to add to the visual information. But where is the information about *amount of turn* to come from? You have to be told the convention that the special angle of 180 degrees is the amount you need to turn to face in the direction opposite the one you are facing now; and that 360 degrees of turn gets you all the way round. Sometimes a clear intuition about angle meaning is coupled with the "wrong" number. For example, 6-year-old Peter answered the question: "How much to turn for a square?" with this reasoning. After thinking a moment, he turned his body all the way round. He then turned 90 degrees and mumbled: "That's a quarter of the way round. Let me see. If the whole is 100, then that will be 25. Let's try RIGHT 25."

Well, why not? 100 is a very good number to hazard. Indeed, I have been claiming that choosing multiples of ten shows some number skill. The whole business of angle is much more difficult and certainly the children playing the target game found choosing inputs for RIGHT and LEFT more difficult than choosing those for the FORWARD and BACK commands (Figure 2.3).

MANNY	PAUL	CARL
RT 198	LT 143	RT 452
LT 198	RT 16	LT 24
RT 189	RT 165	
LT 99	RT 143	
LT 77	RT 13	
RT 25	RT 13	

Figure 2.3. Initial String of Numbers Chosen for Angles

ALWAYS	SOMETIMES	NEVER
Joe	Pat	Hazel
Dan	Paul	
Manny	Carl	
Eliza		
Philip & Matthew		

Figure 2.4. Used Successively Smaller Numbers as Approached Target

Now we look at the effect of the target goal on choice of inputs to the FORWARD and BACK commands. As with Brian's spontaneously adopted task of finding the edge of the screen, a child with a good sense of scale will use larger numbers to start with, and then, as he approaches the target, will use smaller numbers to home in on it. Many of our students did this (Figures 2.4). In addition, some children used multiples of ten as input to the commands, until they were sufficiently close to the target to need single digits (Figure 2.5). In examining the overall strategy and commands used in the target game, Kelly defined a unit and called it an "attack." An attack consists of any number of consecutive turns right and left from one forward (or back) up to, but not including, the next forward (or back). For example, FD 20 RT 7 LT 21 FD 5 RT 2 LT 74 is two attacks. Kelly analyzed responses to the target game in terms of this unit, and drew three conclusions.

1. A smaller number of attacks per target (Figure 2.6) would seem to indicate a "good eye" for lining up two points.
2. A larger number of turns per attack (Figure 2.7) would seem to indicate a lack of knowledge of the effect of particular numbers chosen and their relation to size of turn.
3. A larger number of forwards per attack (Figure 2.8) would seem to indicate a poor grasp of linear scale.

YES	NO
Joe	Manny
Dan	Paul
Hazel	Carl
Pat	
Eliza	
Philip & Matthew	

Figure 2.5. Used Predominately Multiples of Ten

< 2	2-2.9	3 or more
Joe	Eliza	Carl
Manny	Paul	Hazel
Pat	P & M	
	Dan	

Figure 2.6. Average Number of Attacks per Target.

< 2	2-2.9	3-3.9	4 or more
Joe	Dan	Paul	Manny
Hazel	Eliza		
P & M	Pat		
	Carl		

Figure 2.7. Average Number of Turns per Attack

< 2	2-2.9	3 or more
Dan	Joe	Manny
Hazel	Pat	
Carl	Eliza	
P & M	Paul	

Figure 2.8. Average Number of Forwards per Attack

A comparison of the overall performance of individual children suggests trends. As the tables show, Joe did well in the target game. He used successively smaller numbers as he approached the target; chose multiples of ten predominantly; had a small number of attacks per target, a small number of turns per target, and a moderate number of forwards per attack. Kelly described Joe as "very taken with Logo." Judging from his Logo work, he seemed to have good spatial aptitude. He enjoyed learning new concepts, for example, the REPEAT command and subprocedures, and employed them readily and appropriately in several projects. In contrast, a child such as Manny was able to aim the turtle accurately, that is to say, he could judge when the line-up was good, but he had no idea of what numbers to use to achieve that line-up; he was not economical in his number choice to get there. So he took nearly six turns to get to where he wanted the turtle to face, but once there, did not need to turn again; he had lined up accurately. Furthermore, when facing the right way, he then needed six forward steps before he hit the target; he could not fit numbers to the distance he wanted to cover.

Educational Implications

Several themes emerge from the wealth of behavioral observations.

1. Observing a child's behavior in a setting that invites the spontaneous generation of numbers in response to her own goals illustrates the idea of using computer activity as a window into the mind.
2. Skill in choosing numbers reflects, among other things, the extent to which the learner is taking note of the effect of her previous inputs, for example, whether she uses that feedback to get a sense of the scale of turtle steps on the screen. Responding to feedback is part of the information exchange between student, computer, and teacher, an issue pursued further in Chapter Three.
3. The *meaning of the numbers chosen arises out of the purposes being served* by the activity. Relative magnitude is manifested in a concrete way, as is summing two numbers -- the turtle moves forward a distance equal to the sum of two successive inputs to the FORWARD command. Introducing semantics (meaning) into computation is very important. Compare the situation where carrying problems allow the child to cheerfully produce 112 as the result of add 3 to 19.

$$\begin{array}{r} 19 \\ +\ \underline{3} \\ 112 \end{array}$$

4. The goals of the activity came either from the learners themselves, as part of their active engagement, or from the teacher-experimenter. Any learning situation should contain a judicious mixture of the two. This is an important and recurring theme.
5. Characteristic patterns emerge that distinguish children with a *particular flair for working with the graphics screen*. Features to watch include the kinds of numbers chosen, the accuracy of estimation, and skill at spatial alignment. Chapter Four continues this discussion.

Chapter Three

A CHANGING CONTEXT FOR LEARNING

The computer as a learning tool is "not just another piece of technology." Unlike a passive piece of paper, a tape recorder, or a television screen, the computer reacts. It takes account of the user's behavior. Since the communication is affected by the receiver's wishes, an information exchange can take place. Just how we exploit this interactive possibility, just what conversations we invite, will determine the richness of the learning that takes place. Further, one cannot talk about feedback from the machine without considering the role of the teacher, the place for teacher intervention, and the question of who is in control of the learning process. The chapter ends with a consideration of the blurring of traditional categories of teacher and student roles resulting from the new conditions of learning.

An Information Exchange

When interaction with the computer helps reveal the child's thinking processes, it can enhance the quality of the child-teacher interaction. Challenged to observe carefully, the teacher can develop hypotheses about the child's strengths and needs and so structure the next steps for the learner. Up to a point, the questions for a teacher are the same here as in any educational situation:

When should the child be left alone to explore the possibilities?
When should a new problem be posed?
When should help be given, how much, and in what form?

However, these questions take on a different character when posed in a computer setting. In non-computer situations, providing feedback is almost entirely up to the teacher. In the computer case, some of that feedback can be built into the system itself, and the quality of the learning will be affected by just how this is done.

Cognitive Feedback and Learning by Doing

We saw in the previous chapter how activity in the turtle microworld involved trying out something, watching for an effect, and responding to the feedback. All this is more like learning to ride a bicycle than doing arithmetic with pencil and paper. The analogy is between learning a skill via physical feedback and acquiring intellectual understanding via "cognitive feedback."

One of the reasons why active participation, learning by doing, is so compelling is the conviction arising out of one's own experience of the power of direct personal engagement -- the feeling that you really get to "own" a piece of knowledge when you have used it. Looking or listening can be a rich experience, if what you are looking at or listening to is beautiful, interesting, or important to you. But manipulating material objects, like pouring sand or stacking blocks, provides information about how the parts work in relation to one another, information about process and the sequencing of successive stages of the activity. In the case of computer-based microworlds, the central ideas in the subject matter to be learned can be embedded in the activities, so that they can be experienced directly.

Carrying out the activities implies "manipulating the concepts," *and we can think of this as a new version of learning by doing.*[1] For example, an extension of the turtle world has enabled Andrea diSessa, of the MIT Logo group, to take Logo activities into the domain of physics. His turtle is a moving object called a *dynaturtle* (diSessa, 1982), that lives in a frictionless place in which the student can experience Newtonian dynamics directly. This is made possible by building a world that deliberately simplifies the real world in the following way. As the average person surveys and interacts with the real world, familiar objects do not go on moving at a constant velocity until acted upon by a force, as Newton would have it. One reason they don't is the pervasive presence of friction. In the friction-less dynaturtle world, objects really do go on moving as Newton

---

1.   Notice that for some physically handicapped learners this could be their first opportunity to manipulate anything at all, a fact that underlies much of the value of the computer for these individuals (see Chapters Sixteen to Eighteen).

says they should. The computer-based world has been cleaned up for the sake of achieving clarity. When the dynaturtle does not move in the direction your Aristotelian beliefs lead you to expect, you see that it does not, and the arrows showing the forces at play are there on the screen (Figure 3.1). The arrows provide a record of the forces you have applied.

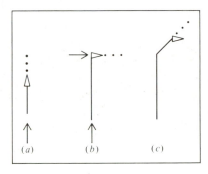

Figure 3.1   Dynaturtle. (*a*) Movement following upward thrust. (*b*) Expected movement when turned right and thrust applied. (*c*) Actual movement.

There is no attempt to replicate the real-world situation exactly: some features will be left out, as part of the educational intention behind the design of the microworld. Ideally, the computer and the real-world activities will complement each other. Indeed, the *computer-based activity can serve a crucial function in revealing the often opaque mechanisms underlying real-world events.* But will this understanding emerge spontaneously, without teacher intervention? Computer-based learning changes rather than diminishes the role of the teacher. As with all project-based work, she needs to find a balance between promoting self-directed learning and making calculated interventions. The enhanced possibilities for self-directed learning in the artifactual world generate new elements to be considered in finding that balance.

Feedback for Teachers

For the teacher, deciding on the appropriate next step in the dialogue with a student has to be based on a scrutiny of the student's performance. In non-computer situations, observing the steps in the problem-solving process may be difficult. Notes scribbled in a random fashion in the corner of a piece of paper are often not very informative. However, some of the private workings of the mind of the learner can be made public in the computer setting, possibly one of its more useful functions in the view of Brookline project evaluator George Hein (Papert et al., 1978).

There is power in having the children's work displayed both on the screen and the display print-out. As Dan[2] goes from child to child he always has available (on the screen) both what they are doing now and what they have done in the immediate past. This is one of the few pedagogic situations where that is possible. Usually you only have the student's latest result and have to guess how the student arrived there. Frequently Dan can keep track of what a student is doing. He can know what to ask, to correct, or to teach, by looking at what is displayed when he goes over to a student. The same principle applies when a student asks a question. The questions are like all students' questions, they refer to what the student thinks he/she wants to know. Dan can look over and say, "That's not the problem; the trouble is that you spelled X wrong in a command farther back." Or he can say, "It still won't work because of XYZ." In this lab, Dan automatically looks at the whole picture, or as much of it as is available on the screen and answers in terms of that.

"But I Thought There Was No Teacher in Logo Learning"

It would be hard to deny that there was a distinct de-emphasis on teaching in the early Logo community. There was strong consensus that *regarding the machine as the teacher was a mistake*. Indeed, that was how Logo differed from the previous approaches to the use of computers in school, where the computer program served as teacher. From the start, Logo had emphasized the humans involved in the interactions, had reacted against the notion that enough was known about human learning processes to enable anyone to write a computer program that would be capable of teaching a child well. The limited instruction considered possible by a machine had little to do with what was envisaged in a Logo learning situation, where the emphasis was to be on enriching the artifactual environment, the computer setting in which the child's learning was taking place.

Attitudes to the role of the teacher became entangled with questions about the need for structure in learning, and this caused confusion. An impression was certainly created that fixed structure in teaching was frowned upon and that there should be a minimum of explicit teaching. Seymour Papert's (1980) vision was focused elsewhere: "Of course the turtle can help in the teaching of traditional curriculum, but I

---

2.   Dan Watt was the teacher on the Brookline project.

have thought of it as a vehicle for Piagetian learning, which to me is learning without curriculum."

This was equated with learning without structuring. Yet a more careful examination of the roots of Logo should dispel some of this perception. Logo had its roots in the artificial intelligence enterprise, and artificial intelligence has to do with making rigorous models. In my view, rigor and structure are central to the spirit of the Logo enterprise, and the question of the teacher's role should be decoupled from the need for rigor and structure in the learning environment. The whole point of the interaction between the learner and the machine rests on the exploitation of the possibility for structure in computer programs.

Control over Learning: Respecting the Learner's Intentions

At its best, the interactive computer experience should drive itself, for at least some of the time, under the steam of the user's intentions. The user should be the initiator, setting goals and taking responsibility for tracking down the errors in her program (debugging). Acquiring some skill at tracking mistakes is part of Logo activity, part of the view that mistakes can be useful, a necessary part of achieving one's purpose, rather than something to be ashamed or angry about. An important test of the skill and understanding a learner brings to a situation is her response to feedback as she tries to discover why there is a discrepancy between what she intended and what actually happened on the screen: "O.K., that didn't go where I expected it to go. Where did it go and why?"

Sometimes students can solve problems and debug programs without appealing for help. But most students are conditioned to think that they have to ask for help every time something unexpected happens. Stepping through their programs, thinking about what each line of program code will do, does not come naturally to beginners. And many teachers are tempted to fix problems themselves. It is easier to do this than to work slowly through the steps necessary to get the students to do it, especially where there is a physical handicap. *Most of the time, in traditional classroom situations, there is a conspiracy between teacher and students to deny the student responsibility, a connivance to reduce the possibilities for arousing intentions in the students.*

Mistakes and Sticking to One's Goals

Some Logo teachers take the view that there are no mistakes in Logo, that anything done is right for something. The liberating effect of this attitude is evident -- the fear of being wrong can be a powerful deterrent to learning.

The difficulty is that it appears to sanction freedom to continually change one's purpose in order to accommodate one's latest "mistake." That is not what I mean by learning from making mistakes. As an example, I remember a child who handled the devastation of failure by denial. James was always ready to change his purpose to fit his latest error. The back wheel of his van came out in the wrong place, because the CIRCLE procedure he used sent the turtle left instead of right (Figure 3.2). His response was to maintain that he had intended the new circle to be the back seat of his van, in spite of his previously announced intention to draw the wheel.

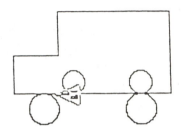

Figure 3.2   James's Van

An ingenious piece of opportunism, you might say, and what is wrong with that? Isn't ingenuity something to be encouraged? There were, however, troubling undercurrents. We discovered that James was never allowed to be wrong. Family life was arranged so that he always won the game. The changing of goal was part of a larger picture of denial that was stifling his development. For James, his fear of being shown to have made a mistake was limiting his progress. It was a great step forward when he learned to tolerate making an error and allowed himself to benefit from the process of debugging that error.

I think a more general issue is involved here. Allowing a constant change of goals diminishes your responsibility to solve the problem you started with. You are not being encouraged to grapple with the problem, to look for the "bug" and fix it, and to learn in the process. The lack of rigor violates the implicit contract of seriousness of purpose that should be present in a learning situation. A balance is required between a readiness to alter ends to suit means and altering means to achieve an end that is held reasonably constant. Both processes are part of learning.

A Cautionary Note: Don't Overestimate the Power of Feedback

There is a difference between what *could be learned* and what *is actually learned*. If during the course of performing an activity, it emerges that your understanding of some aspect is not quite correct, it is, of course, convenient to have your stored knowledge about that activity *accessible and actively mobilized, so that it can be updated*. But there is nothing automatic about that process. Suppose you tell the turtle LEFT 90; it turns, and you see that you should have said RIGHT 90. That does not necessarily mean that you will not make the same incorrect move again next time. There is often an incubation period between bumping into the "corrective" response and spontaneously anticipating it. Long-term cognitive effects are slow to emerge (see Chapter Eight for further discussion).

The aim is to arrange meaningful computer responses, adapted sensitively to the learner's needs. However, a naive user is restricted by virtue of her naivete as to what meaning she will read into these responses. Too often the verbal part of the conversation, the written error message, is not "heard" by the user. In their work with children who have communication disorders, Bull and Cochran (1985) have made a good attempt at providing messages that children might actually read. Older students need standard debugging facilities such as a trace function that prints a record of the procedures executed, so that each step is explicated in more detail. Not all Logo systems have a trace facility.

Teacher-Researcher Cooperation

One fruitful approach to the introduction of computers into the school curriculum involves joint work between academic departments and practicing teachers, with shared planning and training sessions. In a partnership of this sort, the teacher's rich store of informal anecdotal information can be explored and incorporated into the design of materials and activities. The school administration, with suitable financial support, can accommodate the research by appropriate release time for teachers to participate, not as a chore, but as a chosen interest. This is illustrated by the partnership that grew up between the Feltham School (see page 24) and the Logo research team at MIT during the period 1978 to 1982. The enthusiasm of the school authorities took practical shape in the form of a fund-raising campaign for the setting up of a computer center in the school. Computer classes became a part of the regular school curriculum and an integral part of the work in the school resource room.

Cooperative efforts between the Logo group at MIT and schools in the Boston area and in New York are currently in progress. The main flavor of the IBM-funded Headlight project in Boston is provided by a density of computers high enough to allow the student and her teachers to treat the computer as an easily available tool, whose use is to be blended with other learning tools. There is an intimate interaction between teacher and researcher in the exploration of what this does to the atmosphere and activities in the school, the changing role of teacher, the cultivation of opportunities for peer learning, and the development of microworlds for use over the whole spectrum of school subjects. Teacher and researcher come closer; the boundary between them blurs.

Blurring of Distinctions

When significant change in perspective occurs, categories that were well distinguished in the old paradigm tend to become a little blurred. One way of highlighting the nature of the change is to step back and look at these shifting boundaries.

A comparison of computer processes with mental processes leads to a blurring of the distinction between *inanimate computers and animate persons*. In some circumstances, the response of the computer is appropriate enough to encourage some people to treat the machine as though it were alive (Turkle, 1984). For many, the computer becomes "he" or "she," and a sense of quasi-human interaction develops. Dan Watt tells the story of how Tina became attached to a particular terminal, appropriated as "her friend Peter," and became distressed when asked to work at a different terminal (Papert et al., 1979). One student of mine, unaware that his usual QUIZ program was not loaded, became puzzled and frustrated by the stream of error messages that his regular kind of input was provoking. So he tried "You nasty computer" with no better result; then, as if to cover himself, he rapidly followed this with a conciliatory "You nice computer." At that point, and with a rather sheepish expression on his face, he appealed for help.

There is a blurring of the boundary between *knowledge inside the learner's head and that inside the machine*. The talk in a Logo classroom is about working out how you would move to get to a particular place, to help you program the computer to send the Logo turtle to a particular place; about how you would need to turn twice as far to face object X than you would need in order to face object Y. If the calculation is wrong, and the turtle lands up facing in the "wrong," that is, not the predicted, direction, then who has made the mistake, the turtle or you? This blurring of the distinction between what the turtle knows and does, on the one hand, and what the user knows and does on the other, I call identification.

During this child-computer interaction, it becomes an arbitrary matter of interpretation as to who the agent is that is "getting it right." Logo sets out deliberately to exploit this. Whether this is a good thing or not remains to be seen. We have an identification of computer processes with mental processes, in particular with one's own mental processes: "Since the computer is animate and thinks like me, it is something that is capable of being taught" (see Turkle, 1984, for more on this).

During the information exchange between child, computer, and teacher it becomes somewhat arbitrary as to who is doing the teaching; the boundary distinguishing teacher, student, and computer becomes blurred. Who is teaching? Who is learning? A similar shift appears in the relationships among the people in the learning situation. Learners become teachers, especially of their fellow students. Teachers become learners.

I have already mentioned the blurring of the boundary between *researcher and teacher* as part of the exploration of the potential of computer-based activity to enhance learning. In this teacher-researcher spirit, in the next chapter I will use specific case studies to look at some contrasting styles of reasoning.

A Note on Teacher as Learner

Certainly, with respect to getting into programming as a beginner, it helps to have an accessible language like Logo. Since Logo programs are relatively transparent and modular, a first step for a teacher could be to take simple programs, written by a fellow educator or a student, and adapt them for her own use. This serves another purpose, namely, the advantage of being able to tailor a given program to the needs of a particular student, by amending or expanding it. If a piece of software is written in the language she understands, the teacher can scrutinize it knowledgeably and make the appropriate modifications. But Logo is not just about learning to program, and this applies to teachers too. An early step, when thinking about how to make computational environments, is to identify aspects of the subject area of interest that are centrally important. Teachers themselves ought to be the arbiters of the materials they use and will want to be involved in this selection process. But this is not easy for a beginner! How can teachers, who are just beginning move into this complicated activity, also create the necessary computational environments.

Previous educational innovations have not always met with the success they deserved because of a failure to appreciate the need for on-going support systems to nurture the teachers' growing understanding of these new tools. The materials were prepared, found to be good, circulated through the education world, and then left lying, unused, on the shelves of some backroom cupboard. The reasons for these failures are complex. If the new curriculum is significantly innovative, it cannot be treated as a block of self-contained facts and methods, to be simply added, in a linear fashion, to the existing skills of the teacher as though it were another carriage to be hooked on to the existing train. Much of the failure lies in the lack of teacher support mechanisms and staff development, to sustain the exploration and experimentation required. We need micro-worlds for teachers.

Recursion

How about the fairy who offered a child two wishes, to choose anything she liked. Her second wish was for two wishes. . . .

Anon

First, a bare statement of what recursion is and then an explanation. The procedure STAR (page 18) uses BOX as a subprocedure to do some of its work for it. In Logo, a procedure can be used as a subprocedure of itself. For example, the procedure BOX can be called within its own definition. This process of calling a procedure within itself is called **recursion**.

```
TO  BOX  :SIDE  :ANGLE
IF  :SIDE < 0 STOP
FORWARD :SIDE
RIGHT :ANGLE
BOX  (:SIDE - 2)  :ANGLE
END
```

It is as though you solve a problem by finding a small part you know how to solve, then tackling the rest of the problem, which in turn you solve by finding a small part you know how to solve, and then tackling the rest of the problem, which. . . . If the part you know how to solve is the same each time, you can express the solution in a succinct way.

Chapter Four

A CONTRASTING STYLE
OF REASONING

*Some children show a special facility for spatial reasoning, a style of
working that is well suited to the characteristic spatial nature of Logo and
especially easy to observe during Logo activity. Here I set the stage with
two case studies illustrating some aspects of this happy match of working
style and learning environment. The case material provides an example of
the cycle of observation, analysis, administration of probes constructed on
the basis of those observations, followed by further observation. The
chapter ends with a discussion of different ways of representing the same
problem and how that relates to the demonstration of cognitive ability.*

Keith: A Special Facility for Spatial Reasoning

I met Keith at the Learning Disabilities Clinic at the Boston Children's
Hospital. The basis for his selection was quite random; he was one of two
children who happened to have an appointment for evaluation on the day I
brought our computer to the clinic by arrangement with Dr. Martha Denckla.

Keith, aged 11, had been sent to a special school four years
previously with the diagnosis of dyslexia with low motivation and a poor
attention span. The present evaluation was intended to answer the
question of whether he was ready to go back into a school in the public
system. He was noted to be quite "overweight." His record stated:

Neuropsychologically, he presents with a protocol that implicates
difficulty with left hemisphere processing, i.e., he had difficulties in

41

reading, writing and spelling which are language-dependent skills, and in math. In addition, he gave abundant evidence of feelings of inadequacy and poor self-esteem, often present in youngsters who have experienced significant failure.

Keith spent forty minutes interacting with the Logo system. He was introduced to the Logo primitives: FORWARD, BACK, RIGHT, and LEFT. His first step was to determine the size of the screen. For ten minutes or so he moved the turtle around to get the feel of the system. The following conversation then ensued.

Keith: I would like to draw a circle.
Weir: O.K. How could you get me to walk in a circle, using the commands you have learned?
Keith: (Thinks a brief while)
      Forward 10 turn 10 forward 10 turn 10 . . . and so on.
Weir: Right, then, let's do it.

Keith types several forward and right turn commands, stops, and says

Keith: This will take forever. Isn't there a quicker way?
Weir: You can use REPEAT, but you have to know how many times to repeat the forward-turn thing.
Keith: (After some thought) How about 50 times?

Keith tried 50, saw it was too much, so he tried 40 and then 35. The first line of Keith's program (Figure 4.1) shows the sequence of commands he used to execute an almost complete circle. (This corresponds to the lower circle of the body of the snowman.) Keith then made the second circle. He lifted up the pen (line 2: PU -- penup), positioned the turtle for another circle (line 3: FD 90), and took in a lesson on how to teach the computer the new word *circle* (lines 4 through 7). Next he typed CIRCLE (line 8), the computer recognized the new word as meaning the program just defined, and drew a full circle this time. However, nothing happened because the pen was still up. Keith noticed this, put the pen down, and drew the circle successfully this time.

Keith: That looks like a snowman.
Weir: What would you like to do next?
Keith: Put a hat on my snowman.

The record shows how he did just that, without hesitation. In answer to a comment that he seemed to have no difficulty with these maneuvers, he responded, "Oh, yes. I just eye it and then it's easy!"

This boy was impressively productive in his first session with turtle geometry, effortlessly mastering the set of Logo primitives he needed. He showed great dexterity in manipulating the turtle to achieve his graphic purposes, centering the hat on the circular head without hesitation. All through the session his attention was totally engaged by the newly encountered machine and I was obliged to promise him another session before he would rejoin his waiting mother.

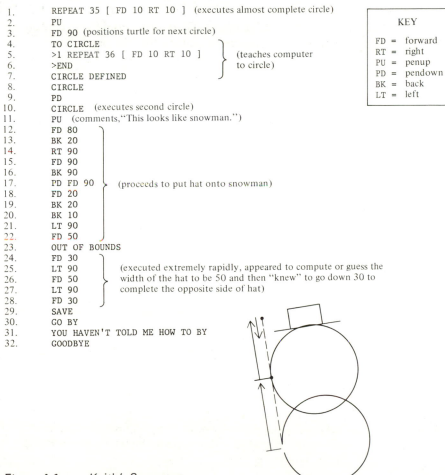

```
 1.       REPEAT 35 [ FD 10 RT 10 ]  (executes almost complete circle)
 2.       PU
 3.       FD 90 (positions turtle for next circle)
 4.       TO CIRCLE
 5.       >1 REPEAT 36 [ FD 10 RT 10 ]        (teaches computer
 6.       >END                                 to circle)
 7.       CIRCLE DEFINED
 8.       CIRCLE
 9.       PD
10.       CIRCLE   (executes second circle)
11.       PU   (comments,"This looks like snowman.")
12.       FD 80
13.       BK 20
14.       RT 90
15.       FD 90
16.       BK 90
17.       PD FD 90        (proceeds to put hat onto snowman)
18.       FD 20
19.       BK 20
20.       BK 10
21.       LT 90
22.       FD 50
23.       OUT OF BOUNDS
24.       FD 30
25.       LT 90            (executed extremely rapidly, appeared to compute or guess the
26.       FD 50            width of the hat to be 50 and then "knew" to go down 30 to
27.       LT 90            complete the opposite side of hat)
28.       FD 30
29.       SAVE
30.       GO BY
31.       YOU HAVEN'T TOLD ME HOW TO BY
32.       GOODBYE
```

KEY

FD	=	forward
RT	=	right
PU	=	penup
PD	=	pendown
BK	=	back
LT	=	left

Figure 4.1   Keith's Snowman

Analysis and Administration of Probes

There are many questions raised by Keith's response, including the possibility of a non-specific computer-prestige effect, but there was no doubting the unexpectedly high level of his task performance. Scrutiny of his protocol reveals features that point to a special *spatial ability*.

1. His very first move was to determine the size of the screen in terms of the arbitrary units provided.
2. Having done this, he spontaneously adopted an excellent strategy for estimating lengths and angles. This involved choosing a standard length (90 units), in terms of which any given span was "too long" or "too short," and a standard turn (90 degree angle), in comparison with which a given turn was, for example, "half as big."

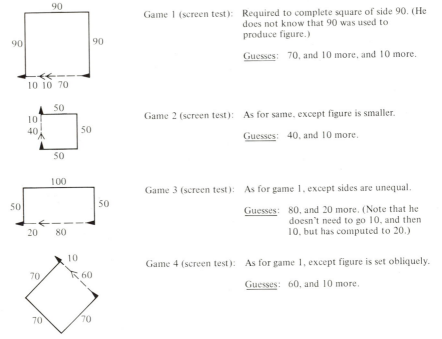

Game 1 (screen test): Required to complete square of side 90. (He does not know that 90 was used to produce figure.)

Guesses: 70, and 10 more, and 10 more.

Game 2 (screen test): As for same, except figure is smaller.

Guesses: 40, and 10 more.

Game 3 (screen test): As for game 1, except sides are unequal.

Guesses: 80, and 20 more. (Note that he doesn't need to go 10, and then 10, but has computed to 20.)

Game 4 (screen test): As for game 1, except figure is set obliquely.

Guesses: 60, and 10 more.

Figure 4.2   Probes of Estimation Skills. The object in games 1–4 was to have the student estimate the number that would send the turtle forward to complete the figure displayed on the screen.

3. He thought in terms of unit-chunks of length (10 units) and turn (10 degree angle). We know this because when he needed to go forward 10 more units he said, "I need one more."

4. His rapid, error-free execution of the snowman's hat included immediately "knowing" that 50 units across would center the hat perfectly.

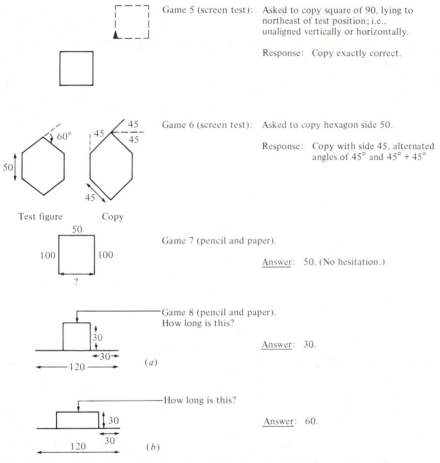

Game 5 (screen test): Asked to copy square of 90, lying to northeast of test position; i.e., unaligned vertically or horizontally.

Response: Copy exactly correct.

Game 6 (screen test): Asked to copy hexagon side 50.

Response: Copy with side 45, alternated angles of 45° and 45° + 45°

Test figure   Copy

Game 7 (pencil and paper).

Answer: 50. (No hesitation.)

Game 8 (pencil and paper).
How long is this?

Answer: 30.

How long is this?

Answer: 60.

Figure 4.2   Probes of Estimation Skills (*continued*). Games 5 and 6 involved copy a figure displayed on the screen In games 7 and 8, the figures were drawn on paper. In game 8(a) the drawing was deliberately misleading.

This led me to ask whether he was using absolutely accurate estimation or whether he computed the numbers required. To probe hypotheses raised by this session, a further session was held three weeks later. A series of "games" was devised in which he was asked to complete figures, without being given any help with the length of the sides in the incomplete figures (see Figure 4.2). It turned out that he did both accurate estimation and some computation. His initial estimate was pretty close, but not absolutely so; he did a substantial amount of very rapid computing and appeared to retain a detailed memory of previously used numbers. Games 7 and 8 were administered with pencil and paper. In each part of Game 8, the answer required by calculation is 60 units. However, the appearance of the line in Game 8a misled him into giving the answer as 30 units.

Why Logo for Keith

The Logo system has a number of special features, two of which were especially important for Keith. Right from the start, he took the initiative -- he was in control and he decided what he was going to do. The second point to notice is that he was choosing among activities that he was able to do very well. That was an unusual state of affairs for Keith, who had spent his time being unsuccessful at things other people were trying to get him to do. Not surprisingly, he lacked self-confidence and had rather a poor view of himself. His spectacular success during this Logo session arose from a convenient match between his own spatial abilities and the characteristic spatial nature of Logo activities.

If you asked Keith what he was doing when he did his rapid-fire choosing of numbers to achieve particular distances, interestingly enough he couched his explanation of his skill in perceptual terms and readily identified it with judgments on the playing field. He said, "I just eye it. I'm good at that sort of thing. When my father plays ball with me, he says how good I am." A great deal of what was involved was not available to his conscious awareness. Indeed, many people, including some highly qualified engineers and computer scientists, are similarly skilled and similarly in the dark about the processes underlying their performance.

Spatial processing is not the only activity relatively opaque to introspection. A surprisingly large amount of our processing has this character, a point that has often been ignored in accounts of the functioning of the mind that equate explicit linguistic expression with thought. More recently there has been a surge of interest in informal or intuitive knowledge and in questions of how such knowledge might differ from knowledge with which we are consciously familiar (see, for example, diSessa, 1983). There are, as usual, several issues that should not be confused. The distinction between conscious and unconscious processing is not the same as the distinction between linguistic and spatial processing; nor are either conscious thought or the use of language to be equated with logical inference-making and the strict application of causal analysis. And then there are all those things which you know without being taught, just picked up as you went along, knowledge you've always used without knowing it; things you never knew you knew.

Franky: Different Ways of Representing the Same Problem

Franky, a 10-year-old learning-disabled child, illustrates the dependence of cognitive skills on how information is represented. His reading and spelling were several years below expectation for his age and grade; he knew some mechanical processes for computation, but these often broke down. He was described in school records as having *behavior problems, a short attention span, and a low tolerance for frustration.* This triad is a familiar refrain to teachers of children with special needs. Each member of the triad is significant, as I hope to show.

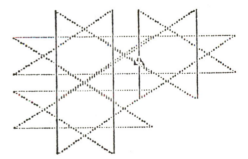

Figure 4.3   Franky's Star Design

In his Logo work, Franky[1] showed unexpected abilities to use numbers appropriately to create relationships in space, to use units larger than 1 as benchmarks for estimating length, and to remember individual commands as well as sequences of commands after a single exposure to them. Figure 4.3 shows an intricate star design which he created from smaller pieces. While creating this design, he needed to move a certain distance on the screen in order to place his next star where he wanted it. The distance was

---

1.   Taught by Susan Jo Russell.

half of 75 -- a problem he was unable to compute using standard arithmetic operations. He looked at the distance on the screen and said, "Oh -- it's about 37." An observer might think this was a lucky guess were it not for the fact that he made such "guesses" frequently. In this example, then, a child could readily estimate half the length of a line in turtle units, but could not divide by two. One can divide a line in half, in a Logo setting, by visually deciding where the half point is, and separately deciding how many turtle units correspond to the resultant line. Nowhere has one actually applied the arithmetic operation: divide the number by two. In addition to a good sense of scale and accuracy of estimation of extent and aim, he displayed a good appreciation of symmetry (Figure 4.4).

Franky seemed to have some of the skills he needed to manipulate numbers when he used a spatial model, but did not have the knowledge necessary to translate this understanding for use in a purely numerical situation. When math was presented as a series of mathematical sentences, such as 33 + 48 = ?, this student showed poor numeric reasoning skills. If he was given a spatial model to figure out a problem, he could use it successfully, but if he was presented only with the numbers, the *idea* of using the spatial model did not occur to him independently. One way to help us distinguish the exercise of spatial abilities from a skill in choosing a good number for the estimate is to ask children to do the same task expressed either as a mathematical sentence or as a picture. The three columns in Figure 4.5 provide three representations: purely visual on the left, mixed numbers and pictures in the center, and purely linguistic on the right.

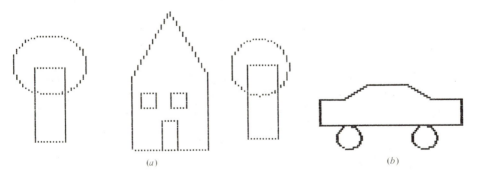

(a)   (b)

Figure 4.4   Franky's Control of Symmetry. (a) His first Logo
                    drawing (b) Note the correspondence between
                    wheel placement and asymmetry in silhouette.

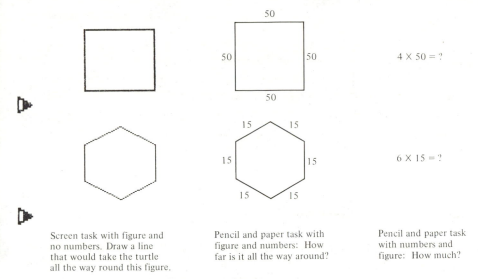

50

50   50

50

4 X 50 = ?

15   15

15   15

15   15

6 X 15 = ?

Screen task with figure and no numbers. Draw a line that would take the turtle all the way round this figure.

Pencil and paper task with figure and numbers: How far is it all the way around?

Pencil and paper task with numbers and figure: How much?

Figure 4.5   Alternative Representation

A child whose computation is spatially based "knows," following a brief exposure to Logo, how far to send the turtle so that the figure will be completed. One child estimated the perimeter of a regular hexagon in turtle units just by looking at it, without being supplied by numbers, but by "eyeing it" (his own explanation, using the same words that Keith used). Yet this same child was unable to answer the equivalent question given as a standard mathematical sentence (column three). The center column gives both the figural and the number information, and here the child who thinks only in linguistic terms is distracted by the visual representation, whereas the "spatial" child is helped by the juxtaposition. A study of group responses to these kinds of problem representations is in progress.

Differences Among Mathematically Able Children

There have been extensive studies on the different problem-solving styles among mathematically able children, most notably among Soviet psychologists. Thus, Krutetski (1968) writes:

> Observations and experiments have also shown that typological differences in the level of correlating the visual-pictorial and the verbal-logical components of mental activity while solving mathematical problems are noticeable at an early age in mathematically able children. Some of them have no need to rely on visual images; "logic" replaces "figurativeness" for them. Others evidently need a visual interpretation of mathematical relations, preferring to solve problems using visual-pictorial means.

Krutetski calls the former the "analytic" type and the latter the "geometer" type and gives an example of how individuals of each type tackle the same problem. The problem concerns finding in one's head, without a drawing, what solid shape is obtained when a right triangle is rotated about its vertical limb. The geometer simply "saw" the rotated solid.

Here I picture the way it is rotated and it is obvious that a cone is obtained.

The analytic type solved the problem in a complicated way by reasoning.

A right triangle is rotated about the leg? Now I'm thinking. . . . The upper point will not be rotated -- it is on the leg. The points on the other leg will be rotated at a different distance from the axis, but each will move an equal distance. Since it is an equal distance, each will describe a circumference, and all together -- a cone. That means, a circle is below, and a point on top. And the hypotenuse, when rotated, connects them. A cone is obtained, right?

My concern is not only with children whose mathematical gifts are clearly evident, but also with those children whose abilities in the spatial domain have not yet been detected or not yet linked to traditional academic skills. Far from appearing gifted, many such children do poorly at school because they have not connected their spatial strengths with academic mathematics. While Logo activities are claimed to have a connection with classroom mathematics, that connection has remained implicit. In the Logo work at the Grove School,[1] we are building explicit connections using a turtle-steps mathworld. Paper-and-pencil and computer activities are integrated to explore elementary school mathematics, for example, REPEAT as multiplication; fractions represented as area; variables as squares (triangles, circles) of increasing size; and word problems as turtle journeys around such shapes (Ary, 1986).

Mobilizing the visual imagination for academic purposes forms an important part of my use of the computer in the classroom. In the next chapter I present a theoretical framework in terms of which to understand this use.

---

1.   A pseudonym has been used for the school to protect the anonymity of the children.

The Button-box

Radia Perlman was the first to use the Logo button-box. Her aim was to demonstrate the accessibility of Logo to very young children (Perlman, 1974). She worked with preschool children using a device "designed so that only a few new concepts are introduced at a time but more can be added when the child becomes familiar with what he has." Her input device, the mother of the button-box family, was planned as an elaborate structure to have five components. Only two were built. The first box had nine buttons: FORWARD, BACK, RIGHT, LEFT, TOOT, PENUP, PENDOWN, LIGHTON, and LIGHTOFF. The second box had all the above commands and an additional row of numbers 1 to 10, and a STOP key. Pressing a button evoked an immediate response from the turtle. When a number key was pressed followed by an action key, the action was carried out for the given number of times. The STOP key interrupted the turtle immediately.

Chapter Five

BEYOND THE INFORMATION GIVEN

The schema theory of mental activity is featured throughout the book as an explanatory theme. Schemas are networks of information representing stored past experience that are used by an individual to make sense of a new experience. Schema mobilization and deployment provide the basis for an account of intuitive thinking, where intuitions are thought of as organized mental schemas. The theory is introduced in relation to a series of examples: a math example from Wertheimer illustrates the role of visual imagination in problem-solving; and a story constructed around a Logo picture illustrates the potential of mobilizing visual imagination in the cultivation of creative writing.

The Exercise of a Visual Imagination

There are many places in the traditional school curriculum where solving a problem involves *seeing* what the next step is -- places where activity traditionally viewed as *perceptual* merges into activity traditionally viewed as *thinking*. Some forms of thinking include the exercise of a visual imagination. Take the problem of finding the area of a regular figure. Suppose the case for a rectangle has been worked through. Now the question is: how can we use what we know about that to find the area of a parallelogram? This is exactly the problem discussed at length by Wertheimer in *Productive Thinking* (1959). A class of children was shown how to find the area of a parallelogram, after they had understood how to find the area of a rectangle. The solution they were given was to cut off the triangle at A and add it to the other end, B (Figure 5.1).

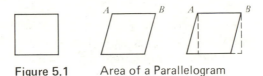

Figure 5.1   Area of a Parallelogram

Wertheimer describes how the class he was observing had learned what to do by rote: drop a perpendicular from the upper right corner, extend the baseline to the right, and so on. So he gave them the figure shown in Figure 5.2a, and they struggled with it. They dropped the perpendiculars from the two upper corners and extended the base line, as per rote instructions (Figure 5.2b) and complained, "We haven't had that yet." Only a few could "see" that the thing to do was to turn the figure on its side and proceed as before.

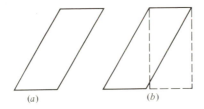

Figure 5.2   Seeing the Relation

In this example, several ways of exercising a visual imagination can occur. One step involves *hallucinating missing lines*: when moving from rectangle to parallelogram, the child is expected to see the triangles at each end of the figure.   Whether or not this will happen spontaneously is the big question. Do *you* see the triangles in the parallelogram? Did you see them before they were pointed out to you? It can be argued that most people would see them only once they know they are there. Once you see them, they're easy to see. How often do our explanations have that character, depending on knowledge which, if present, would mean that the problem was already understood! Seymour Papert tells a story from the early days of Logo. Some fourth graders decided to write a program whose object was to teach first graders simple arithmetic, and during the course of working on the project, there arose a discussion about which multiplications were hardest. Each child offered an example. One suggested 7 x 8, another suggested 6 x 9, and so on. Then one girl made the comment, "None is hardest, 'cos just as soon as you think it's hardest, it isn't, any more, 'cos you know it."

The second visual step in Wertheimer's example involves a *perceptual transformation*: the child is expected to notice that turning a figure on its side reduces the new problem to a previously solved one. This step is prototypical of many problem-solving situations, where what is required is the recognition of the relationship between the shape of the new problem and the shape of problems encountered earlier. Davis and McKnight (1979) refer to a *visually moderated sequence* in mathematical problem-solving: one sees something, which leads to the retrieval and execution of some procedure, which yields a modified visual input, which in turn leads to the retrieval and execution of the next segment of procedures, and so on.

Picture Stories

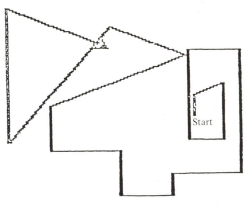

Figure 5.3   Elly's Drawing

The richness of the possibilities in a user-dominated Logo environment is by no means limited to mathematics, to intuitions about numbers and their effects, or to geometric shapes and their possible subdivisions. Quite a different exercising of the visual imagination occurs when a child *sees a story in a picture*. Here is 7-year-old Elly's story to illustrate the point. Her drawing (Figure 5.3) was produced using the INSTANT program. As she made her picture using the turtle commands, she told a story (Figure 5.4):

This is the door.
This is the lake.
This is the place where you get out and dry.
This is the place where the candy machine is.

The INSTANT Program

Logo is an ideal vehicle for making computing accessible to young children, since it has a facility to add user-defined procedures (page 18). This allows one to redefine a single key to have the effect of typing a whole string of keys. Thus the Logo procedure:

```
TO  F
FORWARD 30
END
```

will result in a simplified command, F, which has the same effect as typing the whole Logo command FORWARD 30. Typing one key gives the turtle a command and a constant input. In this way, one can both reduce the number of gestures required and achieve a conceptual simplification -- each button press corresponds to one change in the turtle's state. The INSTANT program listing is:

```
TO COMMAND                          TO INSTANT
MAKE "COM READCHAR                  COMMAND
IF :COM = "F [FORWARD 10]           INSTANT
IF "COM = "R [RIGHT 30]             END
IF "COM = "L [LEFT 30]
IF "COM = "C [CLEARSCREEN]
END
```

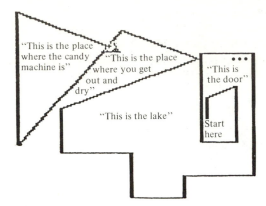

Figure 5.4   Elly's Story

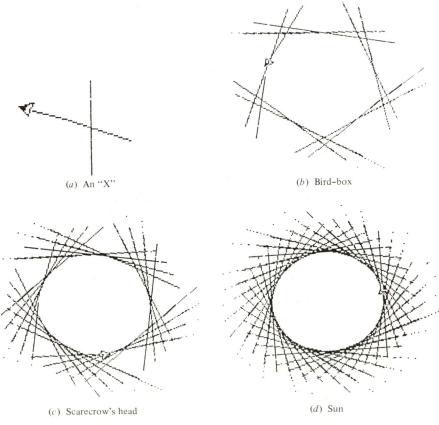

Figure 5.5   Mike and Sam's Sequence

The kind of imaginative leap from picture to story shown by Elly as she invented her story, although by no means universal, is not at all unusual in Logo. It is constantly the case that the users have in front of them half-formed pictures, incomplete drawings, a few suggestive lines that invite completion, that invite a meaning -- suggestive, that is, to some more than to others and in very different ways. For example, having completed their depiction of an "X" for their tic-tac-toe game (see Figure 5.5a), Mike and Sam took a typical side-trip to explore what would happen when they ran the procedure "X" repeatedly. As Mike typed X X X X furiously, Sam sat back and provided a commentary on the growing picture: "Hey, look at that bird box!" (Figure 5.5b); and then, "That looks like a scarecrow's head!" (Figure 5.5c); and finally, "Ah! There's our sun" (Figure 5.5d).

In contrast, Elly used her drawing not as the basis for recognizing what it depicted, but rather as a series of placeholders for the events in her story. This is reminiscent of the mnemonic technique of setting up a house, into each room of which one places a fact to be remembered. This technique makes some people happy and strikes others as a quaint affectation. Pictures and the stories they evoke reveal what sense these children are making of their activity, what meaning they are finding. As they do this, they are seeing something that is not actually there in their pictures. Consider two individuals looking at the same thing, for example, at this.

Each sees an entirely different thing. One sees a cup and the other sees a swing seat. Each finds an entirely different meaning in the picture fragment.

Where do these different meanings come from? The extra something that Elly saw as she made her drawing, that she told us about, that told us what her drawing meant to her -- this extra something came from her organized past experience. As we look at the world and "see" it, our perceptual recognition involves an appeal to category and other kinds of information we already know, to objects, scenes, and events already experienced. How else would we know to call that mass of different shades of gray a picture of our favorite cat? As we respond to the world around us, we construct a description of what we are perceiving. Identifying the object or event before us requires us to relate the description being constructed to information stored in a variety of ways: episodic memory (involved in the recall of specific events related to people, objects, location, and time); category information in semantic memory (involved in the recall of general knowledge about the world); and the like. This presupposes that we have previously stored in our memory a description of that experience in some mental "language," information stored in *mental schemas.*[1] Helmholtz called this process of making inferences from the presence of particular stimulus patterns to the identity of objects *unconscious inference.* "If I see this kind of corner made out of wood standing about my waist level, then I can conclude that I have probably got a table in front of me."

Something about the new experience triggers the memory of the old. The immediately present is the new phenomenon or experience, call it A. The thing not immediately present is the stored schema, or B. Perception would have the quality of connecting A with B. First we start registering the presence of A by making a description of it. In processing terms, a description of the incoming stimulus forms in working memory. Now envisage a process of *search and match*: the search process traverses a collection of stored mental schemas, the organized setting of past responses, looking for a match, for a stored schema, B, to give meaning to the new experience.

If a scene contains details that correspond in great measure to what was stored, then a unique match can be found. If there isn't much there, if the stimulus pattern is too impoverished, something interesting happens. More than one stored schema will be found, each containing one or other component that matches the description of the incoming stimulus fragment. So that, typically, such a matching results in the activation of a number of possible schemas, each of which could be "relevant to the needs of the moment" (Bartlett, 1932). At this point, the information flow starts to go in the other direction. Whereas at first the process goes from outside in, taking the incoming fragment and using it to guide the memory search, now there is, in addition, a process going from inside to the outside, taking a part of the stored description and using it to complete the picture. We can think of this flow from the schema out on to the scene, as *projecting components of the schema on to the scene being viewed* (see Figure 5.6).

This means that there always is a seeing-as process going on (seeing the new as a version of the old), during which we necessarily add information to what is given to the senses. Gaps in the information supplied are filled by information from past experience projected from stored

---

1.   I use quotes to emphasize a particular use of the word "language" here. I am not talking about languages such as English or Spanish. I am talking about the internal language of the mind, whatever that might be. At this point, I will not distinguish between concepts, rules, and codes; between episodic memory and category information; or between cognitive structure and cognitive process. Instead I will use the generic term schema to refer to a closely connected cluster of information, or clusters of processing units.

schemas. For example, we can imagine how things look on the far sides (hidden portions) of objects, even when we are not given that information directly.

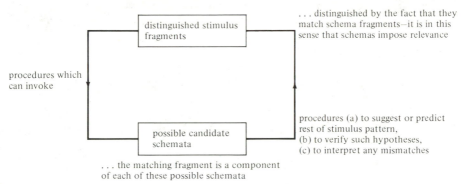

| | distinguished stimulus fragments | ... distinguished by the fact that they match schema fragments—it is in this sense that schemas impose relevance |

procedures which can invoke

| | possible candidate schemata | procedures (a) to suggest or predict rest of stimulus pattern, (b) to verify such hypotheses, (c) to interpret any mismatches |

... the matching fragment is a component of each of these possible schemata

Figure 5.6   Interaction Between Incoming Stimulus and Stored Schemas

We are "hallucinating" the missing parts on to objects. Our eyes and minds "function so as to project their prejudices (models) upon the world" (Clowes, 1973).[2]

> In the Middle Ages when men believed in the physical existence of Hell the sight of fire must have meant something quite different from what it means today. Nevertheless their idea of Hell owed a lot to the sight of fire consuming and the ashes remaining -- as well as to their experience of the pain of burns. (Berger, 1972)

Johansson and His Walking Man

The Swedish psychologist Gunnar Johansson placed lights at crucial points on a human figure, in particular, one on each of the main joints and one on the forehead. The subject was then filmed in dark room. When the film showing the pattern of moving lights is observed, *you see a person walking*

---

2.   This two-way process that forms the basis for stored past experience to influence perception of the new experience constitutes the transactionalist school of Brunswick (1947), Bruner (1957), Gregory (1966), and others. A contrary view that regards all the necessary information as given in the current optical array is held by Gibson and his school. For a discussion of the two views, see Ullman (1980).

along, even though you are only seeing the lights at the joints. All else is dark. There is a compelling universal identification of a moving human participant which is not made when the figure is stationary (Johansson, 1971). When the figure is stationary, then indeed you see nothing but these lights -- a meaningless collection of white dots. The pattern evokes nothing in particular, nothing familiar! When the movement starts up, the human figure springs into action, or rather that is what we think we "see." (Figure 5.7)

Figure 5.7   Johansson Man. Moving dots evoke the
                        walking-person schema.

It appears that the pattern of moving lights, the particular *kinetic* configuration, acts in the same way as the stimulus from a completely visible human form would. It is sufficient to evoke the relevant schema, namely, the *walking person* schema, containing the full description of the complex pattern of movements that constitute this familiar experience. From this schema comes the missing detail, the descriptions of the limbs and trunk, and so on, and the lines joining the dots are projected on to the scene. The moving pattern acquires a *meaning*, and the meaning comes from the evoked schema. Each dot follows a complicated trajectory which is in itself meaningless. It is the fact that a particular pair of dots remain a constant distance apart that enables our perceptual system to reason that they are part of the same object, for example, a swinging arm.

Educational Implications of the Schema-Invocation Theory

Recall how turtle geometry is based on the idea of mobilizing intuitive knowledge already available to the user. We can think of *intuitions as collections of stored schemas*, and the triggering of stored schemas as another way of talking about the mobilizing of intuitive knowledge. Not only is the familiar schema used to explain the partly unfamiliar new experience, but activation of networks of familiar schemas can form the basis of the acquisition of new understanding. An example makes the point. Comprehension of what one is reading entails a linking of incoming information with knowledge stored in memory (Rumelhart, 1977). Reading should be viewed as an interactive process of *bringing meaning to a text as well as getting meaning from a text*. A fragment of a story is read. This triggers a whole story in the mind of the listener.

How can a teacher exploit this process in her teaching? A way of doing this is described in "Probable Passages," by Karen Wood (1984). Students are supplied with a list of significant words taken from a written passage and an incomplete story framework. They construct a probable passage of text from these two sources. At this point they are shown the actual text. An important ingredient of this exercise is the idea of a story structure, a *story grammar*. Just as the grammar of a sentence -- verb / noun phrase -- can generate many sentences, so a prototypical story structure can be used as a basis for story generation. As students compare their own constructions with those of their peers, they have a direct experience of the range of alternative possibilities that such a structure can generate.

What are suitable triggers for story generation? For a language-impaired student, written words or phrases are not the cues of choice to begin with. From an educational point of view, it could be especially advantageous to present language activities in a visual medium for students whose reading skills one wishes to improve. As we saw with Elly, the initial story-triggering fragment can come from a Logo picture. I propose to exploit this possibility by using visual fragments in the form of kinetic sequences to represent story elements (see Chapter Ten).

Learner as Model Builder

In planning our learning environments, we aim to encourage the mobilization of intuitive knowledge by providing *situations to explore rather than problems to solve* (Hoyles, 1985). The student will accumulate fragments of knowledge as she interacts with the materials and encounters conflicts between her existing explanations and her new experiences. Over a period of time, as she experiences the same idea in different ways, these knowledge fragments can become articulated into a rich mental model of some piece of understanding.

During a regular Logo session there is modeling going on at several levels. The child can treat the turtle or the computer as a model of a learner. For the teacher, observing the child program the turtle to carry out a task can supply pieces of understanding to enhance her model of the child's learning. The information exchange can act as a model of communication. For a group of children carrying out a joint programming task or just sharing programs and ideas for Logo projects, the situation can act as a model of cooperative planning and problem-solving, upon which to build future social experience.

These processes can be thought of as steps in the construction of internal models of the world, on the basis of which an individual anticipates what is about to happen and in terms of which she makes sense of incoming experience. These models are culled from experience and determine experience. To the extent that our perception of a situation is mediated by our internal model of the world, two people can construe the same situation differently by virtue of having different world models. This has obvious educational consequences. Teachers need to take account of the differences between individual models of their students. Similarly, when introducing innovative educational technology to teachers, we have to take account of the models they will bring to the experience, often based on quite different experiences. We need to provide explicit models of the kinds of activity being envisaged, so as to allow explicit comparisons with the teacher's existing models (see Chapter Twenty).

To the extent that individuals share internal models, there can be a shared sense of relevance across which communication can take place. At the extreme, impoverished end of a spectrum of shared relevance is the autistic child, whose idiosyncratic sense of relevance severely limits communication. Looking closely at the behavior of disturbed children can help us understand the thinking of "normal" children. In the next Chapter, I describe the computer experience of a young autistic child who was particularly explicit about the link he was making between his experiences with the turtle and his own body schemas. For this child, this linking process provided the basis for a rare experience of shared relevance and communication.

Chapter Six

AUTISM AND THE COMPUTER

Ten years ago I had the opportunity to use Logo with a young autistic boy who benefited from the explicit way that the turtle world highlights what is relevant to the successful performance of the activity. We learned a great deal from his overt demonstration of the connections he made between the turtle's activity and his own body movements. Both these aspects, the issue of relevance and the successful incorporation of new knowledge into an existing functioning system, are of major importance to educators. For our autistic student, these features translated into a sense of shared relevance and understanding, which was accompanied by the onset of spontaneous language for communication.

A Safe Place for Autistic Children

In work with autistic children, I place a special emphasis on two peripheral devices: the physical turtle and the button-box. One can set up situations in which the physical turtle acts as a computer-controlled agent, knocking down blocks of bowling pins, moving between the legs of a chair, under the "bridges" and through the "tunnels" that abound in a room full of ordinary furniture. A commercial building kit or the children's own drawings can be used to construct a little village in which the turtle's activities are incorporated as stories about visits to shops, school, church and the like. Notice that the same considerations apply to younger children, who respond well to beginning Logo with the physical turtle.

Combining the simplicity of the button-box with the concreteness of the mechanical turtle provides the learning environment of choice for low-functioning children: the stage is set for observing their spontaneous problem-solving activity.   Often, autistic children do not relate their own actions to a resultant change in the world around them.   Things seem random and inexplicable. They do not recognize cause-effect chains easily in the unmodified complex real world. We can bring these basic causal connections within their grasp in a simplified button-box-turtle world, where a single key push results in a single action of the robot.   Providing this one-to-one correspondence, clear, predictable, and satisfying, formed the basis for an early study carried out in Edinburgh in 1975.

Donald: Behavior Before Logo Sessions

An extract of our report (Weir and Emanuel, 1976) summarizes the story of a 7-year-old autistic boy prior to his Logo work.[1]

> Donald attended a special unit for autistic children. He presented a classical picture of autism. He was remembered by his parents as a passive infant who didn't reach out for objects, and was unresponsive to "name calling"; he was tested for deafness at 10 months, although his parents knew he could hear since he responded to music. His language development was very slow.   There was little communication with his parents: "He just looked through us." From 4 to 6 years of age he attended a special unit and received structured teaching using a behavior modification approach. At the start of this period he was an emotionally difficult child.   He cried and screamed frequently and for lengthy periods. He resisted physical contact and hated change. Strangers in the classroom upset him. He rarely made eye to eye contact. When he came to his present school at age 6 years, he could carry out simple verbal instructions, and knew some standard word sequences to express his needs, such as "more paper, please." He had learned a variety of skills, including picture-object matching tasks. To quote from a letter written about him by his teacher at this time: "He can sort by color but only knows red and green by name. He can count from 1 to 20 using a one-to-one correspondence. He is learning how to form and recognize numbers 1, 2, and 3."

---

1.   Dr. Sula Wolff of the Children's Hospital in Edinburgh provided access to the clinical notes of this young boy.   Ricky Emanuel, a graduate student in the artificial intelligence program in Edinburgh, was his Logo teacher.

Over the past year in the autistic unit he had learned to read and write. However, his reading was very mechanical in texture, with a flattening of intonation and a loss of emotional inflection, as was his counting. It was difficult to avoid the impression that much of this involved a kind of rote learning, with a real lack of understanding. His parents, teachers, and the psychiatrist in whose care he was shared a concern about his apparent "comprehension blockage." He was quiet and gentle, somewhat inhibited and withdrawn. He avoided eye contact and responded to questions with a stilted high-pitched "unnatural voice." He showed a striking reluctance to commit himself to anything. If requested to point to any particular object, he complied only after repeated insistence.

Logo Sessions: Regularity and Predictability, Cause and Effect

Donald was seen seven times over a period of six weeks; twice the first week, three times the second week, once the next week, and at a final session three weeks later in the sixth week. Each visit lasted approximately one hour and a continuous videotaped record of all his work was made. We used the Edinburgh button-box (described in duBoulay and Emanuel, 1975) and the physical turtle, connected to a Honeywell 316 minicomputer.

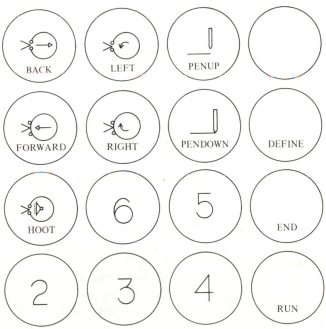

Figure 6.1   Edinburgh Button Box Labels

We used both icons and words to represent the turtle commands. Each button (Figure 6.1) represented a turtle command, e.g., FORWARD, BACKWARD, LEFT, RIGHT, PENUP, PENDOWN, and HOOT. Pushing the button caused the turtle to execute an action, and the button light stayed on until the command had been executed. There were also number buttons which the child could use in conjunction with the command buttons to cause the turtle to execute the command the requisite number of times. Each button push, then, was equivalent to executing a little Logo program. For example, pressing the FORWARD button was equivalent to <FORWARD 10 RETURN>. Pressing a number button, say 4, and then the FORWARD button was equivalent to <REPEAT 4 [FORWARD 10] RETURN> (see the INSTANT program, page 55). Buttons in the rightmost column (DEFINE, END, RUN) allowed one to store a sequence of botton presses as a simple program and then run it later.

During the early sessions we left Donald alone in the room and observed his behavior on the video-monitor in an adjacent room. Later, we were able to stay with him for extended periods without disturbing him. One of the most interesting aspects of this work was the way the behavior exhibited by Donald exemplified some of the claims made for Logo by its inventors (Papert, 1980). Donald's actions make it easier to believe the story. To begin with, only 5 of the 16 buttons were uncovered: FORWARD, BACK, LEFT, RIGHT, and HOOT. The physical turtle was placed on the table near the button-box so that any effect on the turtle would immediately be obvious to Donald, and, indeed, when it moved forward in response to our pressing the FORWARD button, we were rewarded with an "Ah!" "Now you do that, to see what happens." Gingerly, he complied with our suggestion that he press a button. At first his behavior was exploratory, cautious, and nervous. The HOOT button was clearly a favorite from early on and he delighted in imitating, accurately, the sound with a musical "boop." Donald's behavior went through several stages, characterized as follows.

1. Sequence of steps: pressed button, looked at turtle for response, pressed button again.
   Button choice: at the beginning of each session stepped systematically through the available five buttons; after that chose any button, i.e., basis for choice not obvious to us.
2. Sequence of steps: as above.
   Button choice: concatenated single commands into sequences; for example, constructed runs of FORWARD's and so propelled the turtle across the table, and later across the floor toward one of a number of objects scattered around.
3. Sequence of steps: said the action first, e.g., said HOOT or UP, then

pressed the button corresponding to the action just said, looked at the turtle for the response.

Button choice: constructed complex sequences that appeared to be goal-directed; for example, forward to a chosen object; HOOT; back a little; forward again to almost reach the object; HOOT again; back; then forward up to and straight into the object, knocking it over.

4. Sequence of steps: pushed PENUP button, which raises the pen on the under-surface of the turtle, pushed PENDOWN button, which lowers it (both movements accompanied by a rather obvious click), said PENUP, stood up, said PENDOWN, sat down. Immediately after this, pushed PENUP button, pushed PENDOWN button, poked the region of his belly button with his finger while saying "up," stood up, poked his belly button while saying "down," sat down, pushed PENUP button, stood up with his hand in the region of his belly button, pushed PENDOWN button, sat down.

Donald showed an appreciation of the one-to-one correspondence between pushing the button and the turtle's action, as evidenced by the direction of his gaze. Furthermore, on one occasion when he pressed the HOOT button faster than the computer could respond, so that the turtle continued to hoot even when he had stopped pushing the button, he glanced back and forth from button-box to turtle, showing surprise at this apparently unsolicited hoot. He predicted and then obtained an effect, saying "hoot" and then pressing the HOOT button. He did a great deal of explicit acting out, a kind of action conversation. He seemed to make an identification with the turtle in various ways: an identification of his belly button with the PENDOWN and PENUP buttons on the box, perhaps as the instrument of the action; an identification of his body with the turtle as the object acted on; and an identification of his hand as agent in both cases. This action sequence occurred when he was introduced to the very concrete turtle pen and to the commands that control its movements.

In summary, Donald did what Papert hoped children would do, it seems, making connections between the turtle's activity and his own body movements. He appeared to be acting out the behavior of the turtle by reference to his own existing body schemas. The new schemas he constructed while playing with the turtle encapsulated the connection he made between his own actions and that of the turtle. He spontaneously invented ways of showing us this. The striking difference between Donald's behavior in the Logo session and his behavior in his regular classroom appeared to rest, in part, on the clarity of the situation. It was unusual for him to be clear about what was expected of him. It was unusual for him to have such clear expectations of the consequences of his actions. For us, the novel feature was the clarity of his intentions as he used the turtle, in contrast to the more usual impression of a "shutter across his mind."

This is an example of how a process observed in a disturbed child appears as an exaggerated version of an ordinary process. The theory I have described claims that learning involves the linking of new schemas to previously stored ones. How could we know that anything like this happens? The behavior that Donald displayed provides some evidence that, in the button-box-mechanical-turtle case at least, the appeal to prior experience is doing what we want it to do. That is to say, appealing to already existing knowledge about moving around in space provides the setting for the new experience to be linked with the old, familiar schemas. Of course, there is the possibility that our autistic subject Donald was following a deviant path. However, it seems more useful to make the assumption that in this particular regard the thing that is out of the ordinary is the unusually explicit way he "tells" us about his processing. One important feature of the Logo environment for Donald, a feature that is probably playing a major role in the clarity of his perception of the connection between his button-pushing and the turtle's movements, is the explicit way that the turtle world highlights what is relevant to the successful performance of the activity. The issue of relevance is of major important to educators.

Relevance

To help a learner become receptive to our communications, we need both to speak less ambiguously so as to facilitate her perception of what we consider relevant, and to become sensitive to alternative perceptions of relevance she may have. Consider a child in a discovery-learning class, pouring water from one glass container to another. What is she to attend to? The situation is rich with suggestion.

> Wetness -- spillings. Better be careful!
> Does the color matter?
> Changing containers changes the shape of the water. Is that what I should look at?
> Is it because it's glass?
> If I move my head, my finger gets fatter. Would they laugh at me if I said that?

The trouble is that there are so many things around. Among the myriad of objects, events, properties of objects, changes over time, constancies over time -- to which of all these possibilities should she attend? It has been assumed that in making sense of her environment, the child is matching descriptions of her current experience to recorded schemas derived from past experience.   In the container case, she already has many stored descriptions of previous occasions when she met containers and poured things into them; also descriptions of parts of her body, say, half submerged in the bath water, and little experimentations with changing their shape by moving them or by moving her head. The learning situation is intended to *add to* some of that experience. But to which bit of that stored experience is the updating to be made?

How can Logo help in this important issue of relevance, of what to attend to? *Programming in Logo explicitly encourages the user to abstract from the massive amount of detail present in any problem-solving situation, just those elements which require attention.* How does it do this? The difference between turtle activity and the imaginary container scenario is that in the turtle world, *the things that matter are just those things that you have commands to change.* The salient features correspond to the only elements in the turtle's state that you as user can change -- the position of the turtle, using FORWARD and BACK; its heading, using RIGHT and LEFT; and the state of the pen, using PENUP and PENDOWN. Exactly what you are supposed to attend to is writ large by what has been selected as the primitive actions in the system.[2] The nature of the material the turtle is made of does not affect your activity. That which requires attention is more "obvious" in this artifactual turtle world than in the real world, teeming with complexity and confusion.

However, an intrinsic contradiction emerges. We want to simplify the situation so as to keep the salient features uncluttered, so as to enhance the learner's chance of seeing what is relevant. But there is a tension between that desire and the need to embed learning in as rich a situation as one can, so as to enhance the possibility of triggering familiar schemas, of mobilizing intuitive know-how. This tension between rich contextual strategy and stripped-down simplicity is no new thing. Here is Montessori writing at the turn of the century.

I remember being present at an arithmetic lesson where the children were being taught that two and three make five. To this end, the teacher made use of a counting board having colored beads strung on its thin wires. . . . the teacher found it necessary to place beside the two beads

---

2.   As Logo has developed, more elements have been added to the turtle state, for example, the color of the pen, which can be changed by SETPENCOLOR.

on the upper wire a little cardboard dancer with a blue skirt, which she christened on the spot the name of one of the children in the class, saying, "This is Mariettina." And then beside the other three beads she placed a little dancer dressed in a different color, which she called "Gigina." I do not know exactly how the teacher arrived at the demonstration of the same, but certainly she talked for a long time with these little dancers, moving them about, etc. If *I* remember the dancers more clearly than I do the arithmetic process, how must it have been with the children. (Montessori, 1912)

By stressing that there is a need for clarity about what to attend to, I do not mean to imply that everyone needs a single focus of attention. There is growing evidence that different styles of processing are to be found among people with different patterns of attention-focusing (see Chapter Eleven). For some people, identified as having an obsessional type of personality, a single sequence of events is preferred. For others, the hysteroid type, several different foci are preferred and they will rejoice in dealing with many simultaneous changes. Autistic children come at the obsessoid end of the spectrum in this regard. For them, a single focus of attention is what is required and the less ambiguity the better. Indeed, much of their problem stems from the fact that their sense of relevance is idiosyncratic.

The consequent lack of a *shared relevance* is what makes it so difficult for autistics to communicate with other people, and a large part of the advantages of using Logo rests on the explicitly shared relevance it enables (see Chapter Fifteen). The possibility of communication is enhanced in the button-box-turtle setting by the shared relevance it supports. In addition, controlling the turtle can act as a model of communication in that it embodies the idea of communicating a sequence of commands so as to get the turtle to achieve a goal.

Shared Relevance and Communication

Frequent comments in Donald's extensive case notes referred to a striking feature of his school and clinic behavior: "has never made a spontaneous statement to us, except under stress"; "speech has to be prompted every time"; "no spontaneity -- has to be asked again and again." I have already described how in the fourth session Donald made "action speeches" -- pushing his own belly button, saying "up" and standing up; pushing PENUP, pushing his belly button again, saying "down" and sitting down. A little later in the same session, Donald volunteered the remark "Drawing -- me drawing" and proceeded to draw with his finger on his palm. In the fifth session, while pushing the BACK and FORWARD buttons, he again vocalized spontaneously, this time in the form of a comment on the turtle's activity: "Turtle goes backwards and forwards . . . backwards and forwards . . . right" (while pushing corresponding buttons). In the sixth session, he continued in his by now rather deliberate fashion to "tell" us what the turtle was doing, probably aware of just how much we applauded his doing so. After pushing the LEFT and RIGHT buttons, he verbalized the entity "left-and-right." He then linked together all his previous descriptions of the turtle functions and said "Emanuel -- make turtle go forwards and backwards and left and right, up and down, hoot." After this he systematically stepped through the number buttons in conjunction with the HOOT button -- 2 HOOT, 3 HOOT, . . . -- and ended with, "See how it works."

As he vocalized his thoughts spontaneously during his "turtle play," as he volunteered "turtle goes backwards and forwards" and the like, he discovered that, unlike the private nature of his usual monologue, these spontaneous utterances reporting on his turtle activity made sense to us. There are two new things here. The use of spontaneous language, and most importantly, the reporting of his activity to others, with the turtle work providing the basis of this reporting. Neither of these phenomena had been observed prior to this experience. Nor had Donald displayed the active seeking out of social interaction that he showed during his Logo sessions.

It seems that, as the shared sense of relevance and understanding was achieved, so was it accompanied by the onset of spontaneous language for communication. There are probably many factors leading to this behavior. Let us go back to the schema-invocation story to link up the relevance discussion with the stages in the search-and-match process. Recall that there could be several familiar schemas activated by the matching stimulus fragment, each one a possible answer to the questions "What is going on here? What am I supposed to be doing?" Anything that reduces the number of possible candidates evoked by the incoming stimulus pattern will simplify and speed up the recognition process. This is where the issue of relevance comes in. When there is a one-to-one correspondence between what is done and what happens, there is reduction in ambiguity that translates into a reduction in the number of candidate schemas evoked during the search-and-match process. *It is this reduction in ambiguity that forms a crucial element in the success of the approach with autistic children.*

Again, our experience with the autistic child has direct bearing on learners of all ability and of all ages. An interesting aspect of the current computers-in-education situation is that the teacher and her students are learning similar things. Many teachers have mentioned to me that becoming Logo learners themselves has given them insight into some of the difficulties their own students have had. "Learning to tell what is important, how to isolate the action that is going to be repeated over and over again, is difficult when you're at the beginning. My children are at the beginning most of the time, especially with respect to the notation I'm using. I've been too ready to throw a page of problems at them, too soon." The alternative to being confronted with a page of problems in an unfamiliar notation is to participate in an activity where the primitive actions are relatively unambiguous and attention-directing, and where the first stage in the activity is to get clues about what is relevant by examining the effect of one's actions in trying-things-out mode.

Emotional Responses

While pressing buttons to move the mechanical turtle, Donald was clearly enjoying himself. He spoke in a warm, vibrant and low-pitched voice. He smiled. He chuckled. He became rambunctiously excited. He showed total concentration, attention, and a high level of motivation during his sessions. His absorbed engagement during the PENUP belly button incident contrasted rather sharply with what had been going on immediately before that in relation to the introduction of the number buttons. The number buttons were definitely not liked. They had produced a fair amount of negativistic withdrawal. Off went the smile, and back came the barrier, the sad, withdrawn, passive stance. Our speculation was that numbers had a classroom connotation for him and were not part of his new turtle-based play.

To some extent, pressing 4 then FORWARD also broke the one-to-one connection between his action and the response of the turtle: two pushes of a button sent the turtle forward in only one movement and over a longer distance than he had become used to. A similar break in the one-to-one relation occurred later when we used the DEFINE, END, and RUN buttons that allowed instructions to be stored and then run later. No longer was each movement of the turtle directly under his control. Here was the turtle moving without his button-pressing! He was no longer in control! Again, an adverse emotional reaction ensued. His behavior changed. He became agitated, lost his quiet deliberate stance, and began banging keys randomly. In fact, we were so worried we discontinued that activity. It seemed that partial control was not something he recognized.

Partial Control and Models of Self

In order to participate in interpersonal relationships, an individual requires a sense of self that includes two models of self: self-as-agent and self-as-object. It was as though Donald could not understand self-as-agent alternating with self-as-object. Either he was granted total agency or he withdrew. Such an all-or-none stance by an autistic comes as no surprise to us. Typically, autistic children have no idea of "turn-taking," the alternation of actor that forms the basis for conversation. Catherine Snow (1975) describes this understanding of role-taking as already present in infants, but it does not seem to develop in autistic children.[3] This would seem to be connected to a lack of development of a sense of self and other. Itard (1801), when describing the behavior of Victor, the 11-year-old Wild Boy of Aveyron, writes: "He always spoke of himself in the third person. He led people by the hand to show them what he wanted. He was described as unaware of his personal identity."

When the problem concerns an unawareness of self, there are advantages in starting with an activity that focuses on body schemas. The advantage for Donald was displayed transparently by the way he always acted out the behavior of the turtle with reference to his own existing body schemas. The explicit similarity between his own actions and those of the turtle facilitated the connection. Our reward was some quite splendid things he did with the system. The connection he made between his own schemas and turtle programs was spelled out as an action speech. He first moved himself then moved the turtle, looking toward us each time he did this: "Up," he said, pushing his belly button; "Up," he said, pushing the button that lifted the pen.

We expected Donald to enjoy working with our machines and then to experience a problem in transferring the gains he made to his inter-actions with humans. Instead, as he continued with his turtle work, he appeared to be directing his descriptions at us. He behaved as though he was telling us about it. Here is an interaction I had with him.

A short while later, a mixture of actions and words formed a conver-sation. With Weir sitting beside him, Donald shuffled his chair backwards and said, "Back." "Back?" queried Weir. "Yes," replied Donald, and repeated the backward chair movement. Weir answered with a push back of her chair and again said, "Back." Donald laughed, then spelled out, "F-O-R-W-A-R-D," then, "B-A-C-K," and then said, "Spell forward." Weir echoed, "Spell forward." Donald said, "F-O-R-W-A-R-D." Weir said, "Good!" (Weir and Emanuel, 1976)

In this interpretation, I have given the issue of control a crucial role. It was

---

3.   Lack of appreciation of this process could be part of why many autistic children do not change the "you" to "I" in their dialogue: they do not notice the customary alternation in speaker.

rare indeed for Donald to control anything as interesting to him as controlling the turtle, and rare for his control to be as unambiguous. It was even more rare for him to find himself in a situation where what he was in control of was what those people around him wanted him to be in control of, and, most poignantly, rare indeed for his control to be linked with such unequivocal understanding: "See how it works!" His sense of control was both mediated by and in turn deeply affected by the strong emotional responses he had to the activity (see Chapter Ten). Again, the connection with the general learner is clear. The issue of control has several aspects, discussed further in the next chapter.

Chapter Seven

METAKNOWLEDGE

The facts of a given situation are a relatively small part of knowing something. There is a vast edifice of processes embodying knowledge about when to use particular facts and operations; about how to order operations so as to achieve a particular goal. One important difference between "rote" learning and "real" learning is that, in the latter, the student learns how to select the appropriate problem-solving method for a particular kind of problem. Acquiring expertise in a field of activity involves controlling the process of problem-solving by building an understanding of problem-solving itself. Procedural knowledge tells you how to manipulate the factual knowledge you have and is an essential part of becoming a good problem-solver. Problems can arise in the classroom when the need for this knowledge about using knowledge is not recognized.

Knowing What to Use and When to Use It

Since using stored knowledge plays such a central role in problem-solving, we are concerned to understand the processes by which we recognize which pieces of that stored knowledge are appropriate for the particular problem being tackled and how our cognitive systems retrieve the relevant pieces. The problem is that much of this knowledge about how to deploy knowledge is not available to conscious scrutiny. Progress in under-standing what might be involved has come from the attempt to get machines to solve problems intelligently. Precisely because machines are so stupid, all knowledge about problem-solving has to be built into a computer-based system if intelligent processing is to occur (see Boden, 1977, for more on this). Knowledge about knowledge is called *metaknowledge*, and improving one's command of this kind of knowledge is a central part of learning.[1] In order to achieve this improvement, one needs access to this often unconscious knowledge.

A growing child has come to understand how to do certain things. The child's intuitive knowledge of his own body movements as he navigates in space includes such understanding. That whole familiar world of intuitions has structure, in the form of organized knowledge for manipulating information, inarticulate knowledge, informal knowledge. Connecting with existing, naturally developing metaknowledge is the reason why giving the learner active agency is so important and is the purpose behind the "learn it by doing it" school. A reasonable assumption to make is that when previously stored schemas are being actively deployed in some problem-solving process, they are more readily available for updating than is otherwise the case. That is to say, activated schemas make learning possible. If the right connections are made, then what is learned by doing can become intimately interwoven with both the factual knowledge and all the procedural control knowledge associated with those facts. What is learned can become linked into the working system, the "going concern" that makes up the important part of the learner's mind. It is part of the approach taken in this book to postulate that this *knowledge about knowledge* is itself organized in mental schemas.

My son, who is a bright boy, came and said to me, "You see, Daddy, I am very good in arithmetic at school. I can do addition, subtraction, multiplication, division, anything you like, very quickly and without mistakes. The trouble is, often I don't know *which* of them to use." (Wertheimer, 1959)

If one is asked to do an arithmetic problem, it is not enough to know all the

---

1.   Sometime around 1975, the term "metacognition" came into vogue. For an interesting review see Brown (1984), who describes the several different ways in which this term has been used. Some refer to only that part of knowledge-about-knowledge that the individual is aware of, whereas others include all strategy-knowledge, conscious or unconscious; some distinguish knowledge about cognition from knowledge about the regulation of cognition. I will use the more general term metaknowledge for the whole category: both conscious and unconscious knowledge, knowledge about facts and about process.

arithmetic operations. One needs to know what sequence of operations is appropriate for solving which particular problem. One needs to know how to recognize which stage of the problem-solving demands which operation. Typically this could involve a series of recognition steps. The first step could be to recognize the problem as being of a particular kind, for example, a problem about fractions. Then one could recognize the kind of fraction problem it is, say, an addition-of-fractions problem. That could lead to a mobilization of information *about* solving addition-of-fractions problems, for example, information about lowest common denominators. Or it could be that addition of fractions here is taking place with terms containing variables, so that one first needs information *about* how to gather together "like" terms, i.e., terms containing the same variables. All these operations involve representing problem-types and strategy-types as patterns of characteristics that will be matched one against the other. It involves getting more sophisticated about judging similarities and differences between such patterns -- those same processes I talked about earlier in relation to perception. This suggests a relation between the requirements for perception and the requirements for learning, between "recognizing the familiar" and solving problems. An example, quoted by Davis and McKnight (1979), makes the point.

> For some subjects, merely the noun-phrase "A river steamer ..." was sufficient to trigger the retrieval of an appropriate schema, indicated by the subject saying, "It's going to be one of those river things with upstream, downstream, and still water. You are going to compare times upstream and downstream -- or if the time is constant, it will be the distance."

Recall the ways in which the contents of mental schemas dominate what we attend to in a scene. The central process described was the schema-invocation mechanism: the machinery by which schemas are activated is the search-and-match process that yields a number of schemas as possible candidates for the role of Bartlett's "relevant bit of the past" (1932), that would give meaning to the new experience. In the mathematics case, the relevance is to finding a method suitable for solving this new problem. Let's spell this out with a detailed comparison between a perceptual and a learning problem.

> Walking down the street, I pass a woman who seems familiar. I have seen her before. That I know. But I cannot remember where. I can't place the circumstances in which I saw her last. I debate possibilities and decide that it is because she bears a resemblance to someone I do

know and can name. Next day, as I approach the checkout counter at my local foodstore, I recognize the woman checking out customer purchases as the person I puzzled over the previous day. Outside the foodstore I stand talking with a friend. Someone passes. "Who's that?" she asks, "I'm sure I know, but I can't remember." I remark to her that I have just had the same experience.

What is happening? How is all this possible?

I *perceive* a person.
I *recognize* her as a person I have seen before.
I store a description of *a kind of experience*.
I *recognize* similar kinds of experiences.

There are *several levels of processing* going on here. Over and above the simple first level of description, other characteristics of an experience will need to be stored in memory so as to permit these kinds of comparisons to be made. In addition to the ability to describe the current scene, namely, the person I am walking past now, I appear to be producing information about persons in general and to generate comments about who they resemble. In addition to recording the particular detail of the experience, I deduce and record comments *about* the experience: "This is a kind of experience where I can't put a name on a memory" or "Your friend reminds me of my mother."

An analysis of solving math problems in the same terms suggests that as we become proficient at solving these problems, we record similar kinds of descriptions. Corresponding to "This is a kind of experience where I can't put a name to a memory" we would have "That's the kind of problem where it pays to start with all the variables on the left hand side."
Issues of strategy occur in both types of situation -- in looking at people and in solving math problems -- and we would want to add to the stored description, remarks reflecting strategy choice: "How can I find out who this person is?" or "Shall I continue on this track or choose a new operator?" We could also add comments such as "This feels good." or "Goodness, how boring this is!"

Acquisition of Metaknowledge

A common fallacy is to regard teaching as merely the transfer of facts and canned explanations, whereas the student's problem often lies in a failure to recognize the applicability of a particular solution method. The student in some sense may know the procedure required and yet not use it. Where is this procedural knowledge to come from? When you are being taught something new in a classroom, you often don't get this kind of information. What is taught is just the tip of the iceberg. The expert does not mention the rest of the iceberg, because she is not conscious of all the know-how she is using at any particular moment. As Margaret Donaldson (1978) writes, "the better you know something, the more risk there is of behaving egocentrically in relation to your knowledge. Thus the greater the gap between teacher and learner the harder teaching becomes, in this respect at least."

Frequently, a teacher at a Logo workshop will remark on how her own experience as a beginning Logo programmer has given her fresh insight into how her students feel. Part of becoming a good teacher is becoming aware of the things one takes for granted when one knows something, so that one can make these explicit to a learner. Recall the Wertheimer parallelogram: a piece of information was left out by the teacher when the rule to drop perpendiculars was given. The teacher was using the fact that the longest line in the figure she had drawn happened to be horizontal, but she did not give any sign of this to the child.

Learning frequently requires changing the metaknowledge associated with some procedure. When the learner is a passive spectator, the extent of debugging that can occur is limited, since there is no confrontation between the observed actions and the spectator's metaknowledge relevant to carrying out that activity. Typically, you do not see the metaknowledge being employed by the expert when you are a passive spectator. As already mentioned, active use of stored knowledge brings it into working memory, so that stored mental schemas become available to be used in learning processes, to be scrutinized and changed if necessary. This process includes the activation of metaschemas. If it should happen during the course of performing that activity, that your procedural-control knowledge is found wanting in some respect, the appropriate debugging of the already activated metaschemas is possible, since activated schemas are accessible to be debugged.

A good way to learn something is to work with an expert as an apprentice and engage in "guided messing about"(Hawkins, 1974), rather than receive a pure diet of rules, principles and concepts. Young children tend to learn by "messing about" naturally. Unfortunately they are gradually brainwashed out of using this method as they become more sophisticated and subject to social beliefs about "needing to be taught." Computer-based systems such as Logo have the potential for doing something about this, but this potential is not realized automatically. It is necessary to contrive the "messing about" to make it appropriate to particular kinds of experience and so to invite the desired learning.

But more is needed than the opportunity to mess about. As well as doing, we can think about what we are doing. As well as perceiving, we can reflect upon our experience. Piaget called this "reflective abstraction." Conscious self-reflection is slow to develop, and we mature as individuals to the extent that we can look at our own functioning. It must be of benefit to a growing child to be encouraged by the very nature of the learning environment to "look at her own thinking."

An Aid to Self-Reflection

One of the functions of turtle work could be to act as a bridge from what you are actually doing to an understanding of what you know, to a reflection on your learning. Recall the metaphor of teaching the computer, referred to in Chapter Three. The identification of learner with turtle and the blurring of the distinction between what the turtle knows and does and what the user knows can serve a function. Whereas you might have difficulty in examining your own thoughts, you may have more success if those thoughts have been externalized, have become the thoughts of the turtle. That is to say, when you think about how the turtle is achieving some task, you are halfway to thinking about how you would do that task.

Consider what is involved here by analogy with the computer programs shown on page 18. Suppose that after defining the BOX procedure, we type BOX; this will run the procedure, that is, it will draw a box on the screen. Suppose, however, we type EDIT "BOX; this will allow us to scrutinize the code with a view to changing it, that is to say, the contents of the procedure will become the object of our attention. If we use the notion of a computer program as a convenient metaphor for the unit of mental thought, the mental schema (see Chapter Five, page 58), then the distinction is between using a mental schema and looking at it. If the schema contains the instruction to move forward, then using that schema means carrying out that moving-forward instruction, running the schema so that the forward movement will actually take place. On the other hand, looking at the schema has a different result, for example, may see that unless we give the FORWARD command a variable input it will always draw the same size box. Bartlett (1932) called this the ability to "turn round upon" our own mental schemas.[2]

---

2.   This is, in fact, the old philosophical distinction between *use* and *mention*. *Using* the instruction "Close the door" produces a closed door. *Mentioning* the instruction "Close the door," for example, in saying "'Close the door' is an imperative sentence," produces some information about the instruction.

There are two ideas to grasp. The first is that the elements of the turning-around process just described are present in the process of programming the turtle. To reiterate: it is easier to examine your own thoughts if they have been externalized as the "thoughts" of the turtle, so that you are looking at the way the computer achieves a task as a way of thinking about how you would do it. One can use this process as part of introducing a student to the habit of "reflective consciousness" -- the ability to direct her awareness to her own thoughts (Oatley, 1981).

The second component of Logo that is geared to aid the development of self-reflection can be viewed as a blurring of the distinction between concrete operational and abstract thought. Logo offers a world halfway between the familiar real world in which things happen, on the one hand, and the mental world of analysis, mental diagrams, geometry, and algebra, on the other; a quasi-mental, quasi-real world of computational graphics objects, of quasi-real actions. Again, the in-between status feeds into the self-reflective process, since the abstract thought becomes scrutinizable in its concrete form. Logo can be an aid to moving back and forth from concrete to abstract and back again.

These, then, are the kinds of aids to self-reflection that the Logo system can, but does not always, provide. In my experience the chance of this happening without guidance is low. Not only do students not do this, but many Logo teachers do not spontaneously make these kinds of connections either. What is required is a mixture of structured messing about and teacher intervention. The responses of students in diSessa's dynaworld illustrate the possibilities and are described in the next chapter.

Chapter Eight

SOURCES OF CHANGE

The experiences of students are described as they interact with a computational environment geared to create conflicts. Their intuitive theories, culled from everyday experience in the real world, come into conflict with what goes on in the artifactual computational world. A paradigm learning journey takes the student through a messing-about stage, in which she sticks to her existing theories in the early stages of the interaction, makes conservative moves, and confronts the conflict with some discomfort. She emerges some time later with her theories refined and enriched and altered to accommodate the new phenomena. This reluctance to relinquish long-held schemas applies especially to schemas that have a significant explanatory value, to those that play a privileged role in the individual's cognitive system. The way an individual responds to the challenge of learning new things and her reaction to failure depend in part on the view she has of her own ability.

A Dynamics Microworld

Dynaworld is a computer-based microworld designed to provide direct experience of motion in a frictionless world. The intuitive theories being challenged in this world concern what happens to objects when acted upon by a force, theories that are based on experience in the real world, where things remain stationary unless acted upon by a force, and an object moves in the direction of the force acting upon it. The conflict occurs between

82

ideas gleaned from this everyday experience and those arising from interaction with the artifactual microworld, where objects continue to move at a steady velocity as long as there are no forces applied, and where the direction an object is moving at the time it receives an impulse affects what happens next. The claim is that after the artifactual experience, the student will return to a consideration of the physics of the real world with a richer appreciation of the underlying mechanisms. The responses of students were described by diSessa in the Brookline report (Papert el al., 1979), and I use his descriptions to construe the behaviors observed in terms of the explanatory processes that form the thread of this book.

We met diSessa's dynaturtle in Chapter Three. It lives in a dyna-world that is like the turtleworld, but has an additional primitive, KICK, that allows dynamic activity. A dynaturtle, like the ordinary Logo turtle, is a graphics entity that can be moved around on the computer display with commands typed at the keyboard. Like the geometry turtle, the dynaturtle responds to commands RIGHT or LEFT by instantly turning in place. While motion for the geometry turtle is caused by the command FORWARD, a dynaturtle never changes position instantly, but can acquire a velocity with a KICK command which gives it an impulse in the direction it is currently facing. To effect real time control, one normally directs a dynaturtle with keystroke commands, R, L, and K which stand for RIGHT 30, LEFT 30, and KICK 30. The code for the dynaturtle is:

```
TO DT
MOVETURTLE
COMMAND
DT
END


TO COMMAND
MAKE "COM READKEY
IF :COM = "R [RIGHT 30]
IF :COM = "L [LEFT 30]
IF :COM = "K [KICK]
END


TO MOVETURTLE
SETPOS SE (XCOR + :VX) (YCOR + :VY)
END
```

```
TO READKEY
IF KEYP [OUTPUT READCHAR]
OUTPUT "
END


TO KICK
MAKE "VX :VX + SIN HEADING
MAKE "VY :VY + COS HEADING
END


TO STARTUP
CLEARSCREEN
MAKE "VX 0
MAKE "VY 0
END
```

To try out the dynaturtle, type   STARTUP, followed by   DT.

Every time you kick the dynaturtle it is as though you had fired the rocket of a spaceship briefly.[1] The motion changes with each new kick, and the dynaturtle will continue moving with its new motion, which will be a combination of the old motion and the motion caused by the new kick. You can re-aim the rocket by turning the dynaturtle to the right or left. Once you change its heading, you can change its motion by giving it another kick. Since there is nothing in space to slow it down, it will then stay in motion in the same direction until you give it another kick. The fundamental principle is that, instead of the old Aristotelian, plausible but incorrect, notion that a force changes *position*, it is the *velocity* -- which is movement at a given speed in a given direction -- of a moving object that is changed when a force is applied.

Conservative Response and Intervention

A typical early activity offered to the student is a dynamic version of the target game, but, of course, things are not what they seem, since we are in a dynamics world.

Figure 8.1   Target Game

The object of the game is to get the dynaturtle, which appears, blinking, in the lower left corner of the screen, to hit the target, displayed in the upper right corner. The two most commonly used strategies in the dynamic case are the *aim-and-shoot* strategy, that is, to try to aim the turtle where one wants it to go and then kick, and the *corner* strategy, to move the turtle until it is level with the target, turn it to face the target, and kick.

Now the interesting thing to note here is that these are the strategies adopted by students when presented with the standard static version of the target game (Figure 8.2). Notice that the initial configuration in the static target game looks almost the same as in the dynamic game; the only difference is the blinking of the dynaturtle as against an unchanging

---

1.   Spaceships operate in space and space has no friction. Therefore, the word rocket evokes a schema appropriate to motion in a frictionless world.

standard turtle in the static game. The *perceptually dominant* similarity is sufficient to allow the dynamic version to be seen as the standard version, so the same moves are tried.

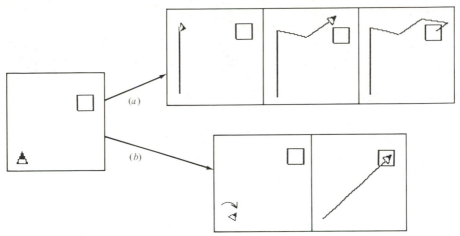

Figure 8.2   Static Target Game: Two Sequences of Play.
(*a*) Corner strategy. (*b*) Aim--and--shoot strategy.

Suppose the student decides to start with the aim-and-shoot strategy. The trouble is that in the dynamic version, the game is set up so that it is not possible to aim directly at the target from the starting point. This is because while each turn step is 30 degrees, the target is at 45 degrees from the dynaturtle's initial position. As we will see, that arrangement forces the user to turn the dynaturtle while it is in motion, and that is the beginning of the conflict between existing schemas and a successful strategy.

The usual response is a conservative one: "Keep the theory. Continue to treat this like the static target game, but try the other strategy, namely, the corner move." This brings the student into conflict between Aristotle and Newton. The Aristotelian expectation is as shown in Figure 3.1. "Kick to the right means move to the right," that is to say, the strategy is simply to aim toward where you want the dynaturtle to go, in this case to the right; then kick in that direction. In fact what happens is that the upward motion produced by the first upward kick is not eliminated by the kick to the right. The effect of the kick to the right is just to *add* motion to the right to the already existing upward motion. *This tendency of an object to keep moving in the direction it is going is called momentum.* A Newtonian strategy, therefore, will recognize that a dynaturtle that is moving upward has *momentum* in the upward direction, and that the dynaturtle will take a "compromise" path, going *up and to the right* at the same time.

Typically, the student continues to be conservative, trying to keep his theory. "His first instinct on failing was to try it again and again," writes diSessa of his 11-year-old student Jimmy. Alternatively, the student seeks an explanation: "complaints that the machine was not working right at this point were commonplace." Another of the Brookline students, Darlene (11 years), tried several other versions of the kick-toward-the-target strategy. In one she started out horizontally rather than vertically (Figure 8.3a), and in another version she used an oblique path and then turned and kicked toward the target (Figure 8.3b).

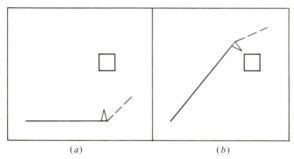

(*a*)   (*b*)

Figure 8.3   Sticking to the Corner Strategy. (*a*) Horizontal
                       Aristotelian Corner. (*b*) Correcting aim–and–shoot,
                       another Aristotelian corner.

Just what Darlene had in mind as she was carrying out the maneuvers depicted in Figure 8.3 is an interesting question. Did she see the experiments as doing the *same* thing or as doing *different* things? Did she start off thinking she was doing something different and then discover that each try was simply a different version of what she had already tried, namely, kick toward target? As diSessa points out, there is indirect evidence to show that some change occurred during this period of trying out possibilities. Before this messing about period, her response to a teacher-intervention in the form of a discussion on Newtonian cornering strategies was quite negative. She did not accept the suggestions made sufficiently to try them out. However, after her own experimenting period, her attitude toward a Newtonian strategy was quite different. She took to the idea readily, made her own conjectures as to how to get it to work, and was eager to try out these possibilities. She seemed to have needed an *incubation period* before she was ready to adopt diSessa's intervention.

The relevant intervention involved inviting the student to concede that she could no longer retain the analogy with the static case as a basis for moves, because in the dynamic case there is this extra thing: the existing momentum of the object needs to be dealt with in some way, needs to be "canceled out." The idea of "canceling out" suggests that a good way of dealing with momentum is to get rid of it by kicking in the opposite direction -- the *anti-kick*. Applying a force of equal magnitude but in the opposite direction leaves the dynaturtle stopped in mid-flight, suspended, with a zero velocity. Once this is achieved, the dynaturtle can be directed around in small steps -- it now does behave like the static case. Sometimes this canceling out step is achieved without teacher intervention, as Alison Cullen found during a Feltham School student's interaction with the dynaworld: "I was called away at the start of the (target) game. When I returned 5 minutes later, I found the student had spontaneously adopted the stop-and-start strategy and had hit the target twice" (see footnotes on pages 20 and 24).

Whichever way it happens, the important point is that, having experienced anti-kick, our student is now in a much better position to understand the whole business of friction. The idea that, once moving, an object will go on moving at the same speed in the same direction is counterintuitive -- not part of our experience. When things like balls and cars move around ordinarily, there is an automatic reverse kicking going on, called friction. Whenever an object moves through the air, it is pushed backward by the air, just as though it were receiving a series of small reverse kicks. If there were no friction, momentum would keep everything moving just the way spaceships or dynaturtles do. Now we can appreciate diSessa's remark that it is only by coming to understand the Newtonian stance that one even acquires a reason to separate friction as a force to be included in the analysis. A Newtonian frame of analysis, continues diSessa, seems necessary to make sense of the notion of friction as a force, rather than as a fundamental and universal phenomenon intrinsic to motion. Friction becomes tractable (diSessa, 1982).

Where Do Changes in Theories Come From?

It turns out that Darlene's approach to the dynaturtle is in keeping with her characteristic style of working with Logo. We can learn more about Darlene from Dan Watt's case description in Part III of the Brookline report (Papert et al., 1979).

Her work was characterized by a large number of short projects, usually involving attractive geometric designs. She very quickly learned a few key ideas in Logo programming and applied these ideas over and over again in similar projects. She tended to reject suggestions that led to longer, more involved projects. Darlene had a lot of curiosity about the Logo language, its commands and error messages. She often carried out "experiments" to test the limits of the language. Darlene had a desire to be self-sufficient in her work. She did not like to ask for help.

What emerges is a distinct tendency to experiment for herself and to avoid suggestions from others. Details from the original notes made by observers on the project make the point clearly.

Session 4 :   Darlene created STAIRS by messing about.
Session 5 :   Darlene was "playing" while exploring different sizes for cat's ear.
Session 6 :   Right before the end, she "fooled around" with FORWARD 90 RIGHT 40 FORWARD 90 RIGHT 40 etc. She called all her old procedures for the purpose of piling them one on top of the other.
Session 9 :   Toward the end of the period Dan Watt showed her recursion with a poly procedure; she didn't seem too interested.
Session 15 :   Darlene resisted suggestion that she make subprocedures, even though she had 63 steps in her castle procedure.
Session 21 :   Darlene just "played around" today.

Darlene had a strong feeling for learning by messing about in her own way, sticking with what she knew in a very determined manner until she was ready to accept help and move forward.

An initial conservative stance should not cause surprise. It is exactly what would be predicted by the schema-invocation theory, which proposes that already existing knowledge structures are mobilized as part of making sense of new experience. All of us, young and old, try very hard to fit new experience into our existing mental framework. Rather than being reorganized in a radical way, the existing schema may be changed by small modifications to allow new experience to be assimilated. As Piaget (1936) said, "Assimilation is the prime fact of mental life." Kuhn (1962) has pointed out that scientists also try to fit new data into the theories and beliefs they already hold: "Normal science, for example, often suppresses fundamental novelties because they are necessarily subversive of its basic commitments." Scientists tend to stay within the accepted scientific paradigm, bending, extending, and otherwise modifying their existing theories in order to accommodate new data.

The tendency to hold on to our current explanations, beliefs, theories, and ways of doing things arises not out of stubbornness or stupidity, but out of the way the cognitive system works. The existing know-how is there to do the job, and it is there because it has worked in the past. Not to take the essential conservatism of the human cognitive system seriously enough is to court disappointment. *The important thing is to learn how to use past experience flexibly*, and this takes time. Making substantial changes is no mean task. This is especially true if our aim is to change significant schemas. What I am proposing is that some schemas are more entrenched than others, reflecting their importance to the integrity of the system. The idea is that these *privileged mental schemas* are enduring, while the peripheral ones are more readily changed. Especially entrenched are those that have explanatory value, that is, schemas that we use to explain others. The extent to which such privileged schemas participate in many explanations is a measure of the degree to which they endure.

For example, the *pushing schema* -- a body moves when it is pushed -- is a pervasive explanatory schema (Figure 8.4). Another example is the *to-and-fro* fragment that participates in many schemas, both as a feeling experience (rocking to-and-fro) and as a visual experience (a pendular movement across the line of vision). Bower (1979) has presented evidence that very young infants expect a to-and-fro movement of an object to continue -- they move their eyes in anticipation of the next movement and show surprise when the object does not arrive at the place it should. At a higher level, the set of schemas that constitutes the individual's sense of self is particularly important and enduring.

We can change such enduring schemas only by repeatedly challenging their explanatory value. And this is what happens in the artifactual world we have been discussing. A conflict is created when the standard pushing schema becomes conspicuously inadequate as a basis for predicting what will happen in the artifactual dynaworld. The claim being made is that the schema is changed not because of what the student has been told, but because she is repeatedly confronted with evidence of its inadequacy during her messing about and because her attempts at reconciling the conflict break down.

The reconciliation process is complex and subtle. When I talk about "changing a schema," I don't mean replacing it. There is evidence that old schemas remain around, attached to old explanatory sequences. New explanations become added on to these old schemas in ways that are not well understood. One can see this well in times of stress, when people fall back into previous ways of looking at things. Several kinds of explanations coexist and are mobilized for different purposes.

If this view is correct, it has strong consequences for education and especially for teacher training. With so much conservatism around, how does change ever take place? It is naive to think that just by writing a few Logo programs, a teacher will lose the old attitudes about teaching and learning that have guided her in the past. These are too deeply entrenched in the sense I have been discussing, in that they control the way she sees and does things. What will push the system to change its stored knowledge? The major point to make is the need to provide time for the kind of confrontation I have been talking about, time for the learner of whatever age to work through this conservative-assimilation phase, this attempt to keep the old ideas (see Chapter Twenty).

Messing About and Knowledge Construction

> *Practical experience also shows that direct teaching of concepts is impossible and fruitless. . . . The existence of associations, however numerous and however strong, between verbal symbols and objects is not in itself sufficient for concept formation.*
>
> *Vygotsky,* 1934

Messing about, play-like access provides the incubation period necessary for this confronting process. The experience can bring to the surface the often unconscious reasoning processes that lie behind the beliefs held by the learner, some of which will need updating to accommodate the new experience. Messing about is presumed to be an in-between stage of understanding, during which pieces from other contexts can be mobilized via the schema-invocation mechanism and used in the construction of a new understanding. Tracking down the steps in this process can be exceedingly difficult. We often see messing about in a Logo context, where the student rehearses old procedures, trying them out in different combinations, looking at the code, running the procedures one on top of the other without clearing the screen, and the like.

It was interesting to observe a transient messing about, apparently aimless phase, in what was the otherwise very planned behavior of Brookline student Donald. Details from the original records described his emerging competence.

Session 2 : Donald had a clear idea of writing a procedure.
Session 3 : He suggested the name BOXPYRAMID for the superprocedure, because "it's a pyramid made from boxes".
Session 6 : Donald supplied the essential idea that a circle could be made by repeating RIGHT 20 FORWARD 20.

Then the tone changed, describing an apparent regression to an earlier level in which he programmed in direct mode.

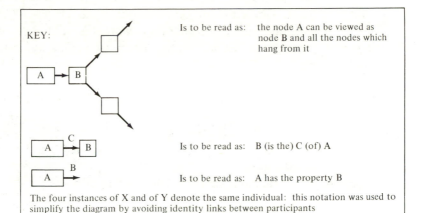

KEY:

Is to be read as: the node A can be viewed as node B and all the nodes which hang from it

A ▶ B

Is to be read as: B (is the) C (of) A

Is to be read as: A has the property B

The four instances of X and of Y denote the same individual: this notation was used to simplify the diagram by avoiding identity links between participants

agent of X

PUSHING

patient of Y

CAUSE

X   agent of   event of   result of   agent of Y

COLLIDES WITH ──precedes──▶ WITHDRAWS–FROM [a]

Y   patient of   patient of X

part of   EVENT-SEQUENCE   part of

X   agent of

APPROACH ──precedes──▶ IMPACT [b]

Y   patient of

a Constraint: if preimpact speed of X < twice post–impact speed, try triggering schema
b Constraint: if duration of contact > 0.2 s, then noncausal

Figure 8.4   Pushing Schema

Session 8: Donald worked for a long time with direct commands today making a city skyline. The teacher intervened, suggesting that he make different sized buildings and then combine them. Donald made one subprocedure, LITTLE ⊓, but then switched to experimenting with his old BOX and TRI procedures. By the end of the class he was trying to draw a face.

The entries in Donald's own notebook as he ended the sessions reflect his own view of the matter.

Session 8: I didn't do much today but tested, but next time I am going to make a man.
Session 9: I was making a man and I am doing good.

For the next twelve sessions, Donald programmed this one project. He had found a topic that lent itself to be broken down into parts, that suited his strong feeling for structured programming (see Chapter Eleven).

A Matter of Self-Confidence

Individuals differ in just how much messing about they engage in, in the way they mess about, and in their reaction to help offered. There is often a great deal of falling back on the familiar. Often the first few steps of the solution are well understood, and thereafter, each time a new step involves uncertainty, the student *starts over again*, does the part that is understood once again, and then tries to move forward from there. Deborah was a Brookline project student, described by her teachers as a slow learner. The Logo teacher Dan Watt (Papert et al., 1979) observed that her patience in one-step-at-a-time operations was quite remarkable. Her format was quite stereotyped.

1. Carry out one turtle step (turn, move or penup).
2. Check to see if it looks right on the screen.
3. If so, write down the step on paper, and continue.
4. If not, clear the screen, retype all the steps previously written down, and try another choice for the questionable one.

The important thing is that this sequence was hers. She invented it, she was in control of it, and she understood it. We may not think much of her method of problem-solving, but with respect to that method she was an expert. During the period in which she used that method, she did not need to ask any one about the next step. She knew what came next in the problem-solving process. Her view of her own problem-solving ability was replete with self-confidence. "I know what I'm doing" was her response to help offered at this stage.

This surefootedness represented a complete turn about from her timid approach at the start of the Logo project. At an early research project meeting we had discussed what Dan Watt could do about Deborah's extreme dependence on his attention. "If she had her way, she would have me sit next to her all lesson, regardless of the needs of the others in the class." The recommendation to Dan was to engage in "supportive silence." He was to remain very friendly, but not continue to be the driver in the interaction, the initiator of the activity.

For the first lesson of this new regime, Deborah sat motionless in front of the computer, waiting to see who blinked first. And Dan Watt, being the wonderful teacher he is, persevered in his plan. Gradually she ventured forth into the unknown. Gradually she allowed herself to type in commands, to continue beyond this move to the next without the permission of the instructor. It took until her eighth Logo lesson to develop enough confidence to use the ENTER key required at the end of each line of instructions, without first obtaining the instructor's permission. From that point on, she explored with two commands, FORWARD 30 and RIGHT 30, achieving a wide range of successful drawings with only these two commands. It was her strategy for survival in a hostile world. Later she expanded somewhat into some of the other available possibilities, but at no stage did she use a great number of commands (see Brookline Report Part III: Papert et al., 1979). Yet the work she did during this period was the first school work she had ever wanted to show her parents. When interviewed by Turkle two years later, it was clear that control had remained a central issue for Deborah (Turkle, 1984). Her concern took a different form. Now, at 13, she thought about things like controlling her temper, her eating, her smoking. She no longer had easy access to the computer, and she chose not to compete against the crowd of talented programmers who mono-polized the machines.

Fear of Failure: Learned Helplessness

The view an individual has of her own competence can play an enormously important role in the kinds of achievement goals she sets for herself, the way she responds to the challenge of learning new things, and the degree of persistence she shows in the face of obstacles. The view she has of herself may be only partly related to her actual ability (Dweck and Bempechat, 1980). Some students see intelligence as something to achieve, something they can increase through their own efforts. These students adopt learning goals appropriate to achieving this improvement -- Dweck's *mastery approach*. Other students see intelligence as an entity or trait that one either has or does not have. These students choose performance goals that fit this belief, the *entity* view of the nature of intelligence. They chose goals that will help to show how smart they perceive themselves to be; or goals that will help hide how stupid they believe they are, so as to avoid a negative judgment. In the face of obstacles, such a student will collapse into *helplessness* (Dweck and Bempechat, 1980).

For girls in particular, a negative relationship often exists between actual ability and performance expectations, so that the more able girls may be the ones who are most likely to underestimate their skills, overestimate task difficulty, and adopt excessively high performance standards.

Examples of negative performance expectancies occur often in the Logo classroom, highlighted by the particular emphasis on user control. Several of the individual profiles in Part III of the Brookline report illustrate this phenomenon. With Deborah, it seemed, we had a marked degree of Dweck's learned helplessness. A second Brookline student, Ray, attended the school learning center for his learning disability. He gave the impression of "having a strong fear of failure, and had adopted a coping strategy of playing the class clown, particularly concerned with not letting anyone know he was trying." He rarely wrote things down, and when asked to consult a reference sheet or an entry in his notebook, "he would usually just sit, and wait for help." These comments from his records are typical of the effect that such a student has on a teacher: "In the next class the teacher again spent a great deal of time with Ray" -- the same refrain heard with respect to Deborah, a prototypical example of fearfulness.

The problems that arise when fear is engendered in relation to meeting entirely new material, then, are part of the story of fear of exposure, of making mistakes, the fear of failure. The major contribution Papert has made is to set up the possibility of breaking into this pervasive cycle of helplessness, creating the opportunity for independent activity. In Deborah's case, she was able to create for herself her own simplified world by limiting the number of commands she chose to use. A useful move in the classroom is to set these boundaries in a systematic way by giving the individual a computational environment in which she feels safe because the world is friendly and the material comprehensible to her. This friendliness is not only a matter of being surrounded by kind, supportive people. Also and most importantly, the structure of the learning situation must take a particular form that supports self-control, self-monitoring, and self-growth. The on-going feedback in an interactive computer environment can provide the context for this to happen. The student can see just how well she is doing and engage in the struggle to get things working in an explicit way. She can understand as much as she needs to in order to stay in control. In the right world, we can all be creative artists; we can all compose! *A microworld is safe and productive for a particular user when it is understood to the point of allowing that user to make predictions in it.* In effect, the student can say:

> Sure it is O.K. to make a mistake, not only because you, the adult in power, say so, but because I, the young learner, feel and know it to be so, because I understand what's going on -- because I can *handle* the mistakes, I can *work* through them. I can be driven by my purposes and not yours. My purposes lead to my rewards, as they do in my street games. My reward can be linked to and emerge out of what I am doing. All this is fine, provided I believe that I can be the agent of my own progress. Putting me into a Logo environment and letting me get on with it is enough only provided *I can see myself in that kind of role*, provided I see my "smartness" increasing in line with my expectations, because I can exploit that famous feedback as part of my mastery view of activity. I might even give it the riveting attention, the lack of awareness of the passage of time that is characteristic of the dedicated computer programmer -- the *hacker*.

But this falling into place is not automatic, and in my experience, it is not happening in many Logo classes at the present time. There are too many socially ingrained attitudes that affect the way children view themselves and the way they view the acquisition of knowledge. Furthermore, the role of the teacher is crucial. If teachers believe in the entity theory of intelligence and judge their students either to have or not to have what it takes to achieve intellectually, their students will get that message and tend to behave accordingly.

As we watch the ways in which students react to the challenge of new ideas and their differing responses to the help they are offered, we come to appreciate some of the powerful emotional influences on learning: the blocks and inhibition of learning that come from a lack of self-confidence and a negative self-image; and the positive effects of an environment that supports self-control for the user. Designing such an environment is considered in detail in the next two chapters.

Chapter Nine

BUILDING GOOD ARTIFACTS THAT STRUCTURE MESSING ABOUT

Messing about sounds like the aimless trying of this and that. But the inventor of the artifact can see to it that this trying-out will be anything but aimless. A basic design principle is to isolate components that are crucial to an understanding of the domain, components that will be used repeatedly, and to incorporate these as primitive actions in the microworld. This means that the structures that get built up as programs will tend to correspond both to the structure of the tasks in the domain and to the key elements in the student's mental representations of these tasks. I look at the possibility of doing this for the language arts curriculum, using the idea of a visual narrative.

The Important Ideas in a Subject Domain

When Papert makes the claim that Logo was invented for learning, he is not referring to a package of *teaching* materials, nor does he have in mind simply a package of materials for *learning*, although these packages could certainly be one of the visible products of the enterprise. The task is to match computational learning environments to the conceptual organization of a subject domain and to a pedagogic theory. What knowledge is needed to build such a microworld? Computer expertise alone is not the answer. Teaching expertise alone is not the answer. There is a third component whose contribution will make all the difference, and this is subject matter expertise. The idea is to provide the means for creating sets of powerful primitives, each set being chosen to support a specific microworld in which the activities of a particular subject area can easily be performed. The user who has an interest in this subject, then, can build her own tools out of these primitives so as to get something done in that area. The tools required to facilitate progress in that subject correspond to the central concepts in that subject. Marrying these important ideas to imaginative computer possibilities requires an interdisciplinary effort.

As has already been pointed out, there is no requirement that the computer-based situation be a real-world simulation. Indeed, the whole point has been *to make the artifact different in principled ways* by isolating the basic components of the activity so as to enhance learning. In turtle geometry, the basic components of the navigating activity are forward moves and turns. The separation of turning from moving forward constitutes a crucial initial step. Notice the effect of this separation. Executing a curved movement need be no more complicated than executing a movement in a straight line. To make a circle, all you need to do is to move forward a very little way, turn a very little bit, move forward a little again. Keep the size of the forward step and the size of the turn constant, and you will get a smooth curve, an arc of constant curvature. diSessa (1980) cites the turtle geometric description of a circle as an example of an important notion in physics: the laws of nature are both local and differential (piece by piece).

```
FORWARD <any small distance>
RIGHT <any small angle>
REPEAT
```

The small local change, repeated many times, is the idea to focus on.

In the dynaworld, several features differ from those present in the real world. The absence of friction has already been discussed in Chapter Eight. A second difference involves an analytic step. In contrast to the continuous control that exists in the real world where we can kick and turn at the same time, there is a separation of turns and kicks in the dynaworld, a separation of the two components of velocity. There is an operator to change the direction of the moving turtle, and an operator to give it a kick. Without the separation, we would lose analytic power. This is illustrated in the case of a problem involving circular motion, where the change in the direction of motion is continuous rather than discrete. White (1981) has shown that students have a great deal of difficulty with this kind of problem.

The components we separate are those that will be used repeatedly, and they are the ones that are crucial to an understanding of the domain. This will mean that the structures that get built up as programs will tend to correspond to the structure of the tasks in the domain. diSessa's achievement is to have found a way to build a computational environment that incorporates as primitive actions the fundamental ideas of Newtonian dynamics. Other environments are suggested by his more recent work (diSessa, 1983), in which he has described other typical explanatory notions in physics, for example, the idea of getting-longer getting-shorter, repeated many times, embodied in a spring.

But the idea is not simply to make a clever computer environment. The intention is that, gradually, the primitives that the educator has implemented will come to correspond to *privileged mental schemas* in the minds of the learners interacting with the computational environment, will come to constitute the key elements in their mental representations of the domain. diSessa (1983) uses the term *p-prim* (phenomenological primitive) to describe such an explanatory schema. As educators we need to become aware of typical collections that students carry around and to develop ways of constructing learning environments that both build on such schemas and reveal their weaknesses. This echoes the Piagetian notion: *It is the conflict generated by the use of inappropriate schemas that reveals the way in which these schemas need to be expanded, refined, and reformulated. Old explanations are displaced or added to by new components.* A good computational environment is one that embodies a large number of privileged schemas, both those that you want the child to have and those she already has that you want to mobilize for the purposes of moving forward her understanding.

Many of the subjects that form the traditional curriculum take the form of a story -- the story of the earth, of the people who have lived on the earth, of animal development -- in addition to the more obvious story understanding and story production that forms the major part of a language arts curriculum. The question for us is how can we cultivate expertise in this kind of subject area.

Stories That Matter

> *To see a World in a Grain of Sand*
> *And a Heaven in a Wild Flower,*
> *Hold Infinity in the palm of your hand*
> *and Eternity in an hour"*
>
> *William Blake*, Auguries of Innocence (1803)

My attempt begins with a widening of the notion of *privileged schema* to embrace schemas with a broader content than the purely cognitive, in particular, to include schemas that are privileged because of the central role they play in the *social, cultural,* and *affective* life of the individual. Much of the unique flavor of an individual's stored past experience comes from the parts of her culture that she has internalized, and this cultural identification plays a major role in the kinds of stories she invents, in the meanings she projects onto her Logo drawings. Here is an example of a culturally rich early Logo experience that makes the point. The writer is Jose Duran, enrolled at the time (1983) as a Fellow with the Community Fellows Program at the Massachusetts Institute of Technology. This is a one-year mid-career research fellowship available to members of minorities -- Black or Hispanic -- who have distinguished themselves in community leadership and development endeavors.

> First I learned to draw a square. Then I learned: TO ARCRIGHT (and ARCLEFT), TO PETAL, TO FLOWER, TO RAY, TO SUN, TO RECTANGE, and TO FLAG.
>
> While drawing the sun and the flower, I was reminded of a similar scene on a pillow my mother had embroidered for me when I was a child. It had a sun, some flowers, and a windmill. I decided to define another procedure: TO WINDMILL. This was easy to do by combining certain procedures I'd been learning along the way. My computer program now had the following scene added to its memory bank which I called DUTCH HAPPY DAY. Then it struck me that I had added a "cultural" symbol to the picture and it took on a special meaning beyond the wonderful memory of my mother's embroidered pillow case (which was a pleasant experience all its own). I am currently working on depicting a "list" of bilingual procedures.
>
> I've created a symbol that resembles a mouth: TO "HABLAR" (talk) and an ear: TO "ESCUCHAR" (listen); when I combine these two procedures, I create: TO "PLATICAR" (converse). For this I combine the lips and ears but I also add a dining room table, coffee, PAN DULCE (Mexican pastry), and DOS COMADRES (two very close female friends) because TO PLATICAR is a custom of sharing and intimacy, of CONFIANZA: which I would display on the Logo screen as two interlocking hearts depicting the confidence and closeness that this word denotes in the Mexican culture. (Duran, unpublished manuscript)

In this example, one sees the self-conscious projection of a sophisticated adult who wants to foster cultural identification in the education of the children of his displaced culture in the United States; who believes that these are the kinds of issues that should be integral to the solution of the minorities question. In the same spirit, and on a large scale, is the interesting Senegalese computers and education project. The project director writes: "We chose Logo because we wanted an interactive computer language that would allow children to create and to program their own projects according to their own cultural feeling and intuitive thinking" (Sylla, 1985). The strong cultural flavor of the work of these Senegalese Logo teachers was shown in a 1982 television program on Logo, *Talking Turtle*, in the BBC Horizon / PBS Nova series. The pictures of houses the teachers had constructed resembled the round mud houses of the countryside around them (Figure 9.1).

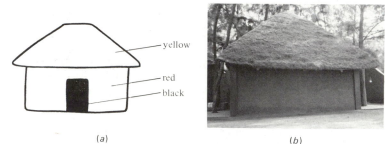

(*a*)   (*b*)

Figure 9.1   (*a*) Logo Drawing of Senegalese Hut.
(*b*) Photograph of a Typical Senegalese Hut
(provided by F. Sylla).

It seems likely that aspects of Logo activity can be used to make schoolwork more meaningful, especially for the population of schoolchildren whose home culture is not the dominant one, so that they can "assume the posture of one who 'has a voice,' who is the subject of his choices," in the words of Paulo Friere (1972). A microworld designed to foster this feature can become a stage on which children of different backgrounds and ethnic cultures can express their own past and that of their cultural group.

Creative Writing on a Word Processor

Providing access to a word processor can enhance personal expression through creative writing, and so encourage cultural individuality. Consider the example of Tina, the Brookline student who saw the computer as her friend (see page 38). The record of Tina's third Logo session reveals her disinterest in turtle geometry. Her dribble file consisted of a line of typing, with an error in it, followed by half a page of new lines where she had typed linefeeds to remove the error from view. "Tina really wants to communicate with the computer. I would like to create a microworld to help her do this -- a simple back-talk type of thing," wrote her teacher, Dan Watt. "Tina is very discouraged by typing errors and seems genuinely offended by the error messages, not surprisingly, since she treats the computer as her friend Peter." During the fourth session, Dan gave her a letter-writing program, which took her step by step through the process of setting up the correct format. She was asked who was to receive the letter, and warned if the name had been used already. Polite messages asked her if she wanted to change anything, and if so which line of the letter did she wish to alter. It turned out that Dan had struck a winning chord. Tina went at the new game with uncharacteristic verve, and produced a series of letters that embodied a rich oral tradition.

Details of how she edited her first draft, changing the vernacular phrase "You doing" to "You are doing," make interesting reading. In her own notebook she had:

How you doing up New **York**

She added "in" while typing the sentence into the computer, obtaining:

HERE IS YOUR LETTER, DORIS.   DEAR DORIS, HOW YOU DOING UP IN NEW YORK.
ENDLOVE LOVE TINA AND PETER.

Next, this was edited to:

HOW ARE YOU DOING UP IN NEW YORK

It seems that the double pass she had over the sentences she had written gave her a chance to recognize the non-standard syntax, acceptable in oral conversation but not in written prose. Note that she used the standard Black English form "You doing," which goes with "right now," to indicate cooccurrence; this contrasts with "You be doing," which would go with "every night," to indicate stretched out time (Dillard, 1972). An interesting outcome of using the text editor and printer is that having one's own production emerge on a printed page provides a distance that makes it easier to adopt the role of reader. With a word-processor, the first effort at composition can become a draft to be edited, rearranged, and improved, and writing can become the *process* that it should be, for the schoolchild as it is for the serious writer (Taylor, 1980). Getting clean copy is a lovely experience, especially for a child whose script is less than tidy. When Tina's work was complete, she used the computer to make as many printed copies as she wanted, each one looking like a professionally typed document. It is hard to get clean copy and polish your prose when your tool is a pen. How many children will undertake the Herculean effort required to change pen and paper writing. The word processor can be thought of as providing a world in which the real-world properties of paper that are not conducive to editing have been left out; properties that require elaborate cutting and pasting, rubbing and crossing out.

In writing a letter Tina regularly asked for spelling and punctuation help. showing a strong commitment to a product that was grammatically correct and in proper form. An interesting change occurred when she shifted from letters to stories. She became less obsessed with spelling and grammar and more concerned with the details of the story: the names of the characters, the places they lived, the sequence of events, and the feelings of the characters involved. My concern is to build settings that will facilitate this transition -- to liberate the student, temporarily, from certain technical issues and allow her to focus on the story as communication: "What am I trying to communicate? What is the logic of the narrative? Will the hearer get what I am saying?" To do this, *I subordinate, temporarily, the use of the word processor to that of the graphic screen.*

From Pictures to Stories

Logo users are constantly confronted with half-formed pictures, incomplete drawings, a few suggestive lines that invite completion, that invite a meaning. When Keith looked at two overlapping circles on the screen, he saw a snowman and proceeded to complete the picture in his "mind's eye," doing what Bruner (1957) called "going beyond the information given." Indeed, much of the joy of Logo is linked to this projection phenomenon that engages the imagination, and it is important to build computer activities whose purpose is to encourage that sort of "seeing." Recall the imaginative leap from picture to story shown by Elly (Chapter Five) as she invented her narrative about swimming and candy. Just as we aspire to cultivate the ability to see "triangles" in geometric figures, so also do we wish to cultivate the art of finding the extra something that Elly sees as her literary imagination is fired by the drawing she makes.

An elaborate story can emerge by combining pictures and words: Elly spoke her words, and they were then recorded for us by her teacher. The example that follows shows us how Chris struggled to get what he wanted and tells us something about the facilities required to encourage this kind of story-telling, to encourage the production of visual narratives.[1]

---

1.   Chris was a student at the Feltham School (see page 24). He was taught by Ann Valente, from whose description this case material is taken.

Chris's words became an integral part of his program -- an example of teacher support that invited visual imagination as part of the story-telling. The prevalence of military elements in Logo stories constructed in the 1980s in the United States bears witness to the truth about culturally determined meanings. I would have preferred a less military example but could not match the spirit of this one!

During the course of his seventh grade Logo work, Chris had been introduced to subprocedures using the familiar example of a program to draw a man:

```
TO MAN
HEAD
BODY
ARMS
LEGS
END
```

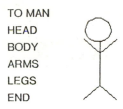

Now in his eighth grade, after several months of Logo experience, Chris retrieved his MAN procedure and set about elaborating it. As he did this, a story began to evolve, and pictures and narrative fed into each other's construction. He added hands and feet to his MAN and varied the perspective, producing profile and front views. He gave each MAN a gun and created a GANG, a lineup of men in profile, each aiming a gun. A second GANG1 sprang into life as the mirror image of the first GANG. The good guys, in GANG, were drawn with a red pencolor, and the bad guys, in GANG1, were depicted in white! With his participants defined, Chris launched on a story that combined text with graphics. He was given a model structure for his story, including, among other things, a hint as to how he could indicate the passage of time, as well as give the viewer a chance to read the words before the screen scrolled on, by writing a wait command that tells the computer to do nothing many times.

```
TO STORY
PRINT some words               TO WAIT :T
MAN                            REPEAT :T []
PRINT some words               END
WAIT 400
PRINT more words
END
```

Using this structure, he created a series of events to constitute a GUNFIGHT.

SHOT shoots lines across the battlefield. After the battle, the bad guys are erased.

```
TO GUNFIGHT
PR [ONCE UPON A TIME THERE WERE FOUR]
PR [BAD GUYS WHO WERE STEALING FROM]
PR [EVERYBODY!!! THERE WERE ALSO FOUR]
PR [GOOD GUYS IN THIS TOWN SO THEY]
PR [CHALLENGED THE BAD GUYS TO A GUN]
PR [FIGHT AT NOON TIME!!!!!! AT THE]
PR [DUST STREET THE BAD GUYS SHOWED UP]
PR [FIRST!!!!]
WAIT
GANG1
PR [AND THEN THE GOOD GUYS!!!!!!]
PU FD 7.5 PD
GANG
PR [THEY YELLED INSULTS BACK AND FORTH]
PR [FOR ALMOST 5 MINUTES!]
PR [THEN A BAD GUY YELLED "YOUR MOTHER]
WAIT1
PR [WEARS ARMY BOOTS!]
PR [THAT DID IT! THE GOOD GUYS OPENED]
PR [FIRE ON THE BAD GUYS!!!!]
WAIT1
REPEAT 2 [SHOT]
PR [THAT ENDED IT! THE BAD GUYS FELL]
PR [TO THE GROUND AND WERE NEVER SPOKE]
PR [OF AGAIN]
WAIT1
PC O
HOME
GANG1
PR [THE END]
WAIT1
END
```

Even though Chris delighted in the exercise, one is struck by the clumsiness of the machinery. So much time is spent on the formatting, the unwieldy syntax, and so forth, that it is hard to retain interest in the construction of a narrative. To support this kind of material, we need an *animation microworld*, described in the next chapter.

Features of a "Good" Computational Environment

We can summarize the features of a "good", that is, well-constructed computational environment.

1. The aim is to incorporate into the microworld principles of subject matter embodied in activities, so that as the learner interacts with environment, she "manipulates" concrete embodiments of the concepts to be learned; she "experiences" the concepts directly, not through language about them.
2. In order to achieve clarity, the microworld often leaves out aspects of the real world. The idea is to juxtapose experience in the real world with experience in the computational world, so that each complements the other.
3. A cluster of activities is made available so that any one concept is met in several different contexts and in different combinations.
4. The activities have a constructive component.
5. It is useful to choose aspects of the environment about which the learner is likely to have intuitions, to have naive theories arising from her "street sense." Such activities invite personal meanings and thus intrinsic motivation, allow subcultural flavors to emerge, stimulate creativity and encourage fantasy, and are just plain fun to do.
6. Activities should cut across disciplines whose separation was historically motivated and is no longer interesting.
7. There should be several levels of formal description, so that a student can move backward and forward from experiential to formal modes of operation.
8. Activities should cater to a range of individual work styles, for example, mobilizing what the student knows through visual means.
9. It is to be expected that there will be some things you CAN'T do easily in any particular microworld.

All this amounts to spelling out what I meant earlier when I referred to "a kind of coherent messing about." The new element that computers bring is to make this easier to do in the sciences in such a way as to make the underlying mechanisms more transparent than they would otherwise be. The dynaworld illustrates another important aspect of this new technology. Logo environments can support both usual classroom activities and some unusual ones, too, and subject matter generally considered too complex to be introduced into a classroom turns out to be readily accessible.

Looking further and deeper, Papert was able to design a system that will help to carry the contemporary expertise of the educational world into the twenty-first century.   This concerns introducing material into the school curriculum usually considered appropriate for much later college level students. (Abelson and diSessa, 1981)

This is in sharp contrast to the view prevailing among many educators that the role of Logo is to get children started, before moving on to "real" languages like BASIC.

Chapter Ten

VISUAL NARRATIVES

Humans possess remarkable abilities to interpret extremely schematic kinetic patterns in causal, affective, and social terms. When kinetic vignettes are combined, viewers often perceive immediate meanings and build elaborate plots around them. This suggests that the activity of building, modifying, and reacting to "visual narratives" might constitute a microworld in which children can learn about a broad range of things, while satisfying their own kinetic aesthetics. The hope is that this might happen in much the same way that turtle geometry brings mathematics to drawing. Used in combination with word processing facilities, work with kinetic patterns has exciting interdisciplinary possibilities. An emphasis on evoking the individual's own personal scenarios allows personal meanings to emerge and serves to mobilize emotional commitment and thereby learning potential.

The Content of Stories: Emotions as Knowledge Mobilizers

A crucial element in a story is the cast of characters. Introducing *animate participants* brings a vitality to the story. Tina's letters were about people, their doings, relationships, and feelings (pages 101 and 134), and both Elly (page 55) and Chris (page 104) tell stories about people and their activities. The gang-fight scenario described in the previous chapter includes a whole world of detail: a set of characters, a series of actions linked into successive events. To generate a story like this, a student needs to access information about typical protagonists in the story, their ways of behaving, their feelings and beliefs. Such information is stored in a complex of schemas called *scripts* by Schank and Abelson (1977).[1] Typically scripts deal with sequences of events. For example, a *restaurant script* might consist of an ordered sequence of standard activities or events such as entering the restaurant, ordering from the menu, eating, paying, and leaving. Scripts provide the skeleton structure of the story, available to both author and reader, so familiar that components can be omitted, assumed, or referred to obliquely.

Central to this idea of a script is a cast of stock characters, the *dramatis personae* of the story, social stereotypes containing definite motifs that crop up everywhere in the myths and fairy tales, the archetypes of world literature, where social reality meets art. Chall writes, "My own personal content preference for first and second graders is folk tales and fairy tales. They have universal appeal" (1967). Much of the significance of these themes derives from the feelings attached to them.

> We are made familiar with the vocabulary of emotion by association with *paradigm scenarios* drawn first from our daily life as small children, later reinforced by the stories and fairy tales to which we are exposed, and, later still, supplemented and refined by literature and art. (de Sousa, 1980)

These paradigm scenarios, then, reflect experiences that are meaningful for the individual by virtue of private past experience and as part of a shared cultural experience. Not only do they provide the target or occasion, they also provide a set of characteristic responses to the situation, responses that come to be thought of as "having emotions." An essential part of education for the growing individual consists in identifying these responses and giving them their culturally defined names. Hence the importance of encouraging this type of content in the visual narratives being constructed.

The important point to make here is that emotions can play a central role in cognitive processing per se. The emotional context in which something was learned can play a part in deciding the affective color of the new experience and thus the quality of the new learning. We can get a sense of this link between the emotional and the cognitive by looking at the schema-invocation mechanism itself. As mental schemas develop during

---

1.   Minsky (1975) used the term *frame* to refer to complex information structures of this sort.

childhood, descriptions of the feelings and attitudes associated with experience being stored become attached to that schema. Each schema records what Piaget (1936) called "the internal history" of an experience. My account requires that this history include, as central components, descriptions of the affective aspects of the experience. The theory requires that *an emotion is a description of a feeling experience.* The development of complex knowledge structures that link certain actions with attitudes and feelings about those actions allows these *feeling components to participate in the mobilization of knowledge.* If the feeling component of a schema matches the emotional quality of the new experience, that match can form the basis for invoking that schema. *It is because these emotion components of knowledge structures can participate in the schema-invocation process so as to direct attention and guide problem-solving that I want to engage them, to harness them to play an intimate and potentially positive role in the learning situation.*

A good place to start is with language arts activity, where archetypal sequences of cooperation, conflict, or competition can be explored, coloring the story telling with a particular significance as they relate to the things that are important to the student.

The Structure of the Story

The idea is to create an animated cartoon strip, a *visual narrative*, that captures the main participants and events in the story in a skeletal form and highlights the dramatic structure. The stress on simple shapes moving in relation to one another is deliberate to focus on the need to find the most essential features of the story. Later the student can expand this sparse framework, can use the word processor to flesh it out into a full-fledged story. The idea of providing a general story structure as a framework for language activity was used by Andee Rubin in her *Story-maker* project (Rubin, 1980), in which a program gave students hints and guidance in their story writing. In Chapter Five I pointed to the need to look at story comprehension and story generation as an interactive process of bringing meaning to a text as well as getting meaning from the text. A fragment of a story triggers a whole story in the hearer's mind, and a story grammar provides the basis for story generation.

A story structure adapted from Project Read is used by David Ary, a language arts teacher working with learning-disabled children (personal communication). The approach involves:

Identification of characters and their interrelationships.

Identification of plot: episodes, rising action, conflicts, climax, resolution.

Identification of a moral (at a later more sophisticated stage).

Selecting the *key story elements* to be depicted helps to clarify what the story is about and focuses attention on what must be retained so as to maintain communication. In terms of our theory, this means isolating key elements to exaggerate their schema-evoking role, to ensure that the picture contains sufficient triggering elements to evoke the relevant mental schemas. These schemas provide the detail to be projected on to the simple figures, the detail from which the richness of the narrative will emerge -- the essence of the cartoonist's art. The scenarios could be represented by a series of stills, like a cartoon strip, or by a dynamic sequence of events. Preferably, these should be in the form of short single-event sequences that can acquire different meanings depending upon the embedding context; collections of kinetic building blocks that can form an animation tool kit.

Kinetic Sequences

A useful way to begin would be to provide some stock animation sequences for the students to work with. Heider and Michotte used the simplest of interacting shapes, indeed those that form the daily fare of beginner Logo drawings -- squares, circles, triangles -- to invent displays that had immediate meanings for their viewers.

To study how people perceive causality, Michotte (1963) displayed two squares on the screen; the first approached a stationary second square and stopped upon contact; the second one then moved off in the same direction as the first had been traveling. When the movement of the second square followed almost immediately after the arrival of the first at its side, the event was seen as the first object's pushing the second object and causing it to move. The kinetic sequence became a cue that activated a pushing schema, which supplied real-world characteristics, turning mere lines on the screen into objects, both inanimate and animate (see Figure 8.4).

When the movement of these simple shapes in relation to one another was slow, the association was perceived to be "gentle and friendly." Rapid movement on the other hand was interpreted as violent; rapid acceleration after contact, following a fairly slow approach, was perceived as one object's being carried off by the other by brute force. The simple shapes took on rich descriptions and were perceived as participants in complex action sequences. What was seen and believed was fed by what was there, but much more was seen than was given to the senses.

The particular interpretation of any one shape depended on the kinetic context. Some of the interacting shapes were seen as human protagonists, participating in actions, with attributions of intention, motive, and feelings (Michotte, 1950). In a similar vein, Fritz Heider and Marianne Simmel (1944) studied the perception of social interrelations, using a 2.5-minute film sequence in which three geometric figures (large triangle, T; small triangle, t; and circle, c) were shown moving in various directions and at various speeds. A large rectangle, R, was stationary except for a section of its outline, d, that could move "open" and "shut" (Figure 10.1).

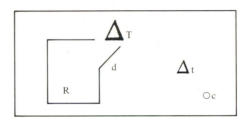

Figure 10.1   Heider–Simmel
Sequence

The interacting shapes were seen as animate objects involved in action-sequences, described as "running toward one another, embracing, pushing each other away or over." Most people saw the triangles as men and the circle as a girl. The attributions were richly detailed, such as referring to the big triangle (T) as the large person, with an aggressive, war-like, angry, dominating personality. Whole stories of aggression and rescue were projected on to the kinetic patterns. Thus, "a man has planned to meet a girl, and the girl comes along with another man . . . the two men have a fight which the larger one wins."

These experiments can form a useful corpus of ideas for creating animation sequences that somehow trigger basic, prototypical action schemas (Weir, 1975, 1978; Kahn, 1979).

To exploit the power of motion as a vehicle for story-telling, we need moving turtles. The sprite Logo extension supports a whole fleet of moving turtles or sprites. Each sprite has a number that acts as its name, so that you can make a sprite appear on the screen by telling it (that is, its number) to adopt a shape and a color. By telling sprite 1 to carry a red ball and sprite 2 to carry a pink face, you can create a scenario about pink faces and red balls. Some shapes come with the system, but you can make your own or change the ones supplied using a shape editor (Figure 10.2). Sprites can be instructed to move at a given speed (SETSPEED 20) in a given direction (SETHEADING 90), so one can have two shapes moving along together, passing one another, moving toward one another, colliding, and so on. Video-game-like primitives called demons can be written that constantly test for particular conditions, for example, a *collision demon* that will be activated when one sprite touches another, so as to initiate the next piece of the action.[2]

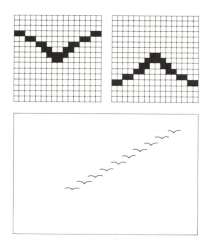

Figure 10.2   Examples of Sprite-Shapes

Classroom Activities

A major goal of the classroom activity I have in mind is to use the animation project as a basis for the development of imaginative communication. The idea is to combine several activities.

1. Teacher-supplied animation sequences will be viewed, described, and analyzed. Students will be asked to suggest modifications, variations, and alternative continuations of these sequences.
2. Students will use animation tool kits to clothe the shapes, to provide a range of background settings, and to create their own sequences. Since any one sequence invites different interpretations, each student can engage in an analysis of what modifications and additions would make her own particular interpretation more compelling for others, to put enough detail into her picture story so

---

2.   Demons come with the system for Atari and Coleco Logo. For other Logo systems, routines that give the desired effect can be written.

that the meaning she sees will be shared by other viewers.

3. These programming activities will be accompanied by the use of a word processor for written descriptions of the visual material. Students will be asked to supply language descriptions to flesh out the shapes: adjectives and adverbs to describe the movements, the characters, and their interactions.

Let's look at an example of the use of a teacher-prepared sequence. In a preliminary exploration, David Ary and I prepared a sprite implementation of a fragment of the Heider-Simmel film. The sequence opens with the large triangle in the rectangle at lower left center stage; the small triangle and circle enter together from the upper right corner; they stop, do a circular dance, after which the little triangle moves down the right side of the screen, "exploring"; upon its return, the door to the square opens, and the large triangle emerges, approaches the smaller one and makes several jerky movements in its direction. The action ends at this point. Ary showed this sequence to a number of children (11 to 13 years) and adults, either singly or in pairs. Viewers were asked to describe what they saw. A few immediately referred to the animation sequence as a story. Others needed prompting. Interpretations came in many forms, hesitantly at first or excited outpourings from the start. Requests for repeated viewings were common. Viewing in pairs provided a particularly fruitful situation.

Several plots were suggested. One proposal contained a combination of two themes: a ball game and a bully on the block. A boy brings his ball in, checks out the neighborhood to find friends to play with, and then the bully comes out to take the ball away. When asked how the story could continue, resolution of the conflict was proposed: "They all make friends and get on with the game." A second suggestion concerned a theft of jewels, interrupted by the FBI. Alternative continuations were proposed: in one, the thief was arrested and put in jail; in the other, the thief got away with the loot. In another vein altogether, a space journey rendezvous was suggested for the theme of the story. There was a tendency to think of the triangles as the active agents and the circle as the passive object in the episodes. The characters were labeled as appropriate to the plot:

The *big triangle* was called: the big triangle, me, the FBI, a spaceship.
The *small triangle* was called: the small triangle, the turtle, a thief, my younger brother, a spaceship.
The *circle* was called: a ball, my youngest brother, the loot, a planet.
The *rectangle* was called: the box, a space station, a jail, Mr. Ary, a whale.

In summary, the attractions of a microworld of kinetic scenarios are many.

1. This kind of fantasy involvement can serve as a powerful intrinsic motivator.
2. It mobilizes intuitions, building on previous personal experience.
3. The content of the activity spans both the sciences and the arts, a desirable feature of a learning environment.
4. It exploits the power of the computer as tool. It would be much harder to do this kind of thing without the computer.
5. It allows the student to come to language activity via the visual mode; for some children this could enhance their chances of making academic progress.

Motion Microworlds

Motion as a topic of study is especially powerful for using the computer to integrate traditional subject matters. We have seen how, in a language arts context, one can develop ideas of dramatic tension, plot lines, etc., using visual narratives. Getting two objects to move in relation to one another involves exploring the mathematics and the physics of relative motion in a way that appeals directly by inviting everyday meanings. Visual narratives could be a good area for activities around social study topics (interpersonal relations) or for an enterprising art teacher to explore as a medium in which to develop imaginative scenarios that combine graphic and text facilities, mobilizing what the student knows through visual means.

Motion has been a productive interdisciplinary theme for a fifth-grade class in the Headlight project (see page 37). It has served to integrate the use of the computer with regular classroom materials such as text, manipulatives, and film. Demonstrations and analysis of the concept of relative motion, discussions on aggression and gender, motion constructions using rubber bands, balloons, and Lego alternated with computer-based simulations of movement. The Heider film of moving shapes inspired the creation of computer-based storybooks for first graders that combined text and animated illustrations.

It could be especially advantageous to use a visual approach to story-telling with students whose reading and writing skills one wishes to improve. The power and the flexibility of the computer allows us to tailor the learning environment to the working style of the student. This is the subject of the next chapter.

Chapter Eleven

LOGO AND INDIVIDUAL WORKING STYLE

A student's classroom behavior can reflect a mixture of her naturally preferred ways of working and the techniques and strategies she has acquired in the classroom. When Logo is used by teachers whose teaching practice is compatible with Logo philosophy, the individual student is encouraged to choose what to do and how to do it. Under these circumstances, a student is able spontaneously to adopt her preferred problem-solving style more readily than is the case under didactic teaching conditions. When students are allowed to work in this way, a wealth of detail about quite divergent styles of working can be observed.

In this Chapter, we look at differences in style of working along several dimensions: preferred mode of representing information; amount of planning engaged in; patterns of attention and emotional engagement; and speed and accuracy of processing. These differences are not independent of one another: particular features tend to cluster together in ways that bear a strong resemblance to the descriptions emerging in recent work on brain-behavior correlations.

Preference for Spatial Problem-solving

Some people lean heavily on pictorial representations; others recognize problems by their linguistic labels and descriptions. Several examples of perceptual problem-solving have been described. Keith and Franky (see Chapter Four) both reveled in the possibility provided by Logo to do spatial

115

problem-solving. "I eye it," said Keith, and he knew what number to use. A similar facility was evident in Franky's work. Estimating half the distance, without dividing by two, was how he proceeded to get the number he needed. This perceptual computation is discussed in more detail in Chapter Twelve. Here we note that a preference for spatial problem-solving is by no means restricted to students with problems. Many talented mathematicians show this mode of thinking. Hadamard, in his *The Psychology of Invention in the Mathematical Field* (1945), describes his own case: "The help of images is absolutely necessary for conducting my thought. . . . I insist that words are totally absent from my mind when I really think." He quotes a letter from Einstein: "The words or the language, as they are written or spoken, do not seem to play any role in my mechanism of thought. The psychical entities which seem to serve as elements in thought are certain signs and more or less clear images which can be voluntarily reproduced and combined" (Hadamard, 1945).

In a similar vein, Freeman Dyson describes the physicist Richard Feynman: "The reason Dick's physics was so hard for ordinary people to grasp was that he did not use equations. The usual way theoretical physics was done since the time of Newton was to begin by writing down some equations and then to work hard calculating solutions of the equations. . . . Dick just wrote down the solutions out of his head without ever writing down the equations. He had a physical picture of the way things happen, and the picture gave him the solutions directly with a minimum of calculation" (Dyson, 1979).

Flair for Rapid Mental Calculation

During the course of their math activity, some children carry out quite complicated processes without consciously recognizing what it is they are doing. They cannot give an account of this unconscious computation, and become flustered when pressed for details. For example, in answer to the query, "What fractions are equal to one over two (1/2)?" John rapidly generated the sequence: two over four (2/4), four over eight (4/8), eight over sixteen (8/16). When asked how he arrived at these numbers, he replied, "I don't know." "Well then," said the teacher, "let's figure out how you did that." "Oh, no, please don't!," came the reply, "I'll get all messed up in my head."

Such a lack of introspective awareness has consequences for learning. When an individual is unaware of the steps in the problem-solving process she uses, she is likely to have *difficulty in incorporating the suggestions of others into that process*. It is difficult for her to use the help her teachers provide. Acceptance of help takes the form of asking for a specific piece of information, but not for the detailed explanation that good teaching would seem to require. As the explanation begins, her eyes glaze over, and she appears disinterested and inattentive. So she is judged to be mindlessly asking for help without thinking things through. She is judged to be a shallow thinker, when, some of the time at least, the problem is just the opposite: *her thinking is too deeply buried in her unconscious to be accessible to the debugging process.* Indeed, the relative difficulty she has in assimilating advice seems to be a question of lack of access to her own procedural control structures. This is connected to the question of planning.

Planner Versus Non-planner

The Brookline report (Papert et al., 1979) provided a classic description of a planner style of working in the student Donald, who programmed the FACE (see Chapter Eight and Figure 11.1).[1] At each stage of the process, Donald would retire from the computer and plan ahead what his next steps would be, as a matter of preference. His notebook shows much evidence of this working ahead.

First Plan   Revised Plan

Figure 11.1   Donald's Face

---

1.   The Brookline report made a distinction between *top-down* and *bottom-up* problem-solving, but the terms *planner* and *non-planner* more accurately describe what is going on.

In contrast, Kevin was not especially given to advance planning. Instead, he went ahead and worked things out as he needed them, trying things out, tinkering rather than planning. He liked building up complex designs from single pieces he had made, trying out various arrangements until he found one he liked, and showing great facility in controlling the turtle in the process.   More recent experience has confirmed the widespread occurrence of these two styles of working. For example, Chris, a sixth grader, was much more interested in making eye-catching designs than in drawing objects.   No planning here, no sitting down and making a preliminary analysis of the structure of a large project, breaking it up into simpler, do-able parts. Rather, he would try out things, synthesizing larger structures out of the elements he deemed suitable, using the repeat command to make designs from the simple shapes he had already defined. Noteworthy was his excitement and energy.   He was impulsive in his choices and enthused by the results of his work on the screen.   Contrast this with Dana, a slow methodical worker, who discovered subprocedures and went on to plan a superprocedure "apartment" composed entirely of subprocedures, involving a careful analysis of the whole into parts.

I have been struck by how often one sees different approaches to the same problem. Here is an example. Dick and Matthew both tackled the problem of drawing a three-dimensional square. Dick worked directly on the screen, "eyeing" his drawing to see what number would turn the turtle so that the oblique line joining the front and back faces of the cube would come out right: "You need to mess about till you get it," he commented in a matter-of-fact self-confident way. It emerged that he was good at deciding when things line up, but not so good at choosing the right numbers to get there. A few days later I came across Matthew, pencil and notebook in hand, working away at the same problem, but in *his* way: "You need to figure out the angles first," was his explanatory remark to me as I looked on, "otherwise it won't come right." And he proceeded to calculate ahead the amount needed to turn the turtle so as to compensate for the 45 degree turn that he had used to get the same oblique line. For all his drawing projects, he made preliminary drawings on a grid of squares which he used to precalculate the numbers he would need for each turtle instruction.

Another lesson I learned while watching a class of sixth graders at work, was that what starts off as a try-it-out approach can turn into a planned approach as the activity generates its own subgoals. This is what happened. I have long been an advocate of turning off the "wrap-around" feature of Logo, which allows the turtle to go off one edge and reappear at a point on the opposite side (see Figure 11.2a).

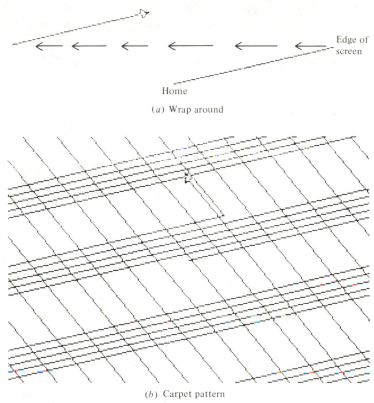

(*a*) Wrap around

(*b*) Carpet pattern

Figure 11.2   Playing with Wrap Around

The effect is a spectacular but not easily analyzable pattern on the screen and, in my experience, has tended to produce a sort of mindless screen-filling, a kind of dead-end "ooh! ahh!" activity, with no particular learning going on, or so it seemed to me. Consequently, I was a little uneasy when this screen-filling turned out to be a favorite activity among the children in a recent project. However, a pair of these children have proved me wrong. Having produced an interesting variegated stripy pattern, "That's a carpet!" (Figure 11.2b), they set about calculating how to repeat the pattern.

As was usual in this game, the trick was to turn the turtle so that it points off the vertical, and then send it FORWARD a large number of steps. On the principle that the larger the number the more spectacular the effect, they had used inputs of 9999 to their commands. As they looked back over the numbers they had selected, they became dissatisfied with the RIGHT 9999. They discovered that large numbers as input to the turn commands simply sent the turtle round and round and, rather than adding to the interest, tended to engender confusion. This led to a discussion about the number that would send the turtle around once, and the number of 360's that go into 9999, and what the remainder means, and there we were into modular (periodic) arithmetic.[2]

Attention Span

In Chapter Four, I described how Keith's usual distractibility disappeared during the half hour he worked with Logo. For Lisa, a bouncy and talkative 8-year-old, Logo provided a similarly attention-holding experience. She was excited and impressed by using the computer, which she approached with a non-planner style. She was provided with a single-key version of Logo that requires less typing and makes it easier for young students to concentrate on the conceptual aspects of the activity (see page 55). Lisa became engrossed and fascinated with moving the turtle and, in contrast to her usual wandering attention, was very focused during this work.

   This effect on attention span is a pervasive finding. Over and over again I hear the same story from Logo teachers: "When I discuss a Logo pupil with his regular teacher, you would think we were talking about two different children. She talks about how noisy and difficult he is in the class, his short attention span, and his poor performance; and I talk about this charming productive, intelligent student who spends weeks on end exploring one situation." Typically, such a child shows absorbed attention, can't wait to get on the computer, and loathes to stop when it is time for the next student to use the machine.

   However, I have observed an interesting quality to this engrossed absorption in a small proportion of these children. Yes, they find computing wonderful. Yes, they spend much more time on a task than they do in any other class. But during the course of a single session they can change focus frequently. Thus, a pair will come into class and announce they would be writing a program to draw a maze. Five minutes into the session,

---

2.   Using a twelve-hour clock is an example of modular arithmetic where the modulus is twelve, and $6 + 10 = 4$ (mod 12).

a glance at the screen shows they have abandoned the maze and are rapidly changing screen colors. Their attention remains engaged, but their usual distractibility is manifesting itself as a rapid change of goal within the same activity.

Emotional Lability

Another striking feature of the interactions of some children is the amount of overt excitement accompanying their computer work, the amount of near-the-surface emotion. I have already mentioned this in describing Chris: "Noteworthy was his excitement and energy, impulsive in his choices and enthused by the results." There is a kind of intensity in the air. A student will jump around on his chair with delight when things go well. If something doesn't work, he is liable to feel angry with the computer or show anger while complaining that the computer doesn't understand something: "Last year it knew how to circle, and now it doesn't ! "

This lability of affect that the computer situation brings out seems to be related to a tendency to change focus of attention frequently, the distractibility already referred to. Sometimes the emotion is largely disappointment: "Oh, I've goofed! Oh, I'll never learn anything!", accompanied by a depressed slouch. By no means all individuals with these characteristics have trouble with academic work, but when they do, it is difficult to say how much of the emotion is secondary to a very real experience of failure.

Projection on to a Sparse Outline

In addition to her engrossed attention, Lisa's work showed another interesting feature. Although the time-consuming and frustrating task of typing the full commands was removed by having single-key Logo, Lisa did not channel her energy into drawing pre-planned pictures. She preferred moving the turtle randomly and *discovering a picture among the lines* -- a characteristic already observed with Keith and his snowman. Both Lisa and Keith show great readiness to project whole pictures on to Logo fragments.

Projection is present to different degrees in different people. Indeed, the Rorschach personality test is based on this property of projection. Similarly, different individuals engage in different amounts of projection during their Logo work. What an individual projects on to the typical Logo drawing plays a large part in determining her choice of projects and her goals of activity. Some children stress the "it-looks-like" aspect, while for others "figuring-it-out" provides the main pleasure and source of fulfillment.

My clinical impression is that non-planners are more inclined to indulge in large amounts of projection than are planners, and that these children are particularly comfortable working in the spatial mode. Moreover, *once they have projected a picture on to the shape emerging on the screen, they show a certain reluctance to break down that picture into parts.* As part of their non-planning, they do not readily subprocedurize. An example from the Feltham project makes the point.

Julie is an eighth grade girl with cerebral palsy. In her first two Logo lessons she readily engaged in an open-ended exploration of the Logo commands, her projects emerging from the shapes created during this trying-out process. She showed good estimation skills in executing a complicated maze-like pattern. She had been programming in Logo for approximately seven weeks, for two hours each week, when her teacher, Ann Valente, wrote this description of her debugging style.

When she looked at a picture which did not exactly match the one she had in mind, she considered the whole picture as wrong. The picture might contain several parts. Some of the parts were right and others were wrong. She needed a lot of help to find the particular detail which was wrong and to see that, in fact, the rest of the picture was fine. This *inability to focus on just one feature of the whole picture* (my italics) was extremely stressful to Julie, and was interfering with her programming. By the same token, once a command had passed inspection it became absorbed in the mass of code. Her idea of programming was that once a command had been written, it had been added permanently to everything else. Her programs grew in a trial and error fashion. She programmed by accretion. There was no top-level plan. The critical components in her drawing were hidden in the code. She knew how to write subprocedures for each part of her picture. But she was not clear about how to use subprocedures to help her understand the structure of her problem. Each step, whether it was a single command or a positioning procedure, was added on top of whatever she had so far. She had just one way of using subprocedures which was to stick them on at the end. (A. Valente, 1983)

Configurational Approach

What I have referred to as Julie's inability to focus on just one feature of the picture is part of a tendency to see the whole picture as a gestalt, to take a global rather than a piece-by-piece analytic view. This approach can have a powerful effect on the way a student tackles a task, as Anne McDougall discovered during a Logo session with her daughter, Kirsty.[3] They were working from one of Anne's books in which the exercises had been carefully graded to form a learning sequence, thus:

Exercise 1.7: Draw three equilateral triangles arrayed around the turtle's central position, as in Figure 11.3a,
Hint: Turn the turtle 120 degrees after each of the triangles.
Exercise 1.10: Spin some squares about the central position to make an interesting design, as in Figure 11.3b.

Kirsty had no problem with the first exercise, but saw the picture for the next exercise as "a completely different thing." In spite of the carefully planned sequence, and the hints, and Anne's guidance in leading her to draw a square and then rotate it, this very bright student persisted in not seeing the repeated square-and-turn pattern. Instead, she tried to draw the outer contour (Figure 11.3c).

Performance on the Rey-Osterrieth task has been used as a measure of *configurational style* (Waber and Holmes, 1985). The idea is to have a person copy the figure (shown in Figure 11.4a), using a series of different colored pens. Of interest is how the individual organizes the picture for purposes of copying: how she breaks it up into parts and which piece she begins with.

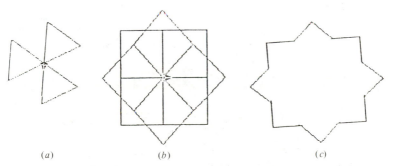

(a)   (b)   (c)

Figure 11.3   Kirsty: Standard Learning Sequence and Configurational Approach

---

3.   Anne McDougall works in the Logo group at Monash University, Australia, and has produced several Logo books. A study of her two daughters as they work with Logo forms the basis of her thesis work.

A typical configurational approach is shown in Figure 11.4b. Notice how the contour and main structures are emphasized. In contrast, the drawing in Figure 11.4c is constructed piecemeal, one part after the next. Further analysis is required to assess the meaning of this configurational style. When it is associated with easy distractibility, where the individual seems to notice everything in the situation, it suggests the presence of parallel processing, a global perception that "takes it all in at once."[4]

In a Logo context, I asked twenty-five students to reproduce the drawing in Figure 11.5a on their computer screens. Several different approaches to the same task emerged: some started with an outer square (Figure 11.5b); some started with an inner cross (Figure 11.5c) or an inner square (Figure 11.5d); and some found a unit by analyzing the figure and wrote a Logo procedure to draw that unit repeatedly (Figure 11.5e).

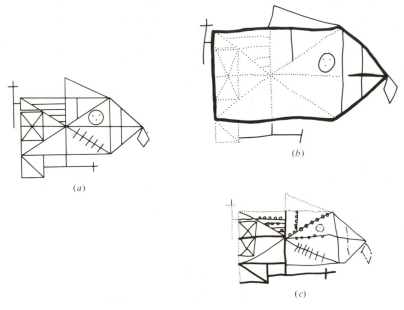

(a)

(b)

(c)

Figure 11.4   Rey–Osterrieth Task

---

4.   This is similar to the work of Witkin and his colleagues (1962) who used a hidden figure task to distinguish between field-dependent individuals, who find it difficult to separate figure from background, and field-independent individuals, who can ignore the irrelevant details to focus on one particular aspect of the situation.

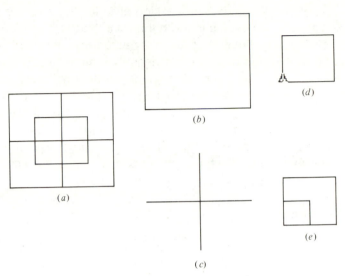

Figure 11.5   Reproducing a Logo Drawing

Mode of Processing and Consciousness

There is good reason to believe that most of our mental processing, thinking as well as feeling, takes place below the level of awareness (Dixon, 1981). It is useful to assume that parallel processing[5] occurs at an unconscious level and that serial processing is accessible to conscious scrutiny, and that all individuals parallel process at an unconscious level for most of the time, and only at particular points in the problem-solving process do parts of the process become conscious and serial. The differences we see between individual problem-solving styles arises in part from where the boundaries between these two processing modes occur, that is to say, individuals differ in the proportion of parallel versus serial processing they use. For example, a flair for rapid mental calculation would imply relatively few of these conscious steps, occurring only toward the end of the problem-solving process. Skill at visual-spatial reasoning, which involves predominantly parallel processing, is associated with an unusually

---

5.   When we look at a picture, we process details from different parts of the picture simultaneously -- this is parallel processing. Spoken words come one after the other and are processed serially.

strong unconscious component.

A predominantly parallel processing style implies multiple focuses of attention. Attending to events in more than one part of the field makes it more difficult to ignore stimuli that are not related to some central focus. An individual with this kind of working style is thus more readily distracted, is described as having a poor attention span. Student reactions to sprites (see Chapter Ten) are particularly interesting. The presence of many turtles all going at once apparently provides a singularly appropriate experience for children who prefer multiple focuses of attention. This observation is tentative and is being explored further at the present time. The challenge is to somehow harness the facility for handling concurrent processes, while at the same time repeatedly refocusing attention to a central top-level goal.

Clustering of Features

There are characteristic ways in which the behavior of an individual along one dimension appears to be related to how she performs on another dimension. I discuss three examples of such clusters of features.

Linking attention pattern with processing mode yields two contrasting styles. One is a slow but reliable working style, with a concern for detail, and piecemeal analytic recognition; this appears to involve a serial style of processing with a single focus of attention. This style corresponds to the clinical psychologist's *obsessoid* personality: slow and deliberate, careful and precise, orderly, parsimonious, obstinately independent, self-effacing, and conscientious (Foulds, 1965; Shapiro, 1965).

In sharp contrast is the rapid working style that combines speed with less attention to detail and a tendency to make global discriminations. This involves a parallel style of processing with multiple focuses of attention. The clinical psychologist labels this personality type *hysteroid* (Foulds, 1965; Shapiro, 1965). Such persons are described as impulsive, given to precipitate action that can lead to carelessness and inaccuracy, emotionally labile with frequent mood changes and displays of emotion, suggestible, overly dependent, manipulative, wanting to impress and gain attention.

In terms of schema theory, individuals of the obsessoid personality type, being more "fussy" and particular, insist on confirming the presence of all (or most of) the details contained in each of the schemas being compared during the schema matching process before calling two things the same. In contrast hysteroids are less fussy, tolerating partial matches as a basis for recognition. Such individuals will be more ready to see analogies, will delight in many possibilities, will have a tendency to take risks. They will be more tolerant of ambiguity.

A second clustering of features is Turkle's distinction between *hard* and *soft mastery* (Turkle, 1984) which rests on the issue of control, the imposition of one's will over the machine versus an open, interactive, negotiating approach. Hard masters like to plan, to deal in abstractions, and to work with formal systems; they are interested in technical details; and they are "overwhelmingly male." "Softs" deal in impressions; their interest is global; their identification is with people rather than with abstract particles; they are interested in sensuous, tactile effects; and they tend to be female.

There is an overlap between the obsessoid-hysteroid distinction and the hard-soft one. The importance of Turkle's formulation for me is the way it emphasizes the issue of control, in a way reminiscent of Dweck's discussion of mastery and control. The gender issue seems complicated since, among the learning-disabled students I have worked with, a large proportion of those who showed a global, impressionistic style (softs in the Turkle classification) were boys (see Chapter Twelve). This issue, among others, is being looked at in more detail in the Headlight project (see Chapter Three).

A third combination of features is typical of the hyperactive child (Connors, 1973).[6] The child is restless and overactive; disturbs other children; fails to finish things; has a short attention span; is inattentive, easily disturbed, and constantly fidgeting; is emotionally labile -- excitable and impulsive; is easily frustrated and demands must be met immediately; cries easily and often; is subject to rapid mood changes and numerous temper outbursts.

This conventional description contains a collection of pejorative terms: impatience, impulsivity, desire for early gratification, dependent and demanding attitude where it is easier to ask for help than to try and figure it out. Having observed the change in atmosphere, the decrease in emotional frustration that can accompany the involvement of these children in Logo activity, I now ask just how much of the situation reflects a mismatch between the traditional learning environment and the natural processing preferences of these children. We might do better by this kind of child when we develop a deeper understanding of different patterns of attention and what that means in processing terms.

---

6.   Recently, these children have been labeled as having an "attention deficit disorder" (Diagnostic and Statistical Manual, DSM III, of the American Psychiatric Association).

Working Style and Brain Lateralization

These descriptions of different working styles are remarkably similar to the behaviors described in connection with types of cerebral hemispheric specialization.[7] It is difficult to believe that this suggestive resemblance is entirely coincidental. What are these cerebral asymmetries? Much of what we know about the connection between working style and the brain was first learned from the study of so-called split-brain subjects, in whom the connections between the hemispheres had been severed as part of the treatment of intractable epilepsy. Recall that the neural pathway from a sensory organ crosses over to get to the hemisphere on the other side, so that input from the right hand (or right ear or right visual field) reaches the left hemisphere first. Communication between hemispheres occurs largely via the corpus callosum, a large sheet of nerve fibers connecting the two hemispheres. In the split-brain individual these connections are cut, so that direct crossing over of information to the other hemisphere does not happen. This allows one to observe the behavior of a relatively isolated hemisphere.

If these individuals are asked to *look* at a pictorial design containing a missing piece, and then to find the missing piece by *feeling* (without looking at) a set of possible pieces, this is what happens.

> When identifying patterns with their right hand (left hemisphere), subjects tended to work slowly and to verbalize their reasoning, giving verbal labels to aspects of the pattern such as number, distance or angle. By contrast, when working with the left hand (right hemisphere), subjects' performance was much more rapid, confident and silent. Performance with the right hand was in all cases slower than with the left hand by 25%. (Zaidel and Sperry, 1973)

What is described is a slow, verbal problem-solving strategy when the right hand is taking in information and sending it to the left hemisphere; and a rapid, non-verbal mode of working when the left hand is feeding the isolated right side of the brain. In both instances the input is non-verbal, namely, tactile information about the shape of the object being felt and visual information about the design to be completed.

The functions of the hemispheres have been investigated using

---

7.   For reviews of the literature on brain lateralization, see Springer and Deutsch, 1981; Segalowitz,1983.

less invasive techniques, and although there is by no means complete consensus on the matter, a pattern of differences is emerging (for details, see Springer and Deutsch, 1981; Segalowitz, 1983).

1. There is general agreement that language processing is a special concern of the left hemisphere, whereas the right hemisphere plays a special role in the processing of most forms of visual-spatial information, as well as aspects of musical ability and emotional responses.[8]
2. Different processing modes characterize the two hemispheres. The left hemisphere characteristically processes information linearly or sequentially, while the right hemisphere typically handles information in parallel. The left hemisphere is essential for recognition of sequences and time relationships, while the right hemisphere is superior for pattern recognition and for the analysis of parallel events.
3. The left hemisphere is dominant for tasks requiring an analysis of the detailed internal structure of the stimulus, while the right hemisphere is concerned with the global characteristics of the task. It has been shown that the performance of those individuals using the left hemisphere is more easily disrupted by obscuring details, whereas those with a right-hemisphere preference are more sensitive to global changes.

The question of hemispheric preference -- complex and prone to over-simplification as it is -- is important for educators to the extent that it can shed light on observed differences in ways of representing problems and in ways of learning.   For example, it is interesting to consider the consequences for classroom activity of the following demonstration of how individuals differ in the strategies they use to solve a sentence-picture verification task.   A sentence is presented and then compared with a subsequently presented picture.   Some individuals seem to translate the sentence into a visual image and then compare this image with the picture, while others appear to turn the picture into a verbal description which they then compare with the sentence (MacLeod et al., 1978).

With respect to learning in mathematics, Patricia Davidson and Maria Marolda, mathematics consultants to the learning disabilities clinic at Children's Hospital in Boston, distinguish two styles.

---

8.   While the right brain does not control speech, it exhibits considerable verbal and written language comprehension. If the left brain is severely injured in childhood (before age 8 to 12), normal language abilities develop but are located in the right side of the brain. However, in spite of this plasticity, the left hemisphere is inherently superior to the right for language function.

In the first, learning style I, the child is better at counting forward than counting backward, and at understanding addition and multiplication than at understanding subtraction and division. These children prefer a step-by-step sequence of operations, seldom estimate and tend to remember parts than wholes. The second general style of math learner -- the child with learning style II -- is good at counting backward, and at understanding subtraction and division. He or she is impatient with step-by-step procedures and is likely to make mistakes while doing them. Such children are good at estimating, may spontaneously give a correct answer without knowing how it was arrived at, and are superior at recognizing large scale patterns. (Davidson, personal communication)

I have described several factors -- spatial-verbal, parallel-serial, detailed (analytic)-global (holistic) in terms of which to think about individual differences in processing. In practice, neurobiological status (hemispheric preference) can conflict with school-generated, acquired strategies. One may do a task in a particular way because that's how one was taught it, rather than because that's how one would have chosen to do it. A third factor is the *nature of the task* being performed. For example, an analytic visual task can turn a right-hemisphere activity into a left-hemisphere one, that is to say, concern for analytic detail interacts with the spatial-verbal distinction.

The computer becomes a tool both for revealing the nature and extent of preferred style and for accommodating these individual preferences. A theme already highlighted is the way computer-based work can help to expose the processing underlying problem-solving so as to reveal unacknowledged ability. In the next section I present a range of students who exemplify the importance of matching learning environments to individual working styles and abilities.

Chapter Twelve

INDIVIDUAL WORKING STYLE AND ACADEMIC FAILURE

Almost from the beginning of the use of Logo, its beneficial effect on children with many kinds of learning disability has been a matter for comment. Characteristically, these children are described as doing badly in school until they start Logo, when there is a change -- they do well at Logo and the teachers see an improvement in other areas. Often, this experience marks a turning point in the teacher's view of the usefulness of the computer or the transfer from using BASIC to an adoption of Logo as the language of choice for these children. A large part of this effect can be linked to the versatility of the computer and its particular aptness for particular individuals who have become labeled as academic failures.

The Class Clown

In 1978, Howe and O'Shea, reporting on the effect of one year of Logo activity on eighteen 11-year-old Edinburgh schoolchildren, describe how a visiting school inspector, unaware of the computer work, expressed surprise at the degree of mathematical aggression displayed: "the most mathematically argumentative class I have ever encountered." We learn that the most dramatic impact on this group of early Logo users observed by the Edinburgh team occurred in a boy diagnosed as dyslexic, who, although receiving regular remedial help with his reading and writing, was making little progress in his classwork.

131

This child had acquired a well-defined role in his class as a buffoon. He would be given easy questions in class, get them wrong and clown for the entertainment of his classmates. Neither his peers nor his teacher, nor he himself expected him to understand anything. After four months exposure to Logo this boy discovered that he actually understood what he was doing. Furthermore, he was able to explain how his programs worked to his classmates, and could help them with their programming problems. His nickname was changed to "teach"; his self-confidence changed dramatically and was remarked on by his class teacher, his remedial teachers, and his parents. His work at the remedial center showed significant progress which his teachers there attributed to his programming activities. His parents reported that he had organized household chores for the family as a procedure comprised of subprocedures for clearing the table; washing up; drying up; putting away cutlery; putting away crockery. (Howe and O'Shea, 1978)

An Academic Liability: the Non-Verbal Problem-Solver

Karl was one of the children attending the school learning center who were included in the sample of sixteen six-graders in the Brookline study. His story was recounted in Weir and Watt (1981).

Karl, aged 12, is a tall awkward boy who has severe learning disabilities, for which he is tutored regularly at the Learning Center. In sixth grade, his general academic achievement was at approximately a second grade level. His attitude toward school seemed to be one of hostile resignation. At this point, Karl was given the opportunity to program a computer during the course of which he overcame severe typing and spelling difficulties to learn Logo. Working over a period of thirty-six hours, Karl demonstrated skills and understandings in geometry, non-verbal reasoning, organization and logical problem-solving that previously had not been evident to his classroom teachers or to his learning-disabilities teacher.

The Logo situation allowed him to use skills that had not been cultivated in his prior school experience. During the interview preceding the Logo work, some significant gaps had emerged between his abilities in tasks that required reading, writing, and verbal expression and those that required solving non-verbal problems, such as those involving number patterns and attributes of different shapes. In the post-Logo interview, Karl was asked to solve the problem of finding all the possible different arrangements of blocks of four colors. Rather than lay out all the blocks and compare color arrangements, the strategy used by most students, Karl slowly calculated that there were twenty-four possible arrangements. When the interviewer confirmed this solution, he picked up the microphone of her tape recorder, and speaking directly into it said, "I'm a brain!" (Papert et al., 1979). Here we have a student who can compute by rule when the items being computed are combinations of perceptual features. This proficiency had not emerged during regular math or other school activity.

Curious to find out more about Karl, I went back to the original data on the Brookline project. In particular, given his skill at maneuvering the turtle and his flair for geometry, I looked to see how Karl had done on a linear estimation task that had been included in the interviews given before and after exposure to Logo. Karl's pre-Logo estimation score was the best in the class, a distinction he shared with a student called Dennis. After his Logo experience, Karl was way ahead of Dennis and by far the best of all the students in accurately estimating the length of a set of lines compared to a given standard. With respect to skill at angular estimation, Dennis had a much better pre-Logo score. However, during his Logo activity, Karl learned about putting numbers to angles and ended up joint best with Dennis in the post-Logo test. This led to an exploration. Who is this Dennis and why is he up there in front? I was fascinated by what I found in his case description, the significance of which had escaped me when I first read it.

A Clever Fellow with a Funny Processing Style

Judged by achievement test scores, Dennis was the second brightest in the Brookline sample.[1] Dan Watt's description of Dennis was written prior to any highlighting of the style of processing I have been describing. It seemed Dennis easily understood the important concepts of the Logo project. He showed an impressive lack of attention to detail and liked to keep all his work in his head. There was a tendency toward inaccuracy, and he flitted from idea to idea, having to be coaxed into settling on one and sticking with it. He was described as excellent at creating designs and showed a good ability at estimating distance. He had a problem with the left-right distinction. He had difficulty with Logo syntax issues; for example, he understood the concept of variables well, but his difficulty with where to put the dots in relation to using variables was marked enough to elicit comment from Dan Watt on several occasions. He was independent,

---

1.   Callifornia Test of Basic Skills scores: reading -- 77; language -- 90; math -- 72; total battery -- 83.

rejecting "helpful suggestions" and insisting on sticking to his own methods even when they were clearly unreliable.

Here, then, was a student with many of the characteristics referred to in the previous chapter as associated with hyperactivity and academic failure, but whose general level of "intellectual" activity was high. He was good at language and had understood intuitively the relation between his spatial talents and doing math so that he could incorporate these skills into his numerical problem-solving and do well at school.

A Preference for Things Linguistic: the Writer

Quite a different set of strengths was cultivated in another of the Brookline learning-disabled students who made significant gains.   Tina was the student mentioned on pages 38 and 101, who had a passionate interest in writing stories, an interest that was finding no expression in her regular classroom activities. Indeed, she was achieving little in the classroom, and national achievement test scores placed her in the third percentile.[2] She has been described in the Brookline report and in *Mindstorms* (Papert, 1980). Here I stress the main points.

Tina expressed a persistent interest in using the computer as a typewriter, rather than programming it. As described in Chapter Nine, when we provided her with editing facilities, her writing became a process that supported self-driven correction. Tina had deep feelings about her subject matter. Her story, Sonny, is typical of her style and intensity of feeling:

> SONNY IS A LITTLE BOY HE LIVES WITH HIS AUNT HELEN IN CALIFORNIA   HE HAS BEEN LIVE WITH HER FOR 9 YEARS. HE IS GOING TO A HOME FOR LITTLE WONDERS 4 WEEKS AFTER THAT TO COUPLE A ADOPTED SONNY HE WAS THE HAPPIEST BOY THAT YOU EVERY SEEN. I GUESS IF THAT WAS ME I WOULD BE HAPPY IF SOME ONE WOULD ADOPT. BUT SEE I AM NOT ADOPT I HAVE MY ON MOTHER AND I AM GLAD THAT I HAVE MY ON MOTHER, BECAUSE THE KIDS THAT HAVE FEELS REALLY BAD.   THAT'S WHY ALL THE KIDS IN THE WORLD SHOULD BE GRATEFUL TO THEIR PARENTS. THE END.

After completing each of her stories, Tina printed many copies to be distributed to her friends, family, and teachers, an indication of the pride and satisfaction she felt in her work.   When the computer teacher, Dan

------

2.   California Test of Basic Skills scores: reading -- 15; language -- 2; math -- 2; total battery -- 3.

Watt, sought samples of her language arts work from her classroom teachers and her learning-disabilities tutor, he found that Tina had not done any creative writing during the entire school year and was extremely resistant to school work in general. Tina's talents, embodied in a rich oral tradition, had remained unexpressed in the classroom. The turning point came about half way through her Logo sessions, when, after a visit with fellow choristers to another city, she used conventional writing materials to produce a long illustrated essay describing this significant event. Her writing continued after the computer classes came to an end. She thinks of herself as a writer and has written and illustrated several small books.

The themes have been met before: the quintessentially process-inducing nature of the medium, the appeal to subcultural sources of creativity, and the beneficial effects on self-image of the activity.

Who Me? I Can't Do It

A third Brookline student, Ray, has a story that makes a pair with the case of the Edinburgh dyslexic boy. Both adopted a coping strategy of playing the class clown, particularly concerned with not letting anyone know they were trying. Ray attended the learning center for special tutoring for his learning disability, and the teachers had become worried that he was noticeably slipping in his seriousness as a student. His sixth grade achievement test placed him in the twenty-fourth percentile nationally.[3] Ray was introduced in Chapter Eight in the section on learned helplessness; he was described there as having a strong fear of failure. He was absent for four of the first ten computer sessions; when he did attend, he rarely wrote things down. When asked to consult a reference sheet or an entry in his notebook, "he would usually just sit and wait for help." Typical of the monopolizing effect that such a student has on a teacher is the comment by his Logo teacher, Dan Watt: "In the next class I again spent a great deal of time with Ray. Not until the thirteenth session, did he come in with an idea of what he wanted to do: today for the first time, Ray came in wanting to work seriously on something." Dan had to wait until the twenty-fourth session for self-regulation in the form of self-initiated record-keeping: "This was the first time Ray typed in things, copied from his notebook without asking."

Yet despite his difficulties, Ray was interested in the computer, showed a good deal of "natural ability" in turtle geometry, and was

---

3.   California Test of Basic Skills scores: reading -- 11; language -- 28; math -- 40; total battery -- 24.

successful at directing the turtle, estimating quickly and accurately. In an interview with Ray's class teacher, evaluator George Hein asked, "Did you notice any thing special as a result of the program?"   The reply reflects the social problems attendant on a disturbed learning situation: "Ray is again working with kids; it is the first time that he has this year. He was isolated in the room before, now he sits with others. The breakthrough for him in Logo, the success he has had, is powerful information for me. He has produced the best piece of writing I've seen from him, either this year or last." (Papert et al., 1978)

This breakthrough came after careful planning on Dan's part. For example, scrutiny of the dribble files showed Ray had been consistently successful in activities that required varying only one parameter at a time. As a result of this observation, Ray was given the procedures POLY and SPI and invited to experiment with different inputs.   Gradually Ray came to focus on the effect of the chosen number rather than on the numbers themselves. And then Ray asked, "Can I put SPI and POLY together?" At the end of that class he spontaneously punched holes in his papers and put them carefully in his notebook.

Here the themes are many. The computer provided the means by which Ray could be weaned from his initial dependence on the teacher. He showed that he could come up with an academically interesting idea of his own, try it out, and store the result in his notebook. When we worked with his strengths in a nurturing environment -- given that he was indeed doing well at spatial reasoning tasks like estimating -- he showed both enthusiasm for the activity and genuine ability. It is important to note that this progress did not come automatically, but needed work on the part of the teacher, just as it does in the non-computer situation. The flexibility of the computer makes it easier to achieve progress by enabling the teacher to offer a range of possibilities, from which the student can take an approach or an idea and develop it further.

A Focus on Spatial Skill and Perceptual Computation

The Brookline project ended in June 1978.   During the summer that followed I saw Keith at Children's Hospital (see Chapter Four) and collected observations on his spontaneous activity and his responses to directed probes during the two Logo sessions he had.   Keith's responses to the spatial feedback he received revealed a *highly developed set of spatial intuitions, an aptitude that emerged particularly clearly and found academic expression because of the graphics screen and the nature of turtle geometry.*   For example, as we have seen, he exhibited spontaneous strategies for choosing units and yardsticks (unit-chunks of 10 units of length and 10 degree turn, a standard yardstick of 90 units of length, a standard turn of 90 degrees angle). He showed an ability to estimate accurately both length and angle of turn. His rapid, error-free execution of sequences involved complex perceptual judgements. For example, the centering of the hat of the snowman involved him in a rapid-fire production of accurate numbers, that appeared to depend on perception rather than calculation -- a perceptually misleading representation of the width of the hat (see Figure 4.2) was sufficient to lead him to an incorrect answer. He showed a readiness to project pictures onto screen objects, and his attention was unusually engaged by the computer activity.

I became concerned to find other children with these features in our Logo classes. One such student was Franky, described in Chapter Four, whose poor computation when presented with exercises in standard notation contrasted with his skill at perceptual computation. Similarly, Kelly's exploration of number choice (see Chapter Two) showed some children better at responding to feedback than others. For example, Eliza was particularly good at homing in on the target and chose predominantly multiples of ten. Here we see her at a somewhat later stage in her Logo activity, as she, Chris, and John each attempted to make an equilateral triangle. Eliza succeeded, Chris came close, as they "eyed" their productions; John, in contrast, stuck to preplanned numbers, in spite of what the product looked like.

	Eliza (14)	Chris (11)	John(11)
Turns	120,120,120	117,117,117	45,90,135
Sides	90,90,90	50,50,50	70,70,100

Eliza never needed to erase a line. She was able to tell by sight if she had the correct angle without taking further steps. She found 120 degrees indirectly by several smaller turns and then summed the numbers to get 120 degrees explicitly. Chris knew exactly what steps were necessary to draw an equilateral triangle and used a method of successive approximations to find the correct angle, beginning with an initial estimate of 110 degrees, and settling for 117 degrees. John attempted the triangle using his known "good angles" 45 and 90 degrees. To compensate for his choice of angles, he modified his plan to get all the sides of the figure equal.

Keith's strategy of using multiples of ten as units to aid estimation of length was seen again by Kelly in the work of her students Joe and Paul (see Chapter Two) and appears to be a characteristic indicator of skill in spatial problem-solving. It was explored further by Patricia Kellison (see page 20), who looked at the number choice of fifteen summer camp students, aged 6 to 10, who had not done Logo before. After a brief introduction to five Logo commands: FORWARD, RIGHT, LEFT, BACK, and DRAW, each student engaged in ten minutes of open-ended Logo activity, followed by two games. In Game One, the student was required to turn the turtle (using the commands RIGHT or LEFT) to face a balloon placed at various points of the compass; while in Game Two, the target was placed at varying distances away from the turtle, and the goal was to use the FORWARD and BACK commands to hit it. In each case a hit was rewarded by a star-like explosion. Each keystroke was recorded in the standard way in a dribble file and provided the data for analysis. Target hitting skill was measured by the number of moves needed to hit the target: the lower the score the greater the skill. Using multiples of ten predominantly correlated positively with lower scores in both the target games. If a child used the strategy of tens at all, she tended to use it across the board with all three activities. There was a consistent increase in the number of moves required to hit the angle target than required for the FORWARD/BACK target (Kellison, 1983). The degree of difficulty in both tasks increased with age and the difference between turn and move tasks held for each age group.

Spatial Ability and Learning-Disabled Children

Next we examined the spatial ability of a group of forty-three middle-school students, aged between 11 and 13 years, receiving substantially separate education at the Grove School for dyslexic children (mentioned on page 50). The sample had a mixture of disabilities: 77 percent were pure dyslexic, 13 percent had known organic disturbance, and 10 percent showed primary emotional disturbance. If we take as our definition of deficiency a score on a standard achievement test of two or more grades below age-expected grade level, nearly 60 percent were oral reading deficient, about half were math disabled, most were poor spellers, but only one-third were deficient in reading comprehension and one-fifth were deficient in vocabulary. The mean IQ was 104 with an SD of 12.52. The sample contained seven girls. The incidence of left-handedness was within the range reported for the general population (8 percent), 34 percent had one or more left-handers among their immediate family members, and 62 percent had a family history of speech or reading difficulties.

Several tests of *spatial aptitude* were administered to the group. The WISC-R *block design* task requires the student to reproduce test patterns by juxtaposing blocks whose faces contain components of these patterns; it tests for the ability to analyze, match, and construct spatial patterns. The *spatial relations* component of the Primary Mental Abilities test involves choosing from a number of spatial fragments the one that will complete a given figure; it mobilizes the student's ability to rotate and match shapes. An estimation of length task was constructed containing 12 items: a random arrangement of four line-lengths (1.0, 1.5, 2.0, and 4.0 inches), each displayed in three orientations (vertically, horizontally and obliquely up to the right). The student was required to estimate the length of each line with respect to a given standard length (1.0 inches) labelled "10 units", without using any aids. An accurate estimate scored a point.

The average scores attained in these spatial tests were within the expected range: the mean block design score was 10.44, the mean estimation score was 6.2, and the mean score in the spatial relation test was 14.26 (the average percentile achieves a score of 14 to 15). However, the distribution of the scores was unexpected. In each case, there was a peak in the below average range and a cluster of individuals at the high-score end of the spectrum, giving a bimodal effect (see figure 12.1). This suggests the presence of two subcategories, one whose members are poor at spatial reasoning and the other containing individuals with a spatial flair.

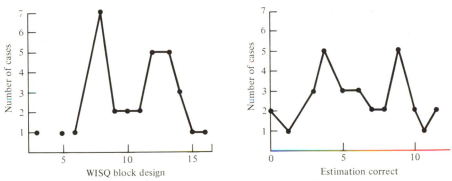

Figure 12.1   Spatial Aptitude of Learning Disabled Children

The response of students in the sample to Logo activity reflected this dichotomy. The students who did poorly on the spatial tests tended to be functioning at a low cognitive level in all areas: these children were helped by the concrete nature of the activity (see Chapter Fourteen), and made slow but definite progress. The response of the spatially talented students was striking. Exploiting the spatial character of Logo, they rapidly achieved a fluency in programming, and tackled complicated multiplication and division problems in turtle geometry that they seemed unable to grasp when expressed in standard notation. Typically, this would happen without the students knowing how they had arrived at the solution (see page 116). The computer screen feedback seemed to act as a series of effective triggers into their unconscious schemas.

All this problem-solving activity translated, when the time came to undergo routine testing, into two or more grade level jumps in achievement. However, we were not sure how to interpret this when we discovered that a similar improvement in test scores had been achieved in classes not engaged in Logo activity. It was felt that a two-week effort to teach test-taking skills throughout the school might have had something to do with the result. However, we did find a significant correlation between the spatial ability of the students and both their Stanford math achievement scores at the start of their Logo experience ($p < 0.01$), and the improvement in their math scores after one year of Logo ($p < 0.006$).

Many of the observations on this group have already been referred to in Chapter Eleven in connection with individual styles of working. In the next chapter, I link my findings with those of other workers and consider their classroom implications.

Chapter Thirteen

LEARNING DISABILITY AND SPATIAL CURRICULA

All through this text I have been talking about a new dimension to learning disability that emerges with the focus of Logo on spatial reasoning. Most of the effort in schools for the learning disabled goes into remedial work in language -- an emphasis on weakness. Most research workers in the field have concentrated on aspects of the reading and writing problems and have not been on the lookout for spatial excellence. Since learning disability is a mixed category, the superior spatial ability displayed by the members of one subcategory can be canceled out by the spatial deficits of subjects in another. Some research workers have indeed reported spatial superiority among the learning disabled, but these findings have had little impact on the education of these students, since it was not clear what to do with this observation in practical terms. The use of Logo with the educationally handicapped child allows us to build curricula that exploits hidden spatial strengths.

Diagnosis by Exclusion

There are many ways to be educationally handicapped. *Specific learning disability* is a label that a child earns when he appears to have an intact central nervous system and a benign environment, and yet still seems to be "going nowhere intellectually, or not going fast enough" (Rudel, 1980). It is a diagnosis based on what children do not have, i.e., when sensory impairment and intellectual retardation have been excluded, when there is no overt neurological disease, and in the absence of a disadvantaged home or school environment. This diagnosis by exclusion can result in a very mixed group.

By far the most conspicuous problem among learning-disabled children is the subgroup who have *difficulty with reading*.

> Developmental dyslexia is a learning disability which initially shows itself by difficulty in learning to read, and later by erratic spelling and by lack of facility in manipulating written as opposed to spoken words. The condition is cognitive in essence, and usually genetically determined. It is not due to intellectual inadequacy or to lack of socio-cultural opportunity or to failure in the technique of teaching, or to emotional factors, or to any known structural brain lesion. (Critchley and Critchley, 1978)

A dyslexic lags behind his peers in his first steps at reading, is late in learning to name the letters of the alphabet, and remains confused as to the correct orientation of individual letters and numerals, hence the numerous reversals, inversions, and rotations that persist long after they should have gone. "This inadequate and labored written work contrasts vividly with his ability to express his abundant ideas verbally" (Critchley, 1981). The errors typical of a dyslexic child's reading include: confusion of mirror-opposite letters; omission or misreading of articles, prepositions, conjunctions; abbreviation of lengthy words; and substitution of similarly spelled words or, interestingly enough, semantically equivalent words. Dyslexia runs in families, and all known evidence supports a hereditary element. It is more common among boys than in girls.[1]

It has been shown that there is a general naming deficiency in developmental dyslexia, with impaired access to the internal lexicon (for a discussion, see Miles and Ellis, 1981). Indeed these researchers propose the name *lexical encoding deficiency* based on the finding that dyslexic persons need somewhat more time for recoding a visually presented letter or word into its letter name or word sound than do non-dyslexic persons. It is not that they don't notice differences in temporal pattern -- they can reproduce a pattern by tapping perfectly adequately -- but when the pattern has to be imitated verbally, they have a problem *finding the name* for that pattern (Bakker and Schroots, 1981).

---

1.   Specific reading retardation is a term preferred by some. The label is applied on the basis of a reading performance at two or more years below grade level.

So there you have it -- a pattern of reading problems that has an enormous impact on the progress of a child through the school curriculum, so much of which depends on making sense of the written word. A student who can neither comprehend written text easily, nor express himself fluently in writing, is at a disadvantage with respect to practically every subject he studies. However, as I have already indicated, observations of the Logo activity of learning-disabled students show that there is much more to the story than the presence of a reading disability. Many learning-disabled students show a particular kind of processing, and, given the right circumstances, can excel at academic activities.

Subclassifying Learning Disability: Sources of Confusion

What has long impeded the study of the disorders is the tendency of educators to lump these people together by their test scores. While children with certain disorders may look similar to a teacher, their brains can look very different to a neurologist.

Frank Duffy, neurologist at Boston Children's Hospital, quoted in the
New York Times Education Fall Survey, 1984.

Reports on learning disability tend to differ depending on the mix of populations studied. Physicians, educators, and psychologists are all interested in why children fail in school. The category is defined, as I have said, by what it is not, and its boundaries can vary with the kind of professional involved. For example, the groups of learning-disabled children seen in hospital settings will tend to include the more severely disabled child referred for evaluation to a particular clinic. The type of clinic selected will match the expertise of the person running the clinic: thus, children with suspected brain damage will end up visiting the neurologist's clinic. This will bias the composition of the group being studied: one hospital sample of 113 learning-disabled children contained 84 brain-damaged children (Mattis, 1981). In contrast, the children seen at a school learning center will be a heterogeneous selection of children failing academically for all sorts of reasons, including social disadvantage and emotional disturbance. When children who are referred to the resource room are described, we will hear more about particular kinds of reading and writing errors made during classroom performance (Boder, 1971).

Many ways of classifying children with learning disability have been proposed (for a methodological critique, see Applebee, 1971). An early basis for subcategorization was the finding of a large difference between performance IQ and verbal IQ (Kinsbourne and Warrington, 1963). My own preference is for the distinction made by Rudel (1980) between two major subtypes on the basis of *the presence or absence of dyslexia.* In Rudel's first group, we find children who fail at reading, who have an impairment of some aspect of language development. They are slow on word retrieval tasks, show disorders in expressive language, and have difficulties in articulation or in writing. They have a short attention span, and, in addition, display signs related to developmental delay, that is, signs such as poor pencil grip and clumsiness that would be acceptable in a much younger child. The familial, so-called pure dyslexics are included in this category, and, most importantly from our point of view, some of these children show *evidence of spatial excellence.*

Rudel's second group of learning-disabled children consists of children who are non-dyslexic and less impaired on language tasks. These children are *poor at spatial tasks*, with a poor sense of direction and a lower performance than verbal WISC (IQ) scores. They are poor at arithmetic and have poor graphomotor (drawing and writing) skills. Rather than signs of delayed development, these children display so-called "soft" neurological signs, signs that can escape routine examination but are detectable by clinicians experienced in assessing this kind of child, signs such as mild motor incoordination, "shadows" of choreiform movements, tremors, strabismus, nystagmus, and asymmetries in reflexes and tone.

Notice how difficulties with reading and spatial ability are dissociated, so that a child can be judged to perform poorly in one area, while showing average or above average skill at the other kind of activity. In contrast to the enormous amount of research on problems with language use, there has been little research on spatial ability among learning-disabled children, except when it has a bearing on poor reading and writing, as in the case of poor visual-motor performance. Nevertheless, some researchers have pursued the matter.

Spatial Abilities in the Learning Disabled

In a seminal paper in 1972, Symmes and Rappaport reported above-average spatial ability in a sample of children with what they called *unexpected reading failure.* Underlying the success of their study was a deliberate effort to exclude all known causes of learning disability -- the "unexpected" is important. The subjects who qualified for admission into the study were fifty-four middle- or upper-class boys of above average intelligence.

These youngsters were given a large battery of tests. They showed a superior performance on all those tasks involving visual recognition and three-dimensional spatial visualization. An additional feature of the group adds interest to the finding of spatial excellence on laboratory tests: their histories contained anecdotal evidence of this spatial excellence, indicating that the result was not just an artifact of the testing situation. Furthermore, among the relatives of these individuals was "a preponderance of strong visualizers," as the report puts it. There were an unusually high number of architects and weavers with superior memory for patterns.

The authors suggest a way in which such a facility for three-dimensional spatial visualization could be a cause of the reading difficulty. Consider the confusion between b, p, q, and d. Suppose one of the strategies that a spatially gifted child might use is to have available "efficient general" spatial representations. This might result, as a side effect, in the encoding of all four of these letters as versions of the *same* three-dimensional form, namely, a circle with a line coming off from one point on the perimeter. That would mean that for these children, the identification of these letters as four distinct two-dimensional forms may be a specially difficult and unnatural one. Symmes and Rappaport conclude: "Perhaps we should be teaching such children geometry before reading readiness."

A second group of researchers, sensitive to the issue of spatial abilities in the learning disabled, tested children of the sort described by Symmes and Rappaport on a route-walking task (Denckla et al., 1980). In this task, subjects are presented with diagrams of paths, as shown in Figure 13.1.[2] Using a floor area marked out with the same pattern of dots, subjects are required to walk in a path that corresponds to the path indicated on the diagram. When groups of learning-disabled children were tested on that task, interesting results emerged. Dyslexic children scored better than other learning-disabled children whose reading was unimpaired. Furthermore, they scored better than did the controls who had no evidence of learning disability at all.

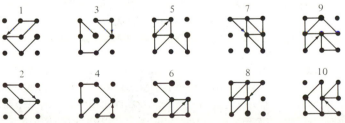

Figure 13.1   Route–Walking Task (based on Semmes et al., 1955)

---

2.   Used by Semmes et al. (1955) to test patients with known brain damage.

Next, the authors separated out the scores of those dyslexic children who had a family history of dyslexia. When these scores were computed separately, the trend toward superiority on the route-walking test was present even more strongly. An important finding was that this superior spatial skill occurred only in those children who had reached their tenth birthday, that is to say, after the corpus callosum matures (see page 128). In this connection there is the interesting result of Owen et al. (1971), who found that, although learning-disabled children were not as good as children in the control group at *reproducing designs*, they were much better at *judging the errors* in their own reproductions than the controls. In fact their judgments were close to the judgments of trained psychologists.

Why hasn't the special relation between spatial reasoning and learning disability been observed in the past? In a recent New York Times Education Fall Survey (November 1984), no mention was made of spatial abilities among the learning disabled, except rather indirectly: "A teacher might give his student drills in distinguishing geometric shapes like triangles and squares, hoping that the student would then transfer the ability to make geometric distinctions into academic tasks;" and "If he is a talented artist or a good athlete, those activities should be encouraged, even if it means somewhat less time for studying." These comments reveal just how little connection is made between spatial activities and academic matters in our culture. Yet the relevance of such activities seems clear, given that certain professions require the use of spatial reasoning. Interaction with engineering and computer science students and professionals gives me an informal impression that many of these have a high incidence of spelling and writing problems and complain about their misery at school, where they performed below their intellectual level.

Cerebral Dominance

The contrast between language and spatial ability takes us back to the issue of hemispheric specialization (Chapter Eleven). Orton's (1925) original suggestion that a peculiarity of brain organization underlies the problem of dyslexia has been much criticized in its detailed claims, but, as Zangwill (1981) points out, the suggestion is not so far off the mark, and it is difficult to believe that issues of unilateral cerebral dominance are wholly without relevance to specific learning disabilities in schoolchildren.

One factor related to cerebral dominance is *handedness*. Most right-handers have left-hemisphere dominance for language. Left-handers can have any one of three possibilities: a few have a dominant right hemisphere; rather more have left hemisphere dominance; while a much larger group have bilateral representation of language (Geschwind, 1984).

The absence of a dominant hemisphere, a kind of *hemispheric ambivalence*, seems to occur more often among dyslexics than among non-dyslexics (Critchley, 1981).

A second factor is the rate of physical *maturation* and *gender diferences*. All late maturers, whether male or female, scored better than early maturers on spatial ability tests (Waber, 1980). Since females mature earlier than males, a slower maturation rate could underly the frequently reported superior spatial skill shown by males. Geschwind (1983) has suggested a physiological connection between some male-related factor (such as the male hormone testosterone) and brain development, in particular, a delay in growth of language-related portions of the left hemisphere and a greater development of the right hemisphere. This would lead to an elevated number of individuals with talents dependent on superior right hemisphere function.

However, interpreting the gender difference is a complex matter, and it is difficult to weigh the relative significance of physiological and social factors. Society expects girls to prefer books and boys to prefer climbing, throwing ball, and building things. Girls are described as not liking computers as much as boys do, especially where there is competition for scarce computer resources (Carmichael et al., 1985). However, when this factor is removed, as in the Headlight project (see page 37), early indications are that girls appear to enjoy Logo and Lego-Logo activity at least as much as boys.

Another factor relates to the degree to which the two hemispheres function independently. Slow maturers show a greater degree of lateral-ization, that is, independent functioning, than do their faster maturing peers (Waber, 1980). Dyslexics also show reduced interhemispheric functioning (Sklar et al., 1972). Recall (Chapter Eleven) that serial processing is associated with the left and parallel processing with the right hemisphere. The idea is that the two types of processing interfere with one another (Levy, 1969), so that the better the separation between the two hemispheres, the more efficient will be the spatial processing.

In summary, then, dyslexia is more common in males, and males show slower maturation, greater lateralization of brain function, a lesser degree of left-hemisphere dominance with less well-developed language functions, and a greater specialization of right-hemisphere spatial skills.

Proposed Subcategory of Spatially Gifted Learning Disabled Children

I postulate the existence of a stable subcategory of learning-disabled children, with deficits in reading and writing, whose members will respond particularly favorably to Logo.   They are characterized by the following features.

> They are spatially gifted.
>
> They display a tendency to emotional lability.
>
> They have strongly lateralized hemispheric processing, with a diminution of interhemispheric processing as compared to non-dyslexics.
>
> They have multiple focuses of attention and a predominance of parallel processing which is performed rapidly and in a form not accessible to their conscious scrutiny.
>
> The characteristic mode of processing tends to run in families.
>
> The characteristic mode of processing is associated with a later onset of puberty than is the case in individuals who excel at language skills.
>
> They fail in a school curriculum that emphasizes language skills, with consequent drop in motivation and secondary adverse emotional effects.
>
> They flourish in a learning environment that allows them to exploit their spatial superiority in formal problem-solving tasks, with a resultant increase in motivation, increase in level of academic attainment, and a dramatic improvement in self-image and mental well-being.

This is the group to which Keith and Franky belong. I do not yet know how many children there are like this. I think that the group is large. Much of the school curriculum is language-based and does not suit their thinking style well. They do well at drafting, they are good with their hands, and they are relegated to the non-academic, vocational track. In the past, their spatial skills have not won them any academic credit. Now the graphics screen is making all the difference to their schooldays. Providing an opportunity for spatial problem-solving *in a formal setting*, in addition to the more usual places like the playing fields and the artist's drawing board, is essential to the healthy academic growth of these individuals -- future engineers, architects, computer programmers -- allowing them to exploit their spatial facility to acquire academic skills.

A Related Phenomenon: Video Arcade Wizards

It would be interesting to know how many of the video game addicts fall into the category of the spatially gifted.   In a recent study of Harvard undergraduates, Diane Gagnon (1985) showed a significant relationship between scores on video games and scores on spatial tests. At the Harvard conference on video games held in May 1983, Patricia Greenfield included among the skills required to play video games successfully a skill at "parallel processing of multiple interacting variables, all operating simultaneously. . . . the ability to integrate discrete spatial information" (Greenfield, 1983). I suspect that some of the video game player's addiction lies in the pleasure of doing well -- at least in part, the rewards are intrinsic to the task. The players are in control of their success.

video game wizards = spatial excellence + parallel processing + control

It is possible that spatial skill underlies the spectacular motivation displayed in arcades, and the intense concentration on focused goals. These people are doing what they do well. Can the video phenomenon teach us something about motivation and dedication to achieving goals that may have application for computers in the classroom? After all, intense interest is not a conspicuous feature of the average schoolroom, and it is certainly not characteristic of the average teenager. Children are failing in our schools largely because they are bored, confused, and afraid. Teachers burn out because they are asked to carry an impossible burden. Encouraging spontaneity while restraining anarchy is enormously difficult, and the counterproductive effect of the classroom is notorious, turning a lively, curious child into an alienated, resentful, uninspired, unresponsive, passive being.

  Cole and his colleagues (1982) report that reading-disabled children who worked hard to *avoid* interactions with teachers during the reading group time were willing to engage in them during computer time, especially when the computer activities resembled arcade games. Here the children showed perseverance, attentiveness, and a great deal of progress from trial to trial and from day to day (Cole, 1982). We need to mobilize skills and develop activities that rest on the individual's strengths.

Computer Activity for the Learning Disabled

The computer can be incorporated into the curriculum in many ways, each with its special advantages. Ideally, the approach to take in a classroom is to embrace different ways of learning: Provide all students, whether officially designated as having special needs or not, with the opportunity to work in their preferred mode.

  1. *Programming*. In the process of inputting their programs and in deciphering the computer messages, students doing Logo can develop their skills in reading, spelling, and typing. The constraints of the situation itself engender a respect for accuracy, since the literal computer cannot understand nearly correct instructions, as humans do. This is a good way to improve spelling -- if not accurate, at least be consistent. There is

nothing like the motivation of getting "that stupid machine to do it."

The theme of programming games in Logo can generate interesting projects for senior students. They can take the program code of existing games and modify it or use it as a model for inventing new games. The Logo procedures used in the games supplied can be considered as a kind of "kit" for this purpose. In the process of this highly motivating game-constructing activity, the student is acquiring more advanced programming ideas and gaining experience in structuring a complex Logo project. Logo games have other advantages over the commercial arcade games that should appeal to teachers, parents, and students. The game can be designed to exhibit particular concepts; it can have a particular pedagogic purpose. For example, when interacting with the dynaturtle, students learn systematic things about what happens to a moving object when a force is applied to it. The fact that the game is written in Logo means that teachers and students can modify the code that runs the game so as to produce variations to suit their purposes. You can't get inside a commercial game to twiddle features -- the innards are mostly inscrutable to all but the really initiated, and, even if you can figure out the workings, they are usually protected from modification. This ability to modify the program is particularly important when tailoring a tool for the special needs child.

2. *Word processing*. Every child with language difficulties should be given frequent access to a word processor. The advantages have already been mentioned. Difficulty in forming letters is often troublesome for learning-disabled students, and the ability to correct errors easily and produce clean copy is a major source of pleasure. Freedom from the need to worry about these things allows the student to concentrate on composing. Donald Graves (1983) has written a wonderfully useful book suggesting activities that build on children's readiness to write from a young age. Children can invent spelling and write before they are ready to read (Chomsky, 1971). The child's own experience feeds into a free flow of writing, helped by the convenience of word processing facilities; students then read and discuss each other's texts. Falbel (1986) has modified the computer-based *Writing to Read* idea of Martin (Martin and Friedberg, 1986) to exploit this possibility.

3. *Images to think with*. Many of the most talented of our thinkers attribute their success to their ability to use images to think with. Here we have children who need our cooperation in allowing them to use images as a way into parts of the school curriculum. I am proposing that the widespread adoption of computer-based learning environments that support spatial problem-solving in schools will actually reduce the incidence of learning disability, by providing alternative approaches to school subject matter. When I talk about mobilizing spatial aptitude in the

service of academic goals, I refer to enlisting schema-based pictorial inferences to participate in problem-solving processes.[1]

Until now research on the relation between instructional materials and differences in aptitude has been inconclusive; no straightforward relationship has been demonstrated between the use of pictorial materials in the form of graphs and diagrams and the learning of students who score high on the visualization dimension (Cronbach and Snow, 1977). This may be because supplying diagrams is only a beginning. To achieve the kind of learning I have been talking about requires a more dynamic approach. Computer-based spatial learning can be procedural and constructive in nature, with all the advantages that flow from that, including the acquisition of *crucial procedural components of metaknowledge.*

Examples of microworlds that directly support spatial problem-solving include: turtle geometry itself; the visual narrative project described in Chapter Ten; the dynaworld, designed by diSessa and elaborated by Dan Watt and Barbara White (White, 1981); and the turtle-steps mathworld mentioned in Chapter Four (Ary, 1986). A preference for visualizing problems can occur at all levels of ability. I would advocate that the above suggestions and others like them become part of the repertoire of all teachers.

We have much to learn about making and using these alternative types of learning materials. This is part of a broader story. The use of the computer to provide diverse learning environments will allow us to make substantially more accurate assessments of the intellectual capabilities of our students. Indeed, computer activity can function as an instrument of diagnosis in these children. For no group is this more true than for those children who function at a low cognitive level. I have already described the response of one autistic boy (Chapter Six). In the next chapter I describe work with other autistic children that illustrates this point.

---

1.   Non-verbal reasoning has its own logic. There is an internal logic in processing pictures, a kind of *pictorial inference* (Clowes, 1973). This suggests that visualizing in mathematics has a lot in common with using logical reasoning in mathematics.

Chapter Fourteen

A STRUCTURED ENVIRONMENT FOR AUTISTIC CHILDREN

Current teaching of autistic children is rightly dominated by the need for a structured environment. The regularity of response and predictability of a machine's behavior suits this need and also allows teachers to combine flexibility with structure. In general, autistic children prefer the physical turtle to the screen turtle. It becomes a navigational device which the child can send to various places on the floor. The importance of bringing together the autistic child and the computer cannot be overemphasized. Experience suggests that low-functioning autistic children respond more favorably to Logo that do non-autists of a comparable measured intelligence. Using a computer with autistic children exploits their fascination for machines. This is no accident. There are striking resemblances between the kind of difficulties that autistic children display and the kinds of problems one meets in trying to get a computer to behave intelligently, resemblances that invite exploration.

The Langridge Project

In Chapter Six I described the behavior of an autistic boy as he interacted with the Logo turtle in Edinburgh in 1975. More recently, I have been able to resume work using Logo with autistic children, this time at the Langridge

School, Massachussetts.[1] The Langridge School works primarily with children who have been diagnosed as autistic, but also teaches children with other emotional and language disturbances. Details of the twelve children involved in a project carried out during the summer and fall of 1981 are given in the table.

Logo	Age	Sex	IQ	Diagnosis	Response to Logo
Moses	7	M	58	Autism	Good
Violet	9	F	53	Autism	Good
Jeremy	10	M	88	Emotional disturbance Primary language disorder	Excellent
Eva	10	F	75	Emotional disturbance Primary language disorder	Good
Theo	11	M	75	Brain damage CP Hyperactive	Poor
Tyrone	10	M	81	Emotional disturbance Primary language disorder	Fair
Roly	11	F	*	Childhood schizophrenia	Poor
Terry	11	M	56	Autism	Good
Marvin	13	M	71	Microcephaly	Poor
Jay	14	M	46	Childhood schizophrenia	Poor
Mark	14	M	56	Autism	Good
Chuck	17	M	65	Autism	Good

*Untestable

The ages of the children ranged from 7 to 17. All had some type of emotional disturbance or developmental disorder, and their academic performance was well below that of most children of their age. These children are very difficult to test. For what it is worth, the IQ as measured by the attending clinical psychologist is given. One child was untestable. The mean figure for the remaining children was 66. The mean IQ of the children diagnosed as autistic was 57 and that of the non-autistic was 73. All the children could read and use numbers. Their typical classroom exercises reflect a focus on the learning of basic life skills, for example, the addition

---

1.   A pseudonym has been used for the school to protect the privacy of the children. David Scrimshaw, a student on this project, was teacher and observer for eighteen months.

and subtraction involved in handling coins. However, the impression one gets as an observer is that much of this is rote learning, and their class teachers agree that often the student's learning does not carry over well into daily life.

Our purpose in introducing computers to this population was to see whether it would make their learning more meaningful to them. The successes or failures, when they came, tended to be unequivocal. In some cases, the children's performance on the computer completely surprised their teachers; in others, little change from their classroom behavior was noted. These responses provided a (subjective) basis for rating progress. Of the twelve children worked with, the five diagnosed as autistic made good progress during the course of their Logo work. Of the seven non-autistic children, five failed to make any progress, either because of their very low cognitive level or because of the extreme degree of emotional disturbance present. Although the numbers are too small to support generalizations, there is a suggestive trend. The non-autistics whose response was described as fair or good had an average measured IQ of 81, whereas those with a poor response had an IQ of 61. In contrast, the group of autistics, who all responded well, had an average IQ of 57. There is the suggestion, then, that the work on machines is particularly appropriate for the autistic group, in spite of their low IQ as measured.

Description of the Logo Activity

The computer was located in a separate room and children were escorted by Scrimshaw from the classroom to the computer room. Sessions lasted fifteen to thirty minutes depending on the child and took place once or twice a week during the year. Owing to the sensitivity and vulnerability of these emotionally disturbed children, we restricted the number of persons in the room to one child and one adult as much as possible. We used both a Texas Instruments 99/4A computer and an Apple II computer.[2]

Exactly as in the Edinburgh and Brookline studies, the aim at the start was to make the children comfortable with the computer. At the time this study was commenced, we did not have access to a button-box, and used a regular keyboard. The children were introduced to the computer using two programs written for the TI computer -- MAGIC and DRAW. In the MAGIC program, the image of a black hat appeared in the lower left corner of

---

2.   Texas Instruments (TI) Logo was the first implementation to go out into the world on a personal computer, and for a time, it was the only computer with the sprite facility. The Apple II allowed the use of the mechanical turtle.

the screen. The user could make rabbits come out of the hat using the PULL command or make rabbits disappear with the HIDE command. The DRAW program was a version of the INSTANT program that required less typing than ordinary Logo (see page 55). These programs were good starting activities, after which the children moved to standard Logo.

In many ways, our experiences with these children raised familiar themes, for example, the way in which work at the computer revealed hitherto unsuspected skills that belied the measured IQ of the student. The 10-year-old non-autistic boy, Jeremy, with a primary language disorder, serious emotional disturbance, and measured IQ of 88, showed considerable skill at using the computer graphics screen. He was seen for fifteen sessions and was one of the few in the study who moved to writing computer programs involving subprocedurization. His spatial skills had been previously unsuspected and, more importantly, were not being used in the teaching he received.

Two themes will be explored in more detail: the importance of a physical turtle and the use of the child's behavior at the computer to provide insights into underlying cognitive mechanisms.

Advantages of Using a Mechanical Turtle

For many of these children, progress was slow until we acquired a mechanical turtle. The dramatic response of both autistic and non-autistic children to this physically present, concrete, three-dimensional object was one of the most striking features of the work with this group of low-functioning children. There was a substantial difference in the responses of three children who had until then been doing turtle graphics on the screen. They showed marked improvement in their choice of commands and numbers, as they maneuvered the physical turtle between and around physical objects to accomplish a goal, than they had shown when using the screen turtle. A fourth subject, Mark, a 14-year-old, had until then shown no desire at all to do turtle graphics. Instead, he had spent his time typing in long and detailed lists of the contents of pop records he had memorized. This student took to the new physical turtle and made good progress, planning his activity, and achieving his navigational intentions with increasing accuracy and progressively fewer moves.

As before, the use of numbers forms an interesting cognitive focus. Whereas numbers in their regular classwork tended to be used in a rote-like fashion, in Logo, choosing a particular number and seeing it do a particular job of work made numbers come alive for the students. Although the MAGIC program allows the number chosen to materialize as that number of rabbits, this seemed less effective in mobilizing number intuitions than did choosing numbers to move the mechanical robot over a specific distance in a particular direction. The rabbit-in-the-hat game elicited "Ooh! Aah!" because of the pretty pictures, but the questions "How many more rabbits do I need to make such-and-such?" or "How many rabbits are left?" did not yield much joy. The situation is reminiscent of our experience with Donald, the Edinburgh autistic; again, lack of success is associated with an interrogatory type of context, where the direct question "How many?" produces a blank stare.

Computing the number of rabbits remaining hidden was a big struggle for Eva (10), as was a classroom exercise involving work with numbers of dollars and cents. In contrast, when we introduced Eva to the mechanical turtle, there was a noticeable improvement in her choice of numbers. Using the mechanical turtle, she began to think about what she was doing. In his research notes, Scrimshaw described the situation: "Prior to this, Eva tended to think only of what had to be done one step at a time. Since she often failed to foresee what the ultimate result of her actions would be, she became frustrated. Now, with the mechanical turtle, she began to plan her moves in advance. She would say: first I'll move the turtle forward, then I'll turn it and then forward to knock down the blocks. She would then proceed to carry out her plan. She became much more interested in having sessions on the computer; her confidence improved; and she more often took action without prompting."

More than one factor would seem to be involved in the success of the mechanical turtle with these low-functioning children. The inventors of Logo treated the physical turtle as much the same as the screen turtle, but *children do not*. For them the physical turtle is a real object that can be touched and handled. It is easier to relate their own body movements to those of the physical turtle. It can be viewed from all sides, so that for example, by standing behind the turtle, the child can mimic its movement, turning her body to see which way the turtle should move. When the physical turtle moves, the entire movement is seen, whereas when the more abstract screen turtle moves it is merely redrawn in a new location. Furthermore, FORWARD for the physical turtle is nearer the usual meaning of forward, whereas FORWARD on the screen is actually more like "up." These considerations are especially relevant to work with very young children (Birch, 1984).

A second set of issues has to do with the functions of the turtle: whether it is used as a navigational object -- traversing a maze or hitting a target -- or as a drawing device, as in turtle geometry. Combinations of forwards and turns are used to solve both kinds of problems. Are we justified in equating the two? Does the level of performance depend on the perceived nature of the task, the intention behind the doing? Will different intuitive knowledge be mobilized depending on whether we are looking at a scene or walking through? One possibility is that the physical turtle is perceived as a navigational object -- "When I move the physical turtle, I am trying to maneuver it to go between those posts or to knock down that tower of blocks" -- whereas the screen turtle is seen primarily as a drawing device -- "I will draw this line above that one." Since moving oneself around in space resembles navigating the turtle around in three-dimensional space more closely than either resembles the activity of drawing, this would mean that navigational activity with the physical turtle would appeal more directly to the student's experience.

There is a particular feature that might be relevant in the case of autistic children. We know from the work of Hermelin and O'Connor (1970) that autistics respond to kinesthetic cues better than they do to visual cues. One could argue that this preference might favor identification of their own body movement and the movement of the physical turtle, as Donald so explicitly showed he was doing. Ornitz suggests that:

> the spontaneous spinning and flicking of objects, the flapping and oscillating of their extremities, and the whirling and rocking of their bodies may be the autistic children's way of making sense out of the sensations in their environment, including their own bodies and their parts, through kinesthetic (sensorimotor) feedback. (Ornitz, 1978)

In summary, then, the experience in this study points to the physical turtle as an important element in the Edinburgh success.

Terry: Finding Meaningful Components

An extremely interesting interaction occurred between Scrimshaw and his student Terry, age 11, with an IQ of 56 and diagnosed as autistic. Terry's enthusiasm for Logo far outshone his interest in anything else he did at the school. His fine motor skills and visual-motor coordination were good. His language development was abnormal, as evidenced by choppy speech, use of sentence fragments, echolalia, and very evident comprehension restriction. His teachers had the impression that he frequently did not understand the relationship between cause and effect. Terry had twenty sessions of Logo, each lasting about twenty minutes. He had the excellent memory for details shown by many autistics and quickly learned the keyboard layout. He also learned two sequences of characters during his first lesson that served him well. He learned to type FD 45 and RT 90 and, from then on, he stuck with those two combinations as the only two he used. They were useful, enabling him to draw a square, which pleased him.

But just what he understood by the two sequences came to be an intriguing puzzle for us, connected with general issues of language usage in autistic children.

Because of the explicit nature of the Logo activity, it was easy to see that his understanding was unusual, to say the least. He seemed to treat the whole phrase "eff-dee-space-forty-five" as a single monolithic entity, saying it rapidly as a continuous string of sounds at the same pitch, typing the characters without error, without leaving out a space ever, and apparently without dividing the continuous flow of sound into meaningful components. The only thing he would occasionally forget was the return key which comes at the end of each command and tells the computer to go ahead and process that command. Evidently, the return key was not part of the entity he had constructed. Once this construction was noticed, various situations were set up to encourage Terry to use different numbers with each of the two commands, so that he would learn to dissociate the two parts, to separate the "forty-five" from the "forward." Tasks were introduced such as drawing a house. To get the sloping roof, it is necessary to use RIGHT with 45 as input rather than 90, as in SQUARE; and FORWARD needs a range of numbers other than 45 to get the different sizes of window, door, and frame. Limited success was reported in that, although Terry continued to use only 45 and 90 as his numbers, he did learn to use each number as a possible input to either command.

This situation persisted as long as he was using the screen turtle. The breakthrough came when the physical turtle was introduced. Whereas throughout the screen-based work, he needed considerable prompting to initiate any action, Terry was one of the children who most appreciated the change to the floor turtle. He became much more self-directed and chose a wider range of numbers. When left to his own devices, he continued to have a small set of favorite numbers which he tended to stick to for long periods of time, but showed flexibility about which particular one he chose. Thus at one point, 5, 7, and 20 made up the privileged set from which he chose his numbers, and at any one session during this period, he would pick two of these as inputs to the two commands he was using, say, FD 5 and RT 7, and stay with these same two numbers throughout that session. When asked to use another number, he would oblige and change his choice, a cooperation that had not been evident at all during the screen-based work, when if anything, he tended to do the opposite of what he was asked to do.

Again, as with Donald, we were struck by Terry's emotional response to the physical turtle, to this real physical object that he could visit, walk around, and touch, as well as control via the computer. Most striking was Terry's response to a successful turtle move. This delighted him and made him laugh excitedly with a display of emotion most unusual for him. Terry became less vulnerable to the presence of strangers. On the day he brought the turtle, the donor, a stranger to Terry, stayed on to observe his reactions. In spite of the fact that this sort of intrusion had invariably upset Terry in the past, this time he went ahead and did well, showing a level of self-confidence and pleasure that surprised us.

What does all this tell us about the underlying disorder in autism? In the next chapter I link these findings with the clinical descriptions of the disorder and discuss classroom applications.

Chapter Fifteen

AUTISM AND COGNITIVE THEMES

Autism, with its combination of alertness and multiple cognitive defects, especially the gross impairment of language, compels attention and defies explanation. I take as my point of departure the autistic child's "insistence on sameness" in his environment. Individuals differ in how much they emphasize the similarities or the differences between objects and events. I view autistic children as occurring at the extreme end of a "fussiness" continuum in that they demand an exact match before they are prepared to call two entities the same. In this respect, there is a resemblance between the thinking of autistic children and the functioning of computer programs. The point is that there are serious consequences for cognitive functioning of this inability to handle any suggestion of ambiguity, implications that can account for many features of the syndrome.

Early Childhood Autism

The term "early childhood autism" was used for the first time in 1943 by Leo Kanner who described eleven children showing a characteristic cluster of features sufficiently distinct from childhood schizophrenia to constitute a new syndrome. The outstanding fundamental disorder in his view was the inability of these children to "relate themselves in the ordinary way to people and situations." In addition to this *failure to develop social relationships*, they showed serious *abnormalities of language development*, and *ritualistic* or *compulsive phenomena*, as part of what Kanner called an obsessive insistence on sameness. Since then many cases have been reported, with various combinations of symptoms more or less closely resembling Kanner's original description, and a multitude of studies have aimed at sorting out the nature of autism (for a recent review, see Rutter and Schopler, 1978).

Some claim that there is no such category and treat autistic behavior as part of other syndromes, but a more generally accepted view holds that a number of associated behaviors arise sufficiently often together, in early infancy, to constitute a separate clinical syndrome. The themes are recurring, and successive authors use the same phrases to describe this uncommon but fascinating collection of phenomena.[1]

Ritualistic and Compulsive Phenomena

The insistence on maintaining sameness in the environment is a feature of autism that has stood out from the first descriptions. The child is described as having an excellent memory for the position of objects in his room which he likes to maintain in precisely the same arrangement. There is often an intense preoccupation with particular objects, which are handled with skill in fine motor movements, but in a manner inappropriate to their designed use. Repetitive behavior is frequent, such as facial grimaces or hand flapping for several seconds at a time. Particularly important are the familiar routines of daily life. There may be dramatic scenes if a new route is followed for the daily walk.

This peculiarity extends to the details of therapeutic regimes used and can affect responses. For example, in using behavior therapy, the therapist sets up a temporal association between some specific behavior item and some particular reinforcement sequence, some specific conditioning. To get conditioning to work always requires maintaining some care in the timing of the reinforcement schedule in relation to the relevant behavior. For autistic children, a consistent timing must be absolutely rigid and unvarying. If these contingency schedules are not strictly adhered to, if the timing is not maintained exactly the same, there will be a disintegration of the training pattern (Kozloff, 1974). In our Edinburgh work, we soon learned to avoid changing arrangements for our Logo sessions. I remember how we once had to go to the school to pacify Donald (described in Chapter Six), who was totally upset by a schedule change.

---

1.   Autism occurs in about 4 out of 10,000 children under 15 years.

Disturbed Interpersonal Relationships

A disturbance in the ability to develop interpersonal relationships is the feature that gave the syndrome its name.[2] Lack of interest in social contact is apparent from an early age. The infant does not adopt an anticipatory posture or lift up her arms to be picked up; the growing child limits eye-to-eye gaze. It is not clear whether this poor social responsiveness is an active avoidance, or rather an absence of expected social behavior because of a lack of appreciation of the multiplicity of roles involved in any reciprocal relationship.

Avoidance behavior typically leads adults to increase their efforts to make contact with the autistic child, which in turn further aggravates the withdrawal (Richer and Richards, 1975). Social avoidance is increased when children become stressed by tasks they find too difficult (Churchill, 1972). Certainly in Donald's case, he assumed appropriate social roles more readily as he understood the situation better. A lack of participation in mutual give-and-take, the so-called turn-taking of social and verbal discourse, is part of a general lack of communication skills.

To ponder why autistic children come to shun humanity as they do is to raise the question of the source of the impulse toward communication in normal children. Wing (1976) warns that the mystery and magic might be illusory. "Autistic children do have a fascination which lies partly in the feeling that somewhere there must be a key which will unlock hidden treasure. The skilled searcher will indeed find treasure, but the currency will be everyday and human, not fairy gold. In return for our attention, these children may give us the key to human language, which is the key to humanity itself."

Abnormal Language Development

About half of autistic children develop no language at all. For those who do acquire some language, development is delayed and deviant. Acquisition of syntactic aspects, such as grammar, is delayed, as in mental retardation, rather than deviant. In contrast, the development of meaning aspects of language goes drastically wrong: language comprehension is deviant. Kanner gave many examples. One child chanted "Peter-eater" every time he saw a saucepan, because once when he was much younger his mother happen to drop a saucepan while reciting "Peter, Peter, pumpkin eater."

---

2.   From the Greek *autos* meaning "self" or "same."

He liked the words, and so he labeled what was for him the salient element in the situation -- the saucepan -- with the words he was hearing (Kanner, 1946). Another child called a bread basket a "home bakery" because that was the label on the store in which he had first seen a basket. He then went on to call all baskets "home-bakery." A phrase is linked to an item in the situation, only unfortunately for the child it is often not a conventionally agreed upon linkage.

If "sit at the table" was learned and understood in the classroom, it is not recognized as meaning the same thing when used in a restaurant. The label seems to be attached to the whole classroom, and, since the new situation does not have those wall charts and desks in it, the words are not given the same meaning in this new situation. Clara Claiborne Park, in her revealing and informative book about her autistic daughter Elly describes how difficult it was to teach her daughter action words, verbs. She had adopted the technique of teaching by drawing an image. Since action requires an actor and often an object acted upon as well, more than one meaning could be abstracted from the simplest verb-picture. "From it, Elly must draw out the right thing -- right not in her terms but in ours. . . . We soon found that the drawing by which we tried to teach 'play' might teach 'swing' or 'girl' instead" (Park, 1967).

Knowing which element in a complex situation to attach the spoken label to is a well-known problem. Quine in *Word and Object* (1969) tells the story. A linguist is in a glade with a native-speaking informant; a rabbit scurries by, the native says "gavagai," and the linguist notes down the word "rabbit" as a tentative translation. The linguist then has to test out his understanding of this new word by offering it under circumstances in which the appropriate stimulus (i.e., a rabbit) appears. But how is he to understand what amounts to assent or dissent? Even if he figures out what is "yes" and what is "no," he would still have a problem. Suppose, for example, the word uttered refers to part of the rabbit and not the whole rabbit. How can the linguist distinguish these two possibilities from the responses of the informant, for each time the rabbit appears, so would the rabbit-part appear, and so the informant would assent to the query "gavagai?" His informant tells him that "gavagai" means . . . well what does it mean? If he already knew which aspect or attribute to look at, he would know what is being named; and if he knew what is being named, he would know where to look. To what aspect of the complex stimulus pattern entering his perceptual field and waiting to be identified should the linguist attend?

This is the dilemma of every learner listening to every explanation, the problem of relevance, of what to attend to. The surprising thing in a way is how a growing child ever solves the problem. A solution for the autistic child frequently involves using the word meant for the whole as though it applied to the part, or vice versa, with disastrous consequences for communication.

An Underlying Explanation: Requirement of an Exact Match

How can we bring the features of autism together under one explanation? Many conjectures have been offered and criticized, most often, as simplistic and biased toward the particular fad-therapy being tried. And I am about to offer another, also based on the particular approach I have taken. First, I would note that complexity of surface phenomena does not necessarily involve an underlying complexity. Consider the classic example of a turtle geometry program, the POLY program.

```
TO POLY :SIDE :ANGLE
FORWARD :SIDE
RIGHT :ANGLE
POLY :SIDE :ANGLE
END
```

This simple five-line program yields a large number of figures depending on the value given to the variables SIDE and ANGLE (Figure 15.1). A small change in the value of the angle produces a large change in the shape. This resembles the situation in linguistics, where a deep rule captures what is common to a large family of utterances; each utterance has a different surface appearance, but belongs to the same family of sentences as defined by their deep structure. In POLY, the program gives the deep rule, and each time we call the program with a specific input, we get a different surface form. In looking for an explanation for the phenomena of autism, it could be that small deviations in a very basic mechanism give rise to a large number of different symptoms. The method adopted is to choose a deviation in a deep rule that will almost certainly be an oversimplification, but which provides some initial mileage as one works through its consequences.

The deep rule I choose concerns the symbolic matching process, introduced in the account of perception given earlier (page 58). This process, I claim, is deviant in the autistic child. I talked of identifying "the thing out there" as a two-way interaction between incoming stimulus patterns and stored mental schemas. Matching a schema to some object out there in the scene being viewed helps break that scene up, segments the scene into its component objects. Since exactly repeated experience is unlikely, much hangs on the criteria for identifying two objects as the same.

Suppose autistic children insist that when any symbolic matching takes place, an *exact* match must exist before two things are called the same. I am proposing that autistic children are at the extreme end of the "fussiness" spectrum I described in Chapter Eleven, when discussing personality differences (page 126). I suggested that individuals of the obsessoid personality type, being more particular, insist on confirming the presence of more of the details contained in the schema than do their hysteroid counterparts. Autistic individuals are obsessoid to a degree that paralyzes their cognitive system.

To make my point, I need to show that requiring an exact match, when two different descriptions are being compared, can account in some degree for the wide range of signs and symptoms of autism, including the disorders of perception and concept formation, the disorders in language development and learning, as well as the insistence on sameness, the withdrawal from people, and the preference of machines to people. The idea is to follow the consequences of the exact-match assumption, in particular, how it leads to a difficulty with categorizing, a difficulty with learning, and problems with ambiguity, analogy, and metaphor.

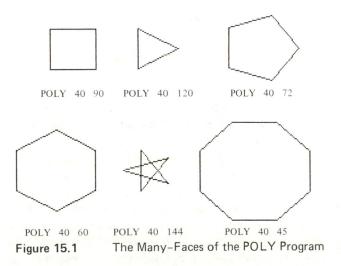

POLY 40 90   POLY 40 120   POLY 40 72

POLY 40 60   POLY 40 144   POLY 40 45

Figure 15.1   The Many–Faces of the POLY Program

Categories

Suppose you have descriptions of the form

John has a beard.
Sam has a beard.
Mike has a beard.

In order to generalize, in the natural way, to

These men have beards.

you need to notice the common features of human men among all of the instances, John, Sam, Mike, and to ignore the fact that Sam is short, fat, and wears glasses, that John is tall, thin, and has blond hair, and Mike has all sorts of attributes that are not shared by John and Sam. In order to generalize from a number of examples, one needs to focus on only the features that are alike in each of the examples and ignore features that are unlike. In short, one has to be prepared to allow for *partial matches* in order to establish the category *man*. What I am claiming is that this is just what an autistic child finds difficult to do. *Either all the properties are the same or the two things are different.* Things can't be alike in certain respects and unlike in others. What then becomes of the process of recognition? Nothing is ever exactly the same as it was before. To the extent that the child cannot use a stored schema to help him find the objects in a scene, so will he fail to segment the scene into familiar components. An autistic child can label but has difficulty segmenting wholes into parts; the label will refer to the whole description, treated as an entity. This should remind you of the "eff-dee-space-forty-five" entity (page 158), where it seemed that Terry was using this label to refer to the whole string of characters that he typed in. We saw examples of this "monolithic labeling" phenomenon in the section on the deviant language of the autistic child. Since the separation of words is not made readily, it follows that a word occurring in two different phrase-entities is not readily recognized as the same word.

In an extensive examination of the language of autistic children, Churchill (1972, 1978) used a basic nine-word language: three nouns -- *block, ring, stick*, three adjectives -- *red, yellow, blue*, and three verbs -- *give, tap, slide*. Low-functioning autistic children reached an impasse somewhere along the course of training. Thus, when prepositions were added, Larry showed certain rigidities in which a particular noun seemed to be preferentially associated with a particular preposition. For instance, any response to "beside" had a high probability of being "beside-cup." It was as though the main effect of the training was to improve one set of associations at the expense of the other, with no progress in integrating the two. When other objects were introduced, even though he knew them well, he could no longer apply the same prepositions to the "new" set of objects. George was taught simple sign language. Although he learned hundreds of associations quickly, there was never any evidence that he generalized from previously learned to novel stimuli.

Learning

The effect on learning of this non-recognition of closely similar but not identical stimuli could be disastrous. Again, we are dealing with an inability to recognize *partial matches*. How is it that a mind can come to understand anything new? During the usual course of events, if the new experience is sufficiently close to an old one, it can be seen as a version of that old situation. Interpreting the mismatch between the two and updating the stored schema accordingly constitute learning. Learning will happen more readily when new and old do not match exactly, but *nearly* match. Instead of recording the description of the new as an isolated event, the learner records the difference between it and the already recorded old event and, perhaps, the significance of that difference. The central process is making connections between experiences and between things; making judgments: about what is the same and what is different; and noting the meaning of the difference. Clearly, such comparisons and updatings are difficult if not impossible for a system that treats things that are nearly the same as two totally different entities.

It would seem that the fascination for machines, so characteristic of the autistic child, is not at all uninteresting or beside the point. It is related to the exact predictability of the machine: thus, given a particular rule and a particular set of circumstances, the machine will do the same as it did last time under the same set of circumstances. All computer-based activity is structured with the kind of regularity that characterizes the thinking of autistic children. Examples of this kind of thinking, which involves an overcommittal to regularity, are given by Park (1967). Using a very good rule, Elly produces *zeroty* and *onety* when told about *twenty* and *thirty*. Computers do not have the notion of the exception to the rule, unless you build it in to your program. Autistics don't either; they like rules without exceptions. Very young children will produce something like zeroty (see, for example, Ginsburg, 1977), and then grow out of this tendency to overgeneralize a rule. Autistic children stay that way.

Language

This demand for an exact match makes for problems when it comes to understanding natural language.   There are a number of places where things can go wrong.

The acquisition of language can be viewed as a process of *mapping linguistic structures onto non-linguistic systems of knowledge,* for example, onto sensorimotor intelligence (action patterns) that the child already has. Using analogy as a basis for mapping across systems is a process that autistic children find particularly difficult, since using analogy rests on being able to handle partial matches. If one aspect of the new task matches an aspect of an old task already known, then by making the analogy between the two, I can mobilize some of the skills I had for that task in the service of mastering this one, remembering to make the changes necessary to cope with the differences. This points directly to one reason why autistic children find it hard, if not impossible, to acquire the use of language.

In addition, there is the failure to segment. In an earlier example, the concept "table" was embedded in the specific instance in which it occurred, in the context of the classroom. To refer to an "it" that is embedded in a context seems to imply that the "it" has been identified. In as much as one understands what is happening, the problem for autistic children seems to be that the "it" is not distinguished and isolated as a separate entity. Either the whole image is left unsegmented or, as in the case of the verb-picture, the part selected for labeling is not the one the adult intended. Knowing where to segment and what to label is part of the recognition problem, in which schema-matching plays a crucial role. It is because this process is disordered that autistic children segment and label idiosyncratically. This is reflected in the strangeness and inscrutability of their language.

Not only do things have to be exactly the same, if the autistic is to give them the same label, but there can't be two possible meanings for any one label. That is just the sort of problem a computer programmer has if she tries to get a computer to understand natural language.   Humans disambiguate the meaning of a word by using the context in which it occurs.[3] To know the meaning of "pen" in the sentence "The baby is in the pen" involves understanding which pen is being referred to, and this rests

---

3.   Translated into schema-invocation terms, the cluster of schemas triggered by an event make up the context that disambiguates that event, and the information in each schema allows us to infer which meaning to choose out of several possible meanings.

on knowledge about babies and what they can and cannot fit inside of, knowledge that must be present in a schema, or built into the language-understanding program.

Social Consequences: Withdrawal and Affective Changes

For anyone who demands an exact match between two experiences before they qualify for the same name, functioning in an everchanging world becomes a major problem. I am suggesting that the degree to which the child insists on an exact match will determine the severity of the affliction. At its extreme, this requirement could be devastating, resulting in the total failure of the individual to make sense of any communications or, indeed, of anything at all in her environment. The less severely affected individual would be helped if things in the immediate environment remained unchanged, and it could be that the little routines autistic children develop of repeating sequences of activity over and over again (ritualistic behaviors, stereotypies) serve the purpose of creating the desired, familiar sameness at times of stress.

Machines do stay the same, much more so in any event than do people. This could underly the autistic child's preference for machines over people, and we were not surprised that Donald liked our machine. We did anticipate having a "transfer" problem -- weaning him off the machine and on to people, but, in the event, it turned out to be quite the contrary. An increase in the predictability of the environment -- "that button always produced that same thing" -- together with the features already referred to that led to a sense of shared relevance, yielded a warmly interacting individual, who made the socially appropriate, turn-taking moves and intercommunicative gestures.

When we met Donald his behavior was typical of an autistic -- the avoidance of eye contact; the flat, high-pitched, and mechanical voice; the withdrawn stance; the lack of spontaneous activity. During the Logo sessions, he rapidly changed from one emotional stance to another, depending on the circumstances. At one moment he would be happily exploring the turtle. Suddenly he would freeze, totally flat, disconnected, apparently showing no anxiety, no affect in any particular direction. He was always unwilling to expose himself to risk. His parents told us how he had refused to try out his new bicycle when urged to by a circle of family members. Several days later he appeared, riding happily. It transpired that he had hidden behind the shed and learned to ride, away from the scrutiny of others. There are two kinds of withdrawal: the *hyperesthetic* form of autistic aloneness, in which the individual is oversensitive to his environment and retreats into an inner fantasy life, and the second *anesthetic* variety of withdrawal into self, of autism, in which there is a lack of affective response without (apparently) any great inner experience. If you can't generalize, if every moment is new, you would necessarily be separated from, not belong to, the normal life around you.

Children had consistently enjoyed doing Logo. This did not prepare us for the major change in affective behavior observed in Donald during his Logo sessions. Indeed, it was his reaction that pointed me to the potential of Logo as a tool for studying the close connections between cognitive and affective processes. Parents of autistic children complain that their children are motiveless. Park articulates the problem in a moving description of her daughter's autism. "It's the sense of purpose that's missing. What seems impaired is not only the capacity for affect, but another capacity perhaps even more fundamental, the capacity for undertaking exploratory behavior and sustaining it. We know little about what we still call by its old-fashioned name of curiosity, still less about the qualities we describe, with more sophistication, as 'motivation' or 'drive'" (Park, 1967). In the spirit of what has been said above, one could speculate that one aspect of this failure to be goal-driven could have something to do with the difficulty of seeing two descriptions as being nearly the same; in this case, the descriptions would refer to two states of the world, the current state and the goal state. Missing would be the goal-directed activity, generated in the normal course of events, by a desire to reduce that difference.

Relation to Existing Theories

My purpose in proposing the exact-match mechanism is to make more specific and to unify some of the general formulations already in the literature. For example, Scheerer and his colleagues (1945) referred to an inability to relate new stimuli to remembered experience among autistic children. Rimland (1964) talked of "stored material emerging unmodified, uncategorized." Menyuk (1978) recognized the basic deficit as one of categorizing and discriminating. Hermelin (1976) refers to the central cognitive pathology underlying autism as an inability to reduce information through the appropriate extraction of crucial features such as rules and redundancies. In fact, as has already been mentioned, the rule-using and rule-creating ability of autistics is a complicated issue. There are circumstances in which autistic children can use rules. What they can't handle, it seems to me, are exceptions to the rules. The rule has to apply in exactly the same way each time.

More recently, Hermelin (1978) uses the Scheerer explanation of a failure to relate present experience to past experience. However, it does not seem to be the case that autistic children can't use past experience at all. Rather, the trouble seems to be that the linkage made between current and past experience is idiosyncratic and comes out as bizarre, until one ferrets out the context in which any particular apparently "meaningless" phrase was originally acquired. Kanner's language examples, given earlier, show a remarkable memory for past experience -- the "pumpkin-eater" experience had occurred many years prior to the use of "peter-eater" to refer to a saucepan.

The explanation proposed here to account for aspects of autism in terms of a disturbance in the mental schema-matching mechanism provides an example of the general hypothesis that children with special needs occur at the extreme end of a spectrum of behavior, where the same underlying mental mechanisms are at work as in so-called normal children. The schema-matching mechanism is regarded as basic to the use of stored past experience to process current experience by all persons. The disorder arises when a change in the matching rules at one point in the process has major consequences further along the process: a small change in the underlying rules leads to a big change in surface behavior.

No doubt the debate will continue. An important question is whether we can make use of any of this in a practical way.

The Computer as a Therapeutic Tool in Autism

The use of computers with autistic children is not new. Colby and Smith (1971) stressed the merits of the machine: a small amount of effort in pressing a key produces a large effect; *the machine is untiring, predictable, always saying the same thing the same way, never angry, never bored.* Colby used computers to stimulate language development in non-speaking autistics. He developed games in which pressing the keys on the keyboard caused symbols to appear on the screen, accompanied by sounds of human voices. Of the seventeen non-speaking autistics he worked with, he judged thirteen to have improved in language development after fifty to a hundred half-hour sessions; improvement meant uttering appropriate intelligible words and phrases in social communication.

Logo-like environments work to the extent that they supply structure as the basis for predictability, yet leave the child in control. I like to use the mechanical turtle to introduce Logo to autistic children, as I do when I work with very young children. My approach is to prepare a wide range of activities to cater to the differing interests and levels of cognitive ability of these children. A recent project illustrates the paths autistic children take through these activities. During the summer of 1984, Patria Leroy, a teacher doing graduate work at Lesley College, worked with ten

Langridge School students aged 9 to 14 years. Of these emotionally and cognitively disturbed children, four were diagnosed as autistic and five had evidence of brain damage. The range of measured IQ was 70 to 90. We planned a repertoire of activities.

1. *Playing turtle*. Before introducing the computer, Leroy spent time in the regular classroom, observing the children, and "playing turtle" with them.

2. *Physical turtle*. For their subsequent sessions, the children were taken in pairs to the gym, where the computer had been set up. Activity began with the physical turtle. Various props were introduced, including piles of blocks, a road marked out with masking tape along which the turtle was to be guided (the road took several acute and right-angled turns), and a set of mazes, drawn on large pieces of paper or plastic. Some children engaged in cooperative activities -- one built a tunnel, the other knocked it down. We saw again the behavior we had seen with Donald, namely, a running commentary on the movements of the turtle -- "and go forwards . . . and turn right." Seven of the ten children worked well with the physical turtle. The remaining three students were less interested in the robot and moved quickly on to screen work.

3. PRINT *command*. One of these, 10-year-old autistic child, Cal, started straight off with the PRINT command, apparently in response to his evident pleasure in saying "Hello" to the computer. This child, whose measured Verbal IQ was 70, spent ten half-hour sessions using PRINT and REPEAT. He readily mastered the syntax, read and copied out error messages, and produced this letter during his ninth session, refusing any help from the teacher.

```
TO LETTER
PRINT [DEAR, SNUFFLE-UPAGUS]
PRINT [WHAT ARE YOU DOING IN YOUR UNDERGROUND CAVE]
PRINT [WELL I:M MAKING A SNUFFLE-PARTY]
PRINT [IAM GOING TO INVITE SNUFFLE-UPAGUS AND BIRD WILL BE THERE AT
THE PARTY]
PRINT [SIGN ME AND SNUFFY]
PRINT [GOODBYE]
END
```

Karl, a 12-year-old autistic child with a measured IQ of 89, had successfully driven the robot through the mazes provided, crawling around with the turtle in an involved way. In his seventh session, he asked to "Write a program with words." He used PRINT with much concentration to produce the following:

```
TO FAMOUS.PEOPLE                    TO TELEVISION.STATIONS
PRINT [GORGEWASHINGTON]             PRINT [CHANNEL 2]
PRINT [LENARDBRESHNEV]              PRINT [CHANNEL 4]
PRINT [ARTHURFIEDLER]               PRINT [CHANNEL 5]
PRINT [JOHNWILLIAMS]                PRINT [CHANNEL 7]
PRINT [SERGEPROKOFIEF]              END
PRINT [DEBRA]
END
```

4. *INSTANT*. Eight children used a simple version of the INSTANT program with one key for each Logo primitive: F, B, R, L, and E for erase. Five students used an enhanced INSTANT, with keys for a square, a curve, a triangle, a flower, a sun, and grass.

Karl, whose teacher described him as "the artist," used both versions of INSTANT to produce several drawings. He called his first drawing "Serge Prokofief" and a later one "The world" (Figure 15.2).

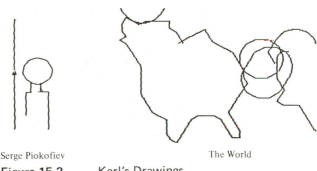

Serge Piokofiev   The World

Figure 15.2   Karl's Drawings

Max, a 9-year-old autistic child with a measured IQ of 58, was introduced to the simple version of INSTANT during his fourth session. He was told only that it worked like the floor turtle and he said, "I'll try F," showing that he could draw the parallel between the floor turtle and the screen turtle. He drew the shape ⌐→ , said "Down," and pressed D, using the rule: type the first letter of the command you want. He was told that this turtle only knew F, B, R, and L, chose R, and went on to complete his shape, saying "Box". At one point, he said, on his own and to himself, "Make my decision" (about what to make next).

5. *Standard Logo*. By the end of the summer three children had used standard Logo commands, including some elementary procedure

definition.   In his eighth session, Max used standard Logo to make a
procedure MAX.

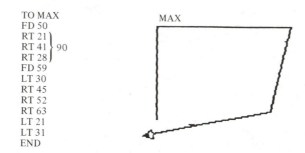

```
TO MAX
FD 50
RT 21 ⎤
RT 41 ⎬ 90
RT 28 ⎦
FD 59
LT 30
RT 45
RT 52
RT 63
LT 21
LT 31
END
```

        6.   *Animal program.*   A Logo implementation of the Animal
program, an interactive game in which players are invited to guess the
name of an animal (described in Abelson, 1982), was attempted by seven
children.   The program allows players to add their own animals and their
distinguishing characteristics to the initial set given in the program, and
those chosen by the children were sometimes idiosyncratic.   For example,
rather than think of animals, two (non-autistic) children thought of famous
people, and, in answer to "Can it run?"   when the person in mind was
Mondale, one replied gleefully, "Sure, he can run for president."
        It is interesting to note that these two non-autistic children were the
only ones in this study who did not respond well to Logo.   For the rest, the
computer became a means of expression, unusually revealing to us, and
rewarding for them.   I attribute our relative success largely to the strategy of
making a range of activities available through which the child and her
teacher can find their own path to productive engagement.

Chapter Sixteen

EDUCATING THE PHYSICALLY DISABLED

Give a man a fish, and he will eat for a day. Teach him how to fish and he will eat for the rest of his life.

Chinese proverb

The next few chapters present the Logo experiences of children who suffer a serious physical handicap. Estimates developed from the 1977 Health Interview Survey (reported in Technology and Handicapped People, 1982) tell us that one and a half million people in the United States are affected by paralysis, two and a half million have impaired upper extremities, and seven million have impaired lower extremities. The computer will play an enormous role in the lives of these people. For them, Logo can serve as a toolmaker, allowing the construction of diagnostic, remedial, and research tools. There are particular reasons why, for this population, the enabling function of the computer serves a liberating role. As will become clear, the impact on the school we worked in has been far more than just the introduction of another subject into the curriculum. Further, the lessons learned have implications for the non-handicapped.

The Computer Can Change Lives

Imagine you have grown up never using a pen or pencil. You are capable of sophisticated intellectual activity, but have to do it all in your head.

Someone comes along and offers you a chance to "write it down."

You are accustomed to sitting around waiting for someone to be free so that you can get on with your learning, which is only possible with them around. Someone comes along and arranges things so that you can now get on with it, when you want to, without disturbing any one else, at your own pace, for as long as you feel moved so to do.

You are used to someone else's taking the initiative, while you sit passively. You don't really expect any action that you take will make any difference to the world out there. Things get done *to* you, rather than *by* you. Someone comes along with the most powerful piece of technology known and puts you in control of it. You get to choose what project you will do, what you will "teach" that "dumb" computer.

When a handicapped individual does not engage in the ordinary range of motor activities, one of the things that is missing from her life is the important experience of seeing the effect of an action she takes. There is a lack of explicit confrontation between actions performed and the consequences of such actions in the physical world. This has several profound effects, emotional, cognitive, and social. There is a distortion of the processes that ordinarily support the development of a belief in one's power to affect the world, a sense of self-competence and self-esteem. One of the most moving aspects of working in this area has been the extent to which we have been able to make a difference to the lives of such individuals. The superintendent of the Feltham School (see page 24) wrote in a letter (March 12, 1979):

> Since Project Logo we have seen a remarkable change in Mike. With the development of these new skills, Mike is now "somebody!" . . . He has developed a wonderful sense of self-worth, and his personality has improved remarkably. He now has a more positive attitude, has developed poise and shows more confidence in his ability to contribute. The "bottom line" is vocational placement. That is the purpose of the school, and Project Logo has opened up a new avenue for us to explore when planning for our more severely handicapped students. (Weir, 1981b)

Missing Schemas

What happens if the interaction between schema and experience is disturbed? Consider the unusual childhood of an individual handicapped from birth. If the handicap is sufficiently severe, the child will not have handled objects as part of growing up, and the question arises as to the effect of this lack of manipulative experience on the development of the mental schemas of these individuals. If you have not had the opportunity to put things together and take them apart, to draw, mold, or build shapes, structures, or likenesses; if your opportunity for finding out about spatial relationships in the environment has been restricted by your dependence on others for mobility; if all this has been your lot, then what chance is there for you to develop a coherent system of spatial understanding? What can we learn from a study of the consequences of such deprivation about the development of cognitive processes in general, and what are the educational consequences of such a disruption in opportunity? What happens to the pedagogical principle of surfacing existing knowledge I have been stressing when the experience needed to acquire that existing knowledge is missing?

Educational Plans

In planning the education of individuals with cerebral palsy there are several factors to consider.[1] Beyond the obvious motor disability, specific cognitive deficits can occur as a secondary consequence of restricted experience, and our efforts should be directed to reducing these effects. It is as well to remember, however, that a pure motor disorder is rare since the various causal agents of cerebral palsy do not necessarily recognize functional boundaries and cognitive deficits can result from direct damage to parts of the brain other than the motor areas. Since one cannot easily determine the extent to which improvement will be limited by irreversible brain damage, there is always a purpose to be served in pursuing the possibility for improvement

My own experience is confined to observing the responses of children in the Logo environment, and in general, I have been surprised by the amount of learning that can take place. My observation is that most handicapped children are functioning below their capacity because of the lack of interactive opportunities in their lives. With lowered expectations, there is a danger that the educational situation will be perceived as a holding operation; that too little challenge will be presented; that too much will be done for the disabled, rather than making the arrangements necessary for them to do things for themselves. The resultant poor self-image and passivity in turn perpetuates poor achievement, a vicious circle justifying and intensifying the lowered expectations. Jose Valente

---

1.   Cerebral palsy is a disorder of movement and posture resulting from a permanent, non-progressive defect or lesion in the brain occurring before the end of the first year of life.

writes:[2]

> The first thing we see when we approach a physically handicapped person who is trying to do something on his own is the heroic struggle this person goes through in order to accomplish the task. Our immediate reaction is to help. With the best of intentions we help by fulfilling all his requests. We are motivated by the affective aspect of the human relationship and become trapped in that role. Our tendency is not to consider a more effective way to help, nor to provide that person with means to overcome his physical problems in order to be more independent. Instead we create dependency. . . . I was once approached by a teacher who said that I did not need my "computer paraphernalia" to teach the physically handicapped, what I needed was "to love them." When I asked her what she would do if her students told her they wanted to write or draw something, she said that if their physical handicap prevented them from doing it she would write or draw for them. It is interesting that it never occurred to her that possibly her students were not interested in the final product but rather in the act of producing the drawing or the writing for themselves. Her "love" was preventing her from finding ways in which these children would be able to accomplish certain tasks on their own. (J. Valente, 1983)

One is reminded of the demonstration of the major role played by teachers' expectations in determining the achievement of their students in the 1968 study by Rosenthal and Jacobson. Twenty percent of the children in a certain elementary school were reported to their teachers as showing unusual potential for intellectual growth. The names of these twenty percent had been drawn by means of a table of random numbers, which is to say, the names were drawn out of a hat. Eight months later these unusual or "magic" children showed significantly greater gains in IQ than did the remaining children who had not been singled out for the teachers' attention (Rosenthal and Jacobson, 1968). The change in the teachers' expectations regarding the intellectual performance of these allegedly "special" children had led to an actual change in the intellectual performance of these randomly selected children.

Something almost as strong might be going on in the classes of handicapped children. It could be that the care and affection and intense solicitude that the caretakers of these children bestow on them, the degree

---

2.   Jose Valente was a member of the MIT-Feltham project.

to which things are done for them, and the reduced expectation of levels of achievement -- all these things conspire to produce an actual lowering of performance.   Equally misguided would be too high an expectation, assuming too much potential in those children where the brain damage has gone beyond the boundaries of the motor areas and places definite ceilings on achievement.   My approach is to both improve assessment and create opportunities for each child to show what she can do.   Current assessment facilities provide an inadequate basis for prediction and will need to be enhanced by computer-based tasks that support active involvement. Indeed, performance during Logo activity itself is often a good test of what the child is capable of.   This means the child's regular teacher can play an integral part both in the assessment process and in tailoring the computational environment to the needs of each child.

An Information Prosthetic

It is important to stress that the role of the electronic device in the situation I am describing is somewhat different from the usual function of electronic communicators.   The computer is not simply acting as a bridge from the child to some other activity, as prosthetic devices usually do.   The electronic system is acting as a communication device, but *the emphasis is on giving handicapped individuals the facility to have interesting, exciting, and creative things to communicate about* (Weir, 1981b).   The power of the electronic system lies in the information processing that it supports, comes from the fact that it is an *information prosthetic*.   The central purpose is to encourage and facilitate cognitive and social interaction and the development of language for communication (Weir, Russell, and Valente, 1982).

The overall situation aimed for is, as always, one that is simple enough to engender security in the child and yet challenging enough to engage her interest and problem-solving capabilities. Progress is invariably slow because of the presence of the physical handicap, and one aims to steer a middle course between reducing the effects of the motor restriction and stifling initiative by overdoing the help. Making things too easy rarely works. How much do you help with a crutch and how much you leave the child to struggle? Notice this is exactly the same question we ask in relation to the education of all children.

On the whole, a handicapped person prefers not to use special help if he can possibly get away without it. The more the arrangements resemble those for normal children the better. It feels good to be able to manage. The more in control and the greater the sense of independence, the happier the outcome. All the children with whom we worked could type.

The DELETE key was invaluable since unintended keys were hit annoyingly often. The effort required was reduced by the use of simple devices for reducing the number of gestures required. We used a button-box for the younger children as well as for the more severely handicapped, both for pedagogic reasons -- beginning Logo is easier when each push of a button results in a single action -- and as a way of speeding things up for those students whose slow typing made learning anything at all too difficult. For example, for their work with the first through fourth graders, Susan Jo Russell and Eileen Kiernan used a hardware button-box, indeed, the original button-box used by Perlman (1974), revived and modified by Valente.[3] The Boston button-box, like the Edinburgh one, is a plastic box with large, well-spaced buttons to prevent unintentional keystrokes, troublesome when involuntary movements are present, as is often the case with cerebral palsy children. A similar effect can be achieved by single-key Logo (see page 55), in effect a software button-box. Larger primitives can be defined in the same way, e.g., a ready-made square, a quarter-circle, a triangle, each available at the push of a single key. It is a good idea to record each keystroke as it is made, so that the user can name the picture she has produced and can then use that named picture as the building block for a more complex design (Figure 16.1).

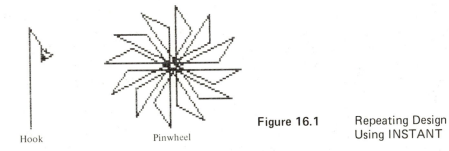

Hook   Pinwheel   **Figure 16.1**   Repeating Design
                                                                    Using INSTANT

Exercising the affected hands and fingers was a side effect of all the typing and resulted in unexpected improvements in fine motor control. In many ways there were advantages in living with the slowness. Requiring the typing became a therapeutic tool, whereby an intrinsic interest in the computer-based activities themselves provided an intense motivation to

---

3.   Valente rewired the Perlman device so that it could be linked to the Apple computer via the paddles for use as the input device for younger cerebral palsy children.

perform the movements. Children mobilized their own tools, for example, several used loosely gripped pencils to depress the keys.

It should be evident that decisions about the role of the computer are multidimensional and have to do with more than just the content of the lessons. Again, this is just what has been said about the role of the computer in the education of non-handicapped children.

The Feltham School

Experience over the years 1978 to 1982 at the Feltham School for Handicapped Children leaves little doubt that the computer-based Logo activities we have designed have had a considerable impact on the children with whom we have worked. The question of whether Logo activity has a place in a school curriculum for cerebral palsy students can be answered with a resounding "yes." Much of the work described below is taken from the records of the MIT research project. Since this ended in 1982, the school has continued to provide access to Logo for every child who comes into the school.

We began our project with an initial lecture-demonstration, attended by the entire staff of the Feltham School, at which we explained the Logo philosophy, demonstrated the activities, and outlined our reasons for wanting to use Logo in the education of the physically handicapped. Following a consultation with the superintendent, his administrative officer, and the head of the math-science department, it was decided to work intensively with Michael M., who was the most severely handicapped student in the school.

Since then, we have worked with many other children and with the staff of the Feltham School for four years. The range of activities covered a wide spectrum. More than ever, each child is a law unto himself. The use of the computer as a notebook-cum-scratchpad of ideas has replaced the need for *doing it all in the head* and has given a new lease to the intellectual life of these students. An important element in the observed success at the Feltham School is the way problem-solving experience is built into the daily Logo activity in a direct way, allowing the student to make hypotheses about likely outcomes of one or other course of action, test these ideas, and refine the hypotheses in the light of experience. In short, there is an opportunity for *sustained* problem-solving that is really difficult to achieve when the presence of physical handicap prevents the recording of intermediate results, upon which later problem-solving steps can be built.

All in all, the sheer fact of this whole new world of knowledge, and of their own independent management of the activity, has had a profound effect on the intellectual life of these students. Aside from the educational impact, the human and social consequences of the experience have been dramatic. As I have said, the impact on the institution has been profound, far more than just the introduction of another subject into the curriculum. The teachers have noticed this sudden access to all kinds of problem-solving activity that was not possible before. They have noticed the changes in their students -- the increase in confidence, the improvement in self-image, the increase in motivation -- with students arriving at school half an hour early and cutting lunches to get time on the machine. Indeed, it was their observation of this impact that led them to join the program and to begin their own training.

However, that is not to say there were no problems. Indeed, there will be years of working through the many nuances and unexpected turns of event connected with the use of this radically new tool. Here is an example of a short-term gain that turned out to be very counterproductive. Both for purposes of conceptual simplification and for purposes of overcoming motor restriction, we used the software button-box with several of the middle school Feltham pupils, sometimes with complicated results. Arlene was a 12-year-old student with cerebral palsy who was ambulatory with the help of a walker. She had some athetosis (involuntary movements) and paresis (weakness) of all four limbs. She made good progress using the software button-box. Using sequences of F's, B's, R's, and L's, she built up some complex and satisfying drawings. At what was judged to be the appropriate moment, she was introduced to regular Logo. Now for the first time she had to supply the inputs to individual instructions; now she had to calculate the required number, rather than rely on the number built into the single key. She found it depressingly difficult to achieve in standard Logo the complex drawings she had rolled out previously. We had inadvertently left the intellectual crutch around for too long, an especially risky thing to do, given the tendency towards passivity already present.

Quite a different situation occurred in the Michael M. story, which we will look at in the next chapter.

Chapter Seventeen

DETERMINATION AND A WILL TO ACHIEVE

An intelligent, spirited individual, grossly limited in the fulfillment of his potential by severe motor handicap, showed what could be accomplished with a computer. He moved from being a source of frustration to his teachers, who were unable to meet his needs and felt particular concern at the lack of available vocational outlets for him, to undertake a promising college career in computer science.

The Challenge

Michael was 17 years old when the project began, a quadriplegic cerebral palsy (all 4 limbs involved) following birth trauma. His disability was more marked on the right side, with sufficient residual motor power on the left to control his wheelchair, but not a writing implement. Involuntary movements caused his arms and legs to flail around and produced grimacing and drooling. His communication was extremely limited, since dysarthria badly garbled his speech, making him difficult to understand. His "written" work had been the dictation recorded by his mother. Academic progress had been grossly hampered by the consequences of his weak grip, depriving him of a scratchpad to record his working results.

We met Michael on our first day at Feltham. Bright he certainly was. In particular, he seemed to be very mathematical, but he was doing it all in his head. He had the use of a typewriter and a calculator, but had tremendous difficulty operating these devices. The school superintendent said, "You take him; I'm stuck. If you can get somewhere with him then I'll take you seriously." We were delighted. He was our first subject.

In my first report to our funding agency, I summarized the reasons for accepting Michael into the study. His high intelligence, as surmised by the staff, meant that he was likely to be able to exploit the intellectual power of the Logo environment.[1] He had a methodical approach to his work, a liking for challenges, and an enormous drive. This gave us a bias toward a favorable outcome, which was what was needed to get us going on this innovative track. His teachers were concerned that his motor and language disabilities were handicapping him. There was a gap between potential and realization, and the staff felt at a loss as to how to fill this gap. There was particular concern expressed at the relative paucity of possible vocational outlets, which in view of his age was becoming a pressing problem. This made him a paradigmatically suitable candidate for our work.

A Major Effect

Mike spent approximately ten hours a week at the computer from the onset of the project until he left school three years later. The story of Michael's interaction with the Logo system represents a classic example of the enormous effect this technology can have on the education and the life of a handicapped individual. Recently Michael attended the laboratory to participate in a videorecording session. There was a striking contrast between this energetic, purposeful, productive young man nimbly maneuvering the controls of his specially fitted car[2] and the student we had met four years previously, frustrated and deprived, in spite of his own efforts and those of his parents and teachers. A particular advantage of gaining access to the computer world for Michael was the way the activity had spoken to his strengths. One strength emerged unintentionally, namely, his extraordinarily powerful memory. Early on in his programming life, he lost several weeks work because of a machine failure to store his programs. Nothing daunted, he proceeded to type the whole set in again from memory!

Michael was brought to the Logo laboratory weekly during vacations when the computer at the school was not available to him. This gave his mother an opportunity to watch him at work. "Oh, so that's what

---

1.   At age 12 years and 4 months, he was tested on the WISC and the Peabody vocabulary tests and achieved a verbal score of 115. The performance tests could not be done. It was clear to us that this measure of his intelligence did not do justice to his ability.
2.   A mobile frame can be lowered and raised under his control, enabling him to "ride" into his car in his wheelchair.

he talks about upstairs at night, before he goes off to sleep!" She had heard but not understood his discussions with himself as he lay in bed solving Logo problems in his head. He produced a massive amount of programming code -- Valente calculated he filled 27 disks, each of which has the capacity to hold 512,000 characters. His typing speed improved from 9 characters per minute at the start of his Logo work to 23 characters per minute one year later.

After many months of intensive typing, he happened to attend the hospital for a routine checkup. His physician noticed an increase in fine motor control, inquired about what changes there had been in his life, and was told about the computer work he was doing. She subsequently visited the school and was delighted to receive a demonstration of his work from her patient. At the time of writing, there has been a continuation of this physical improvement, with fewer athetoid movements and much less salivation and grimacing than when we first met him. Shakey was his login name, and with characteristically robust good humor, he relished reading an account of a Stanford University robot, also called Shakey because of the poor motor control early programmed robots had.

On that first day, as he is fond of reminding us, as we sat in a huddle discussing what form of physical prosthetic he would need, he quietly wheeled himself up to the computer and "just got on with it." He invented a way of steadying his hand by curving his fingers around the top edge of the keyboard and gripping it, leaving his thumb free to type. Trouble came with the need to hold down two keys at once. This he was at first unable to do, and Valente would assist by holding one key down for him. A short while later, he appeared with a non-slipping weight that he had arranged for the school shop to make for him. This now meant that he could achieve simultaneous key depression in three moves. For example, if he needed CONTROL-P, he could first place the weight on the CONTROL key, then press the key for P, and then remove the weight. As time progressed, he learned to use two fingers together and brought his weaker hand into the activity, gradually exercising and reviving residual muscle potential.

Michael was offered virtually unlimited access to the computer, and, twice a week, Valente would spend two to three hours working with him. For the first few months, he was the only one at the school who was allowed to use the computer. His activity engendered much envy on the part of his classmates and led to a request from him for permission to run a class in which he would teach five fellow students. Soon, he was spending so much time on his teaching that he had no time left to pursue his own computer studies. An additional burden on his time was a consequence of the success of the program. Mike was the one who gave the demonstrations when visitors came to see our work. He was sensitive about the fact that it was taking him forever to type, and that this slow typing reduced the amount of material that could be demonstrated to the visitors. Characteristically, he did not rest with fretting about it, but produced a creative solution that advanced his programming skills.

He had noticed that, when doing our screen tasks (described in Chapter Eighteen), our system displayed a menu from which to chose the next task, and we were able to move from one task to the next by simply pressing a single key. Emulating this example, he wrote a program, Big Show, that gave him similar control, leading the visitor through a repertoire of available options for display and scrutiny. A print message addressed the visitor by name and invited her to select from a hierarchically arranged set of menus, the item or facility, procedure, or display she wished to view. The selected program was then automatically loaded and run, or parts of the computer code were displayed as requested. Mike's showman style and feel for effect was evident in his choice of a name like Winter Wonderland, a program of increasing complexity of rotating and interlocking shapes all constructed out of a square and a pentagon (Figure 17.1). Michael showed the end product first, had the visitor guess how many different shapes were used in the program, and then carefully explained the constructive process.

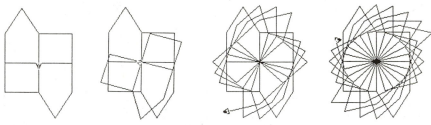

Figure 17.1   Michael's Winter Wonderland

Michael's Programming

Several points central to the Logo position are illustrated by Michael's story.

1. Logo is a serious programming language. Michael acquired a sophisticated knowledge of programming, as evidenced by the degree of control over his programs that he displayed during his demonstration of the Winter Wonderland example. He had progressed from simple programs with a flat sequential structure to programs with a more complex flow of control, using conditionals and subprocedures (J. Valente, 1983). A feature of these later programs was the prevalence of sophisticated programming concepts such as recursion, the use of list and array data structures, as well as the incorporation of algorithmic solutions to problems.

 2. *The student needs good models upon which to build his progress.* In order to accommodate his progressively larger programs, Mike was obliged to learn all the tricks that experienced programmers use to cope with memory restrictions. He carefully observed the programs that the MIT project members used for their various activities, and used the expertise embodied in those programs to achieve his purposes.

 3. *Logo drawings can act as a bridge into standard classroom work.* Drawings happened to be the objects that captured Michael's attention and evoked his hitherto untapped resources. Largely within the context of producing drawings, Michael's programming illustrated well the principle that achieving a drawing can involve much along the way. His programming became a tool with which to build bridges into standard academic activity.

 One of his projects concerned labeling a stop sign in his Copley Square program (Figure 17.2a) so that visitors would not confuse it with a drawing of a tree. Instead of simply writing the Logo procedures to draw the S_T_O_P, using the dimensions required by this particular picture, Michael decided that what was needed was a program for the general case. His new project, which lasted several months, was to write a procedure to draw each letter of the alphabet and the numbers 0 through 9. Each letter was placed in a rectangular envelope (Figure 17.2b), so the required size could be specified by giving the width and height of each letter. These variable input procedures were relatively easy to write for some letters, for example, the letter G in Figure 17.2c. But in the case where the letter has an oblique line, as in the letter R (Figure 17.2d), the slope changes with the proportion of height to width, and the angle of the slope could not be specified ahead of time as a fixed number. It had to be supplied as the trigonometric function: the ratio of the length of the side opposite the angle to the length of the side adjacent to the angle (Figure 17.2e).

 Not long after Michael completed his alphabet project the rest of the class embarked on their own versions of the project, each receiving an introduction to practical trigonometry via the project of his choice. The school until then had not included trigonometry at that stage of the curriculum, since it was regarded as too difficult for the students. Here we had classroom mathematics growing straight out of these fun projects, one answer to those who say "Who cares about drawings! Let's get to the serious stuff."

 This finding is, of course, not restricted to the work with the handicapped. In the past two years, careful accounts of how mathematical ideas emerge during Logo sessions have been reported by workers coming out of the traditional mathematics education world (Hillel, 1984; Hoyles et al., 1984; Hoyles, 1985; Leron 1985; Noss, 1985). For example, Noss showed a significant improvement in the understanding of geometric concepts following twenty to forty hours of Logo activity, especially with respect to angle conservation and angle measurement, in a group of eighty-four students aged 8 to 11 years, when compared to a control group of ninety-two students of matched mathematical ability.

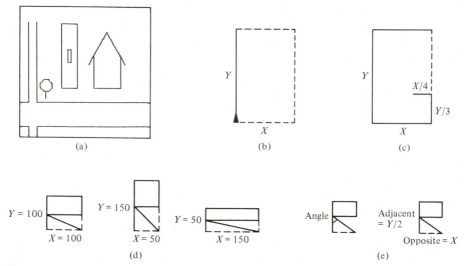

Figure 17.2   Michael's Copley Square Project. (*a*) Original drawing; (*b*) rectangular envelope for letters and numbers; (*c*) the letter *G*: (*d*) different inputs for the letter *R*; (*e*) calculating the slope of the line.

4.   Remedial software can be generated with Logo programs. Michael noticed that Valente was using a paper-drawn clockface with a student who was having trouble with selecting numbers for turning. "Why not do it on the computer?" he asked, and proceeded to write a program that told "the real time" by accessing the internal computer clock. For the clockface, he used the programs for generating numbers he had written for the Copley Square project.   He incorporated his recently acquired trigonometry knowledge into a program that reset the hands of the clock at the correct angle after the elapse of each minute.   The time shown on his clock corresponded to the time given by the internal computer clock.   He discovered that the time information is represented in the computer as a list of numbers, and he arranged for his program to go around a loop looking for a change in the numbers in that list, at which point it updated the position of the hands of the clock.

His clock program became a piece of remedial software, an example of what Michael called his "middleman" role in the project, helping us to work with other handicapped children.

5. *Logo can be used to develop application programs with vocational relevance*. The opportunity provided by the work with Logo for setting one's own tasks gave all the senior students a chance to look for application programs to help them get direct vocational experience. Problems in *business programming* suggested by the manager of the school print shop (a commercial venture which handled outside orders) yielded programming tasks of the sort he would need to know in order to hold down a job. Michael's estimate program involved estimating the cost of printing orders. A record of an interactive session using this program is shown.

```
HOW MANY JOBS ARE YOU GOING TO ESTIMATE AT THIS TIME? ...." # "    1
WHAT KIND OF STOCK PAPER? ...."W"                    INDEX
WHAT IS THE LENGTH OF THE PAPER? ...." # "      11
WHAT IS THE WIDTH OF THE PAPER? ...." # "       7
        MAX  WASTE       17
        SIZE             22.5 * 35
        WEIGHT           182
WHAT JOB NUMBER IS THIS ONE? ...." # "              12
WHAT TYPE OF JOB IS IT? ...."W"          1
TYPE A WORD
WHAT TYPE OF JOB IS IT? ...."W"          LETTER
HOW MANY PIECES OF PAPER? ...." # "      1000
HOW MUCH IS THE PAPER PER 1000 ...."$"          12
HOW MUCH IS THE NEGATIVE? ...."$"               5
HOW MANY NEGATIVES? ...." # "            1
HOW MUCH IS THE PLATE? ...."$"           5
HOW MANY PLATES? ...."3"                 1
HOW MUCH IS THE PRESS PER HOUR ...."$"                  35
WHAT IS THE RATE OF THE PRESS PER HOUR? ...." # "              3500
HOW MUCH IS THE ART PER HOUR? ...."$"                  39
HOW MANY WORKING HOURS WILL IT TAKE TO DO THE ART? ...." # "     .5
```

The interaction continues in this vein, dealing with amount and cost of ink, cost of cutting, trimming, folding, collating, stitching, and ending with the letter detailing the final estimated cost. A profit of 30% is added.

JOB NO. 12
             LETTER

```
COST OF PAPER PER 1,000 IS ....$12.00              $16.20
COST OF NEGATIVE IS .... $5.00                     $5.00
COST OF PLATE IS ....$5.00                         $5.00
COST OF INK IS ....$15.00                          $1.50
COST OF ART WORK IS ....$39.00                     $19.50
COST OF PRESS IS ....$35.00                        $10.00


THE TOTAL COST IS ....$57.20 * 1.30                $88.66
```

IF YOU WANT A PRINTOUT PUT THE PRINTER ON LINE AND PRESS "P"
IF YOU WOULD LIKE TO ESTIMATE OUTHER JOB, PRESS THE SPACE BAR.

This programming project involved writing routines for truncating and rounding off decimal numbers (not supplied as system routines in Logo), a further exploration of the way numbers are represented in the machine, developing an algorithm for choosing the size of stock paper appropriate to a given order so as to minimize wastage, and formatting routines to professionalize his output. The program Michael wrote enabled the print shop manager to carry out in a few minutes the cost estimates that had previously taken him several hours.

Planning for the Future: Communication Needs

Michael began to plan for his future, a future that now looked very different from the prospect he had faced previously. Vocational access is the "bottom line" for the pupils at Feltham, and the school runs an active program training students in various branches of the printing trade. As already mentioned, the school print shop operates as a commercial enterprise, taking in orders from the outside. There was no possibility, however, that an individual as disabled as Michael could participate in that program, and his schooling had not had much focus. He was now spending more and more time in the computer room, and he decided he wanted to earn his living working with computers. The school superintendent's hopes were being realized. Together, Michael and his teachers began to examine his needs for such a career. Michael had not written anything ever, since he could not hold a writing implement. If severely handicapped individuals are to hold down a job, the quality of their writing is important. Career access is enhanced by an ability to express oneself verbally. No one knew just what kind of text he would produce if left to himself. Prior to this, his caretakers had recorded his thoughts for him, turning these into "proper" prose in the process.[3] At first Michael was extremely reluctant to expose himself by trying. However, he was persuaded by the formula that always worked with him: "We need to have you try so that we can learn how to help people like you." His first piece of creative writing echoes our pleas. Notice how he has been arrested at the "spoken word" stage. This looks like spoken English which has been written down.

> I ment Dr. Sileva Where, Jose Valente and Gary Drescher on October 5, 1978 at 9 : 32 : 47 AM. which the compuer I was so excized it like being it a waitting & maternace room at a hospiltal whiting to fine if oot's a boy or a grail.
> We had a and we whont you to do it fist for us. I am Logo number "1" ginny pig. When they get a new idse they say to hel, michalel we had a and we whont you to do it fist for us. like a nice guy I do if I wont to or not. I do and then I give my por and con on the idse. I tell them why I came up for a allturative.
> Why you mite ask? Becose I know how the person on the arther end feel. Becose I am the middle man betwee M.I.T. and handcap people.
> I also teach five stundts. No tow lean at rate. Some ask then I know they are intered in leaning about logo. Then the one that take for granted. I can tell. When I teach I lean form my standt. as well or bedter then form a book. I call that on the job training.
> My fist and every day experreance with the compuer when it cash and it lost but it keep on losting all that I have tort it but keep no teaching it overy and over agian when I bring back to live."

Many questions arose: How much was the quality of his writing due to lack of experience and how much to damage to the relevant language-processing brain area? Were the errors random, resulting from inaccurate typing, thinking faster than he was able to type, lack of spelling experience, and the like? The important point to note is that without experience of writing, he seemed to have become stuck at the oral-speaking stage. There was much phonetic spelling -- "ginny" for guinea and "whont" for want. There were errors in the use of tense markers -- "feel" for feels, "handicap" for handicapped, "take" for takes, "cash" for crashed, "keep" for kept. However, these errors could conceivably have been due to his misper-

---

3.   Inserting all those "minor," "trivial" markers, etc., whose presence or absence is of diagnostic interest.

ception of the spoken words, upon which he was basing his spelling. Notice that he wrote "fine" for find. Misperception could also cover the instances of letter omissions that occurred, especially "r" that is not sounded before a consonant -- "fist" for first, "lean" for learn.

Haste or lack of experience or brain lesion could conceivably have accounted for the numerous omission of words -- he left out "idea" twice, writing "we had a and we" for we had an idea and we; "it like being in" for it was like being in; "at rate" for at the same rate. There were reversals of letter order -- "por" for pro, "tow" for two, "form" for from, "no" for on. Combinations of errors occurred: letter reversal and typing error -- "idse" for idea; omission and reversal of letters -- "stundts" for students.

In order to investigate and treat this problem, a *focal remedial program* was set up. In collaboration with his English teacher, we arranged that all his English lessons took place in the computer room, using the text editor, instead of a scribe whose activities were masking the true situation. He wrote his own book reviews, essays, and the like on the computer. In addition, a series of remedial writing sessions with a visiting teacher was instituted, involving specific exercises based on weaknesses shown in his writing, in order to assess how much improvement could be achieved. Early indications were that a great deal could be achieved. Some months later, he wrote a letter in response to a query about Logo from another victim of cerebral palsy. This was the first version of that letter.

17 Sendon Crescent
Notown, Mass. 00001
February 6, 1981

Mr. John Smith
Bush Farm
1000 Acacia Rd.
Granby, N.C. 20000

Dear John,

My name is Michael M. I am the person whom your mother saw on "PM Magazine". I attend the Feltham School in Boston mass. I have been work with the compuers for about two and a half years. The name of the system is "Logo". It has open many new doors for me. Now I can draw picture on a cheen ane write letter like this one.

I was the first C.P. person in the U.S. to tired the "Logo" system. Inclose I will send some of my work.

Sincerely Yours,
Michael M.

P.S. I would be greatful if you could send me a piece of your art.

A College Career

Michael's programming achievements confirmed his high intelligence, and, with our encouragement, he decided to apply for, and was admitted into the computer science program at a New England college. Jose Valente kept up his close relationship with Michael, acting in an advisory and supportive capacity. A computer science professor describes Michael's performance during the first year, and reflects on his transition from the Feltham School to University:

> Our environment was a bit of a shock for him, I suppose. He came from a school where the total population was not much more than 100 children, whereas we had 100 in that one computer class. That threw him. It is difficult to get personal attention in that class, but fortunately Michael is not shy. He made up for it. He would come around and ask questions and make sure he understood. Altogether, the students wrote 25 programs, of which about half were non-trivial. In other words they had a very heavy work-load. Michael survived that quite well. A lot of students didn't. We have a drop-out rate of 50%. I would say he is an average programmer with an above average grasp of principles. If I had to rank him in the class, I would place him in the upper third.

An English professor reported on the need to provide explicit help for Michael in the organization of his ideas, a need that was particularly acute because of the lack of consistent previous experience in organizing his work or any other aspect of his life. At present Michael is scoring above average for his computer work, getting good grades for his English, and working away at plugging those gaps in high school mathematics that are holding him back. Here is how he commenced an essay recently, writing as always from the heart, and in his intensely personal way.

Trapped Intelligence

Trapped intelligence is a phrase which is used to describe people who have normal or above normal intelligence but are non-verbal or slow-talking and society assumes that these people are stupid. Project Logo and the computer have changed this meaning. It has allowed people to show what they can contribute to society.

Personal Development: Self-image

Michael M. had indeed become someone, managing his own life and achieving intellectually in a way that had been denied him prior to his use of the computer. In all this progress, the importance of self-image cannot be overstated. There is no doubt that the special role given him as a result of his participation in the research project played a large part in the changes observed, in particular in his view of himself. Patiently he introduced turtle geometry to his fellow students at the school. He has become a model for his handicapped friends. He has taught Logo at a computer summer camp and runs an ongoing class from his home. He is determined to help others along the path he has taken. And that path is for him, as he puts it, "a whole new world." When assessing the effect of Logo, he quips, "I have learned a few things about myself, too."

Introducing a computer into the learning environment of a severely handicapped student can revolutionize his life. Students whose intelligence has been inaccessible because they cannot communicate what they know, either because they cannot write or because they cannot speak or because they can do neither; students who in the past would have remained totally dependent on others, financially and otherwise, can now look forward to a measure of independence, to the possibility of earning a living, to the possibility of enjoying a future with dignity.

I have not personally worked with the hearing-impaired, but the experience of Dr. Battro in Argentina leads to the conclusion that for that group also, the computer is an indispensable educational tool. The students he has worked with have made major intellectual progress and undergone profound changes in self-perception associated with their computer activity (personal communication).

The ultimate goal is to allow the physically handicapped person to enter into the life of the community as an independent agent, as far as this can be achieved. Increasing basic skills in reasoning, mathematics, problem-solving, and understanding spatial concepts contributes to the fulfillment of the individual in as much as it helps that individual to attain productive self-sufficiency. It is important, however, not to raise false hopes. Michael is blessed with an above average intelligence. Careful assessment of the abilities of each physically disabled student will be necessary to provide realistic guidance. And improving assessment techniques is part of the computer story.

Chapter Eighteen

ASSESSING THE COGNITIVE EFFECT OF CEREBRAL PALSY

Physical handicap makes assessment by standard methods a problem. By reducing interference in processing from motor difficulties, the computer can become a diagnostic instrument to improve the accuracy of assessment of a child's conceptual understanding. Children who grow up without adequate opportunities for manipulating objects are at risk with respect to the development of spatial concepts, and computer-based activities can serve a remedial function to supply some of the missing experience.

Development of Spatial Concepts

We are interested to know what effect lack of manipulatory experience has on cerebral palsy children's understanding of space. There is controversy about the role of experience in the development of concepts. Piaget assigns a central role to early sensorimotor activity in the conceptual development of children (see, for example, Piaget, 1936, 1937). Central to his account is the notion of *egocentrism* in infants and young children, who decide on the position of things around them in terms of their own position; they use a self-referent system. In *The Construction of Reality in the Child*, Piaget claims that the development of the concepts of object and space are inextricably linked. The classical Piagetian position is that, initially, an infant experiences objects as extensions of her own actions, so that when an object is removed from her sight, it is regarded as non- existent. As the infant experiences her world, there is a gradual separation of objects from self, with a growing appreciation that objects continue to exist even after they have been removed from view. Space is an ordering of objects. So an understanding of space follows from a growing understanding of the concept of object.

Recent work has challenged this account, suggesting that some version of the object concept is present at birth. In particular, evidence has been presented to challenge the Piagetian claim that the infant totally lacks the concept of *object constancy* (Bower, 1979; Spelke, 1985).[1] These researchers believe that the infant already has a notion of object existence and object persistence, claiming that infants do show surprise when an object hidden behind a screen isn't there when the screen is removed, and do expect an object to persist as a unit when it moves. The claim is not that infants possess a full adult knowledge of all there is to know about objects. Rather, it is thought that the neonate comes equipped with an elementary object concept, and that the important role of experience is to expand that limited understanding.   For example, experience provides specific knowledge about particular sorts of objects and their behavior: we learn that the size of an object decreases as it recedes[2] and that the shape of an object changes during rotation. We learn this as we watch things move, as we manipulate objects. One would expect on this theory that an individual with restricted motor experience would have developed the object concept, but not the concept of size constancy. Two empirical studies are relevant.

Piaget described the last stage of object concept as normally reached by 18 to 24 months. Décarie (1968) studied the development of the object concept in thalidomide children, who have absence or shortening of the long bones and are judged to have minimum opportunity for "manual prehension." She found that the majority of the limbless thalidomide infants, the oldest aged 31 months, had already reached the last stage of object concept by the time she tested them. Decarie, herself a Piagetian, was surprised by this lack of substantial delay in the development of the object concept, in spite of the deformity and consequent restriction in manipulatory experience. This finding, of course, would conform to the

----

1.   The concept of object constancy involves questions such as: Is the object I see now the same as the object I saw in that same place a moment ago? Is the object I see in this place the same as the one I saw over there a moment ago?

2.   This is known as size constancy: understanding that the change in size one sees as one moves away from or toward an object does not reflect an actual change in the size of the object which stays constant.

views of Bower and Spelke.

In a second relevant study, Wedell and colleagues (1972) found that there is a relation between the amount of independent mobility experienced by an individual with cerebral palsy and the development of the concept of size constancy. *The longer a child with cerebral palsy has been independently mobile, the better an understanding of size constancy she develops.*

The Role of Experience

I agree with the Bower-Spelke argument that the child is born with a rudimentary object concept, which is then refined and elaborated by experience. I regard the provision of computer-based activities as a way to begin to fill the gap in experience suffered by individuals who are handicapped from birth.   The particular virtue of the large spatial component of standard Logo activities for this handicapped population is that it allows us the possibility of supplying manipulatory experience at one remove.   The lines on the graphics screen can be seen as objects (AS-IF objects), and we can arrange matters so that these "objects" can be manipulated by a minimum of motor effort -- by simply pressing a single key. These manipulations are AS-IF actions (Papert and Weir, 1978). The child can use the turtle to explore a defined and manageable spatial world and in doing so can learn about shape, length, angle, size, position, and number.

As pointed out earlier, when prescribing learning environments for these children who have both motor restriction and possible brain damage in other areas, there is always the problem of knowing how much of the conceptual deficit present comes from the brain damage and how much comes from the lack of manipulatory experience. If we give a handicapped child an exposure to intensive computer-based spatial problem-solving, we can use this as a *diagnostic instrument*: an improvement in performance would show that the deficit was due, at least in part, to the lack of experience. Further, it would suggest that this kind of activity should be started at as early an age as possible.

Nicky: a 7-year-old with Cerebral Palsy

Nicky was one of the students whose computer work was the outcome of the close cooperation between Susan Jo Russell, of the MIT research group, and Eileen Kiernan, the resource room teacher at the Feltham School. In general, Feltham students who attend the resource room for specific problems receive a detailed assessment of their abilities in the area for which they have been referred. In Nicky's case this assessment was repeated at the start of his work on the computer and confirmed the presence of many deficits, including an inability to count accurately more than four objects, to match a small group of objects one-to-one, and to conserve number (know that the number of objects had not changed when their arrangement was changed). It was decided to use the INSTANT program (see page 55). Notice that the INSTANT program is written in Logo and is relatively accessible to teachers to modify to suit the particular purposes of the moment. Russell and Kiernan developed several versions of the program for children at different levels of performance. Nicky worked with the standard INSTANT program as supplied by Terrapin, Inc.

At the start of his work, Nicky used only a small portion of the screen and had difficulty turning the turtle in the direction he wished. He was unable to make square corners;[1] he was unable to match sides of figures; his drawings were typical of a much younger child; and although he attempted to achieve closure and succeeded in doing this most of the time, he had trouble getting a good square or circle (see Figure 18.1). Nicky's working style resembled that of many beginning Logo users and, especially, very young children. He did not decide on an object to draw and then draw it. Rather, Nicky would begin by working until a shape emerged, and then label it after the event. He made small shapes which appeared to be unplanned, and at the completion of the drawing he would announce that it looked like a such-and-such, and name it accordingly. The examples in Figure 18.1 were his first named pictures.

As his work progressed he began to plan more, and during the sixth session he decided to draw a staircase. This turned out to be a very difficult task for him. The task's difficulty lay in having to turn the turtle a full 270 degrees clockwise at points A and B since there was no way to turn counterclockwise in the system he was using (Figure 18.2). The session was one long struggle for him and ended without his having achieved his goal. Interestingly enough, at the beginning of the next (seventh) session, he produced without hesitation and without mistakes, the steps he had been unable to do during the previous session. It seems that the solution occurred somehow between the sessions. Not only had he made remarkable progress in finding the solution, but here he was actually setting himself a task, predicting ahead of time what he wanted to have as his end product, and deliberately planning the sequence of commands needed to achieve that product.

---

1.   In the INSTANT program, each R turns the turtle 30 degrees to the right, so that it requires three presses of the R key to turn 90 degrees.

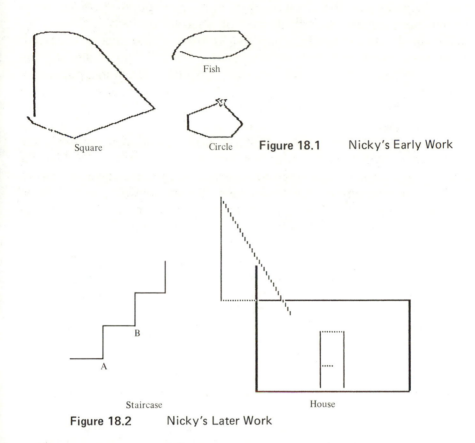

Square   Circle   **Figure 18.1**   Nicky's Early Work

Staircase   House

Figure 18.2   Nicky's Later Work

During the next (eighth) session he took another major step forward. He produced a house, which showed several noteworthy characteristics: consistent use of three turns to make a 90 degree angle, matching of the lengths of opposite sides, use of a large area of the screen (both left and right halves), and a deliberate planned sequence to complete the picture symmetrically, for the most part (Figure 18.2).

The Computer as Diagnostic Instrument: What Exactly Is Missing?

We see in Nicky a progressive acquisition of visual-spatial skill over a relatively short period of time. It is possible that everything he needed to achieve these tasks was there all the time, and we simply gave him a way of getting it out; that rather than promoting conceptual development, we allowed already existing understandings and cogitations to see the light of day. Providing a means of expression, an effector tool that the individual did not have before, is certainly part of what we do with our computer environment. Just how big a part that is will become clearer when our assessment procedures improve. And there's the rub. The validity of using standard assessment tools as a measure of competence in this population is open to question, since the very presence of motor difficulties affects the assessment process itself.

A good demonstration of this was given by Zeitschel and his colleagues (1979) who showed that the same cerebral palsy individual scores lower on tests of visual perception when the test has a high motor component than she does when there is no motor component; the score decreases as the motor aspect increases. Again, cerebral palsy children often fail on the block design reproduction task of the WISC, a task that involves motor activity. When the motor element is removed and they are required to choose one correct design out of three possible solutions, these same children improve their performance (Bortner and Birch, 1962). When the assessment consists of a purely motor task as in the Goodenough draw-a-man test, it is not surprising that cerebral palsy children perform badly. This is not evidence for their poor body image, as has been claimed, since they also perform equally badly when asked to copy very simple figures, suggesting that the difficulty lies in the act of drawing per se (Abercrombie and Tyson, 1966).

Computer-Based Assessment Tasks: an Extension of Logo

Clearly, it is important to try to get an accurate assessment of a child's conceptual understanding without the interference of motor difficulties. Exploiting the possibilities of a computer-based, interactive graphics situation can provide a significantly novel way of assessing persons with motor restrictions.

We made a preliminary step in addressing this possibility by developing an extension of the existing Logo system, which we could use to replicate standard assessment tasks on the graphics screen and invent new ones.[4] The cursor was the *hand* that could be moved by four directional keys on the keyboard and used to pick up, carry around, and drop graphics

---

4.   Gary Drescher wrote the Logo code; he and Jose Valente were the principal users of the system.

screen objects. It was a general purpose system for implementing a wide variety of tasks, and new tasks could be added with relative ease. A feature of the system allowed one to keep an automated record of the moves made by the subject, complete with a time marker and a facility for using this record to drive a rerun of the task for purposes of analysis.

The possiblities of the system are illustrated by three examples. The first one shows the usefulness of the automatic record and, most importantly, demonstrates the rich possibilities created by a situation in which the student can remain active in the problem-solving process and show us her intermediate steps, giving us a better chance of exploring the details of her deficits than would a multiple-choice response to possible outcomes supplied by the investigator. This is even more true with respect to the mobilization of hidden strengths enabled by this approach as shown in the second example. The third example describes a graphics screen task that replicates the Piagetian seriation task, and how this helped us follow the progress of a student receiving computer-based remedial activities.

Integrating Spatial Information over Time

Severely physically handicapped persons can readily acquire visual information about shapes and spatial configurations. It is the information from manipulatory experience that is not easily available to them. Manipulation of objects involves a coordination of several different kinds of information:

Visual information

Haptic information -- information obtained from touching the objects

Kinesthetic feedback from the muscles in the upper extremity -- information about successive positions of the hands and fingers as they move with and over the objects

Data from the motor component, i.e., the coordinated instructions to muscle groups that correspond to particular movements.

Normally, identification of objects by touch (haptic identification) develops more slowly than visual identification. A possible explanation for this is that the various features of the object being explored by touch are not available "all-at-once" as they are in the visual case. They have to be searched for and integrated over time. This means accumulating information in appropriate data structures. Haptic identification has been shown to be significantly impaired in brain damaged children (Rudel et al., 1974). Since it is difficult to test children's skill at palpation if they cannot move their hands and fingers over the object, we decided to use our system to allow us to separate out the difficulty with palpation from another possible source of the deficit, namely, an inability to integrate information over time.

The task we invented involved finding a hidden figure on the screen, using pieces of contour information obtained sequentially. Shape identification was made by moving a cursor and "revealing" the hidden contour in the following way:

1. Single-key commands moved the cursor in the four compass directions.
2. The location of the boundary of the hidden figure could be discovered by moving the cursor around and watching for its shape to change, indicating that it was crossing an edge of the hidden figure.
3. At this point, the user could inspect the configuration of the edge just crossed by pushing the PEEK key. This caused the display of a small piece of the contour for a short period, after which the screen was again blank, and the search for the shape could continue.

The task allowed the subject to accumulate pieces of evidence about what the shape looked like at various points on its contour -- whether edges were curved, straight, horizontal, oblique, pointed, and so on. Exploration of edge shape at different parts of the hidden figure in a sequential fashion could lead to a recognition of the hidden shape. The set of possible shapes was taken from Laurendeau and Pinard (1970), who used wooden versions of these shapes to investigate haptic perception in 2- to 12-year-olds. A board displaying the twelve shapes, as in Figure 18.3, was available for scrutiny during performance of the task.

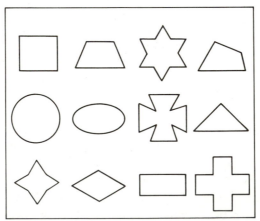

Figure 18.3   Shapes for the Hidden Figures (taken
                    from Laurendeau and Pinard, 1970)

Seven of these were chosen as the test figures, namely, square, triangle, trapezoid, circle, maltese cross, diamond, and four-star, and were presented in that order. We were interested in whether the hidden shape would be recognized and what problem-solving strategy would be used. First we tested non-handicapped children and found that the mean scores of the number correct increased with age.[5] Seven handicapped students between the ages of 12 and 17 tried the task, a small sample which nevertheless yielded interesting trends. The three students (17 years) who had full use of their hands scored 6 or 7 out of 7. In contrast, the four individuals with restricted hand movements found this task extremely difficult. One (12 years) was unable to do the task at all and had no correct answers. One 13-year-old and two 17-year-olds had only half correct.

In addition to the number of correct solutions they obtained, we were able to study the way the students carried out the task. Since the program had a facility for recording each keystroke as it occurred, it was possible to rerun the whole sequence of moves, at the speed they were made or speeded up. This allowed us to study aspects of the student's behavior at our leisure. The non-handicapped students showed an increase in sophistication of search method from the 9-year-olds to the 11-year-olds, as measured by a number of features: entertaining alternative hypotheses about what the figure could be; searching for particular features that would disambiguate two competing alternatives, thus allowing for systematic elimination of possibilities; contour following; and calculating the extent of the figure, required, for instance, to distinguish between a square and a rectangle.

The handicapped students with restricted use of their hands were much less systematic in their search for evidence, going over the same territory several times and often seeming to stumble on useful evidence. An interesting behavior trait shown by these students was a tendency to match only on the fragment immediately under consideration, rather than on the basis of all previously seen fragments of the contour of the hidden figure. This was shown by the way they would shift from one possibility to another, apparently not storing any of the information derived from contours seen earlier. For example, suppose the child first saw a "< " and decided correctly that this acute angle fragment favored a triangle as the hidden shape. Upon moving down and across, she later saw a " __ ". At that point she would claim that the hidden figure could be a square, a reasonable

---

5.   Sixteen children, four at each age between 9 and 12 years, were tested. Their mean scores, out of a possible 7, were as follows: 9-year-olds, 3.5; 10-year-olds, 5; 11-year-olds, 6.25; 12-year-olds: 7.

possibility on the basis of the straight line, but one which should have already been ruled out by the angular fragment seen earlier. It could be that the lack of experience had somehow delayed the development of appropriate data structures (and their associated operations), in which incoming information of shape outline could be accumulated and coordinated. Given an inadequate memory of the past fragments of contour, the student was forced to rely on the current one.

In summary, then, among the small number of students with motor restrictions we tested, there appeared to be a low-level *specific* deficit in shape memory, as well as evidence for a more general lack of problem-solving skills, as shown by unsystematic search strategies. We need to provide computer-based activities for all children with cerebral palsy from an early age to counteract the development of these deficits as far as is possible.

Eliminating the Motor Element in a Standard Task

The next example continues the theme of computer-based activity as a revealer of the problem-processing strategies of individuals whose cognitive systems have suffered injury. James (13 years old at the time of testing) was a quadriplegic whom we have already met in connection with number choice for his Christmas tree project. He was grossly restricted in the movements he could perform. Every movement took a great deal of concentration and a great deal of time. He had to devote resources and conscious attention to an aspect of the task that would have been done automatically without any thought by non-handicapped children. So for James the conceptual aspects of the task did not get their share of attention. In the computer task, the motor hurdle was removed. All the user had to do was press a button, a minimal movement of the finger, to achieve movement of the object. The line on the graphics screen became an object and the cursor became a hand, used to pick up an object and do with it whatever was appropriate for the task.

James's performance on Piaget's topographical task was revealing. In this task, the child and the experimenter each have identical physical models of a scene containing a few houses, a pond, a road, and a railway line (Figure 18.4 shows a screen drawing of the model). The experimenter places a doll at successive locations in the scene, and, for each placement of the doll, the child is required to place his doll in the same position on his own model. Nine positions of the doll, A through J, are used. These locations vary in their difficulty of description, i.e., in terms of proximity to particular objects such that the description accurately localized them. The task has two parts. The first time around, the models of experimenter and child face the same way, are in the same north-south orientation. In the second part, the experimenter's model is rotated 180 degrees, while the child's scene remains in the same orientation. James's strategy in performing the task was to copy the physical movement of the experimenter. He made it clear that he was doing this by asking the experimenter to repeat the action slowly so that he could copy it exactly. That worked quite well when his board was oriented in the same direction as the experimenter's board, but was, of course, no use at all when it was inverted; the result was a series of wrong placements, with only three out of nine correct placements.

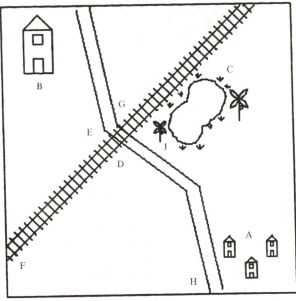

Figure 18.4   Piaget's Topographical Task

We then did a screen version of both parts of the experiment, in which the experimenter used the same physical model as before, while the student worked on a *screen drawing* replica of the model (shown in Figure 18.4). Again, in the first half of the experiment, the models were aligned in the same orientation, and in the second part, the experimenter's model was inverted, while the student's layout remained upright. In the screen task, the doll was the cursor that could be moved around the screen (scene) by pressing appropriately labeled keys on the keyboard. In the computer version, all James had to do was to press one key at a time to guide the cursor to the desired spot on the screen picture. Now his energies were free to solve the conceptual problem. His performance improved substantially, and he achieved a score of eight out of nine correct placements.

As usual, there was an added interest for us in observing the way he did the task. When he was presented with the physical model, his poor place-finding motor skill led him to use a relatively unsuccessful copying strategy. In the computer task, he began to talk himself through the task, describing the position of the doll in words. Now, "free to be himself" as it were, he adopted a strategy that rested on his well-developed linguistic skills. He succeeded in turning the computer version into a linguistic task about spatial relations, for which he had the appropriate linguistic metaskills. There is evidence in James's case of a discrepancy in skills across domains. The issue is taken up further in Chapter Nineteen.

Seriation on the Screen

Consider then what we have here. The motor handicap leads one to suspect the presence of a deficit in conceptual development. That same motor handicap makes the assessment of any deficit difficult. The thing that you want to test in a person is the very thing she couldn't do in the first place. Because performance tests are notoriously difficult to administer to this group, they have traditionally been turned into multiple-choice format. For example, to test how well children with severe motor restrictions can *seriate* (order by length), the tester lays out a set of possible final configurations from which the child chooses the correct solution. However, turning the task into a set of multiple-choice alternatives supplied by the tester has the regrettable effect of putting the student back into the passive role. A virtue of computer-based tasks such as the two just described is that they allow the child to be an active participant. This is true also of the third graphics screen task to be described, a two-dimensional version of Piaget's (1941) seriation task.[6]

In this task, a set of randomly oriented "sticks" (represented by graphic lines) were clustered in the upper half of the screen. The goal was to transfer these to a "tabletop" located in the lower half and to arrange them in serial order along the tabletop (Figure 18.5). Since the sticks were

---

6.   This task was used extensively by Jose Valente (1983) in his doctoral research.

"carried" using the cursor "hand," the action was achieved by the coarsest of gestures, namely, pushing a key. Four directional keys were used to direct the cursor until it touched the particular stick of interest. At that point, pushing the GRASP key caused the "hand" to "grasp" the stick. Once the stick was grasped by the hand, pushing the directional keys moved both the hand and the stick; pressing a rotational key rotated the stick clockwise or counterclockwise. When the stick had been moved to the desired position, it could be dropped by pressing the DROP key.

Before performing the screen version of the seriation task, Valente's subjects were asked to do the standard Piagetian task with wooden sticks, referred to as the "real" task. To eliminate the problem of fatigue, only four sticks were used for each version of the task. If these were ordered successfully, additional sticks were presented for insertion into the seriated row, as is the usual practice in this task. For the graphics screen task, Valente first allowed the subject to become familiar with the directional keys, using a two-stick display. After this practice session, the test proper was carried out.

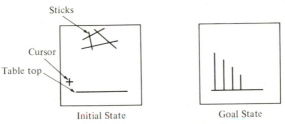

Initial State   Goal State

Figure 18.5   Seriation Task on the Screen

What emerged was the following: the removal of the current motor difficulty solved some but not all of the problems involved. There was something missing as a result of the long-term deprivation of experience. This is how 13-year-old James fared using the system. He failed to seriate the real sticks, and, articulate as ever, he complained bitterly because he knew that what he was producing with the physical sticks was not correct. Frustratedly, and almost in tears, he exclaimed, "I don't know how to make it come right!" In contrast, when presented with the screen task, James was able to do the required ordering. But he was not able to insert extra sticks into the row he had constructed.

James was one of thirty-two handicapped children between the ages of 11 and 19 tested by Valente on their seriating ability. Of these, twenty succeeded in the real task and twenty-three succeeded in the screen task. Overcoming the manipulatory difficulty was enough to change the outcome in three (9 percent) of the subjects tested. On the basis of the real task alone, these three students would have been called non-seriating. However, there remains the problem of the nine handicapped individuals who could not seriate even in the screen task. Removing the current motor difficulty was not enough to change the outcome for these students. The absence of manipulatory experience had left its mark. This is discussed further in Chapter Nineteen.

Comparison with Non-handicapped: Patterns of Error

Finding non-seriating teenagers was unexpected and disturbing. In a sample of thirty-five non-handicapped children tested, all those who had reached their seventh birthday could perform both the real and the screen seriation tasks. There is a real difficulty in choosing an appropriate control group when investigating performance problems in individuals with cerebral palsy. Since the 7-year-olds could do both the real and the screen seriation tasks, it was decided to use a group of 4- to 7-year-olds as the non-handicapped comparison group. The screen task was more difficult than the task with real sticks for this younger group. Of nine children between 4 and 6 years of age tested on the seriation task, eight succeeded in the real seriation task, whereas only five were able to do the screen version. (The four who failed were the child who failed in the real task and three more.) The important point is that these younger children found the screen version more difficult than the real task because they became so tied up with mastering the computer moves that they could not concentrate on the conceptual aspects of the task itself. This is a reversal of the situation for the handicapped persons, where the screen task avoided the physical difficulties that, in the real seriation task, tended to prevent them from concentrating on the task demands.

Non-handicapped persons have sets of automatic routines that take care of movements, routines that do not reach consciousness, and so take up fewer resources than they do in the case of individuals with motor restrictions: "In addition to thinking about size comparisons, and where on the board am I going to put this stick, I have a third thing to think about, namely, how am I going to get this hand of mine there and how am I going to make the right movement so that I will be grasping this stick and letting that one go."

This difference in perceived difficulty was reflected in an analysis of the errors made by each group during the process of seriation. The younger, non-handicapped children tended to select screen sticks on the basis of their proximity to the "hand," picking up the easiest and nearest object. So pleased were they to actually get the stick to the table and place it in the correct orientation, that they then let well alone and tended not to go on to rearrange any sticks that were out of order. In the real task, they selected sticks in order of size, for the most part; consequently, less subsequent correction of the line of sticks was needed. In contrast, handicapped subjects seemed better able to select by size in the screen task than with the real sticks. The conjecture is that, in both cases, the difference in error patterns is related to the incidental difficulty of the actual manipulations to be made, rather than to the conceptual problems underlying the task.

The Potential of Computer-Based Assessment

We have seen how computer-based tasks can be used as diagnostic instruments to clarify the nature and extent of deficits in cerebral palsy children. I have no doubt that computer-based assessment will become popular for non-handicapped children, too, as school psychologists realize the potential of the technology. The list of virtues is long and includes the advantages of automatic recording of the student's moves and automatic timing; the emphasis on process; the exposure of problem-solving strategies as the student responds to feedback; the ease with which a range of modifications of a problem can be generated, and the ready availability of alternative modes of problem representation. Different modes of presenting a problem can be especially revealing, as we seek to show what a student knows and can do already (diagnosis) and make predictions about what she can come to know and might come to do, with the right help (prognosis). To the extent that what a student knows is organized in terms of her own individual needs, goals, and feelings, it is clear that standard testing arrangements do not facilitate access to that knowledge.

Chapter Nineteen

LEARNING POTENTIAL

The argument about testing in schools is not whether it is important to find out what students know; the point of disagreement is how to do it. There is a tension between allowing the student to set problem-solving goals and the need to develop standardized assessment procedures. Unexpected successes and surprise failures are particularly informative in building up a picture of the current status of a child's understanding and her learning potential. I use the work of Kate, James, and Grace to illustrate aspects of procedural control knowledge and present the ideas as a series of principles that link our experience with the handicapped to the mainstream of Logo work.

Missing Metaknowledge

Principle: Procedural control knowledge is deficient when there is insufficient opportunity for active doing.

Kate's responses during a turtle-driving task represent an extreme example of the effect of a lack of active doing: she seemed not to know when to stop one action and start another and was able to change to a correct operation only when reminded to do so.

Kate, a 13-year-old cerebral palsy girl, resembled James in that her language skills were much better than her spatial skills. From her school record, we learned that Kate had a measured IQ of 79. She was described by her teachers as having difficulty with abstract reasoning; she needed to work with concrete objects in order to be able to comprehend. But manipulating concrete objects was not easy for physically handicapped Kate. She was the kind of child who had a hard time at school, since she did not seem to do anything but chatter away in what was perceived to be a "shallow, mindless" way, frustrating to her teachers (and to us).

In contrast to this ready flow of linguistic material, Kate's performance in the spatial domain was very poor. She was unable to do a computer-based mental rotation task (adapted from Marmor, 1975, who used this task with five-year-olds). She could not be tested on this task because she did not meet the required level of performance during the training stage. She scored zero on the hidden-figures task and could not seriate four sticks. Her control when navigating the cursor around the screen was poor. Indeed, watching her perform the screen tasks made it difficult not to be skeptical about her intelligence.

In spite of her poor performance, Gary Drescher, intrigued by her verbal fluency and considerable curiosity, decided to introduce her to the INSTANT program (see page 55). The four basic turtle commands were explained to her, and she quickly memorized which keys were to be used for which commands. She was given the task of getting the turtle from the lower right corner of the screen to a target, usually a drawing of a house, in the upper left corner of the screen. She was quite unable to drive the turtle to this given destination. She invariably went off in the wrong direction and made no midcourse corrections. A typical interaction is illustrated in Figure 19.1. At the start of the session, the turtle faced the upper right corner, so that to get it to the upper left corner containing the house required a change in direction, to be achieved by a turn key. Kate pushed the F (forward) key and continued to move forward unconcernedly until she had almost reached the top of the screen (at A in Figure 19.1). At this point, Gary asked, "Are you going toward the house?" Kate's response was to change direction. She turned around clockwise, stopped short of where she needed to be, and again moved forward until he asked the same question (at B in Figure 19.1).

Figure 19.1   Kate's Poor Procedural Control

Only if Gary took the driver's seat, took control of the process, was Kate able to "solve" the problem. When left to her own devices, she made no attempt to correct direction and used the question "Are you moving toward the house?" as a cue for when to stop one action and start the next. Drescher's notes describe how he probed her goals: "I sometimes reminded Kim of the objective of reaching the house, suspecting that she had abandoned that task and was amusing herself with another game. But she assured me that she *was* trying to reach the target. She appeared aware that her commands were unsuccessful, but said she didn't know what to do to correct the situation." Kate's problem would appear to be not so much that she did not have a given schema, but that she did not know when to activate it or how to choose the most useful of several possible schemas. She gives the impression of having small local packets of knowledge, without the appropriate spatial procedural knowledge of how to fit these into any particular solution path.

One can express the situation in terms of knowledge-organizing knowledge (Chapter Seven). It would seem that procedural control knowledge is a kind of metaknowledge whose development is crucially dependent on active participation in the carrying out of actions. The reduction in manipulatory experience during the childhood of a cerebral palsy individual leads to a disturbance in the development of this kind of metaknowledge. This is an extreme version of what happens during the learning of normal children whose educational setting provides insufficient hands-on, manipulatory experience of the concepts they are meant to acquire. The computer can support direct interactions with concepts in ways that are difficult if not impossible to achieve without it, particularly in some areas of the science curriculum.

Moral: Don't expect an individual to understand material they have not personally confronted in an interactive mode. Don't expect to distinguish among the many possible reasons why a student cannot give the right answer to a multiple-choice test question administered without regard to process issues. Don't expect a student to show an understanding of the appropriate use of operations (procedural control knowledge) on the basis of a demonstration of the solution of a typical problem, without providing appropriate "manipulatory experience."

Sometimes She Can and Sometimes She Can't

Principle: Performance can depend on mode of presentation.

We saw how James had been able to mobilize his linguistic understanding on his own initiative, talking himself through the topographical task (see Chapter Eighteen) by describing the position of the doll in words.   Kate was not able to make the spatial-linguistic transformation herself, but did so when we provided the right circumstances.   Taking a hint from James, we provided Kate with a setting that would encourage her to use her linguistic ability: we embedded the navigation task, which had so defeated her in its pure spatial form, in a story context.   Together, Gary Drescher and Kate created scenarios based on topics suggested by Kate.   For example, she chose Mork and Mindy, characters in a television series, and decided which of the characters and activities in the story would be represented on the screen.   The activity consisted of having the turtle visit each character in accordance with a script that Kate herself developed.   Both for the Mork and Mindy story and for the Flintstones, another television series, Kate was able to provide a wealth of detail from her television watching to support a rich commentary on the turtle's journey.

Now the fascinating thing that happened was that, in this context, her control of the turtle improved to the point where she was able to guide it on her own toward the desired place on the screen.   When the goal was "take character A to visit character B" her aim improved, and she readily made appropriate midcourse direction corrections without any prompting, choosing the correct sequence of actions to achieve her purposes.   When the problem took the form of a verbal task, both Kate and James showed appropriate metacognitive skills.   They knew what to do when processing was to be controlled in the linguistic domain, but the relevant network of metaknowledge was missing when processing occurred in the domain of pure spatial manipulation.   In James's case, we have other evidence of his verbal expertize.

James's intelligent conversation had suggested the presence of oral verbal skills, but, like Michael M., James's motor disability had prevented him from producing written materials prior to his work with us. He was introduced to a text editor and chose to produce a newspaper.   This became his favorite project, and he planned it carefully.   He first generated the section headings and then went back to fill in details, taking each section heading and expanding it, beginning with the easiest and not with the first -- an excellent problem-solving strategy.   There was a ready flow of ideas and good organization.   He chose the following categories: comics, sports, social, horoscope, school reports.   His spelling was phonetic, as in Michael's case.   When working on his newspaper project, James exhibited intelligent, top-down planning, and yet he showed little such planning ability when programming a drawing.   Indeed, in his Logo work, James was not able to progress beyond the use of the primitive commands controlling the turtle, and programmed a simple drawing of a car step-by-step and painfully slowly, with no evidence of planning ahead.   In addition, he functioned at a very low level when given our screen-based spatial tasks. At 14 years of age, he failed on a mental rotation task that 5-year-olds can do. He could seriate four screen sticks but not four real sticks. He could not perform the insertion step in the seriation task (Chapter Eighteen), either in the real or the graphic version of the task.

There was a dissociation of metaskills: James could plan activity and solve problems in the linguistic mode -- language function was spared; whereas damage to spatiomanipulatory function extended up to include a lack of planning and procedural control. For Kate and James, knowledge-organizing schemas are not all general-purpose -- some are tailored specifically to the particular task to be performed. For them, domain specificity is not restricted to low-level procedures, but extends to a high level of metacognitive mechanisms. It remains to be seen to what extent a finding in brain-damaged persons applies in the general case. One would need independent evidence from the behavior of individuals with intact nervous systems.[1] At the very least, one can be a little skeptical of explanations involving *general sequencing difficulties* for someone like James: he can order letters skillfully, and one would expect there to be separate procedures for spatial sequencing and letter sequencing.

Moral: We need to provide choices for our students in the learning environments we offer. We need to match learning environments to student idiosyncrasy, so that they can show us what they understand and what they can do. It is important to exploit the spatial nature of graphical problem-solving. The same requirement applies to testing methods. We have to find a way to provide choices in mode of problem-solving during assessment. Only then can we be sure that we are obtaining a true picture of what our students know.

Context-Dependent Learning

Principle: One can know a fact, a concept, or a procedure in one part of one's conceptual system and appear not to know it in another.

Context-dependent learning, where understanding is restricted to the context in which the task was learned, has been called contextual welding (Brown, 1984). This was a particularly strong feature of Kate's learning. Once again, the special needs child highlights an interesting phenomenon.

---

1.   Fodor (1983) believes that domain-specific modularity is restricted to low-level processing. Drawing conclusions from deficit to normal functioning requires care, but our findings are suggestive of a modularity that extends to a high level in the cognitive system.

Kate was a highly sociable young lady, and while she worked on her navigation narratives, she carried on conversations with anyone at hand, including her classmates who were busy working on standard Logo drawings at computers near her. One day, Kate asked if she, too, could "draw squares that get bigger and bigger," and indeed "making a square" is just what she proceeded to struggle through, guided by Jose Valente (1983). She was gradually introduced to elementary Logo, and learned to define shapes and even to use them as subprocedures of more complex procedures. What she lacked in mental agility, she made up in persistence: she spent twenty-two sessions of approximately an hour each, working on different projects using squares (Figure 19.2).

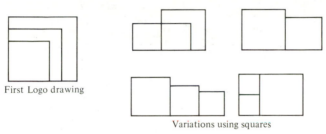

First Logo drawing

Variations using squares

Figure 19.2   Kate's Squares

She was told and rote memorized that RIGHT 90 gave her the correct square shape. Her earliest Logo drawing is shown in Figure 19.2. She spent a great deal of time on this drawing, and gradually developed an appreciation of how the numbers she chose for the input to the FORWARD command would have an effect on the sides of the square that resulted. She also learned that each side of the square had to be drawn with the same input to FORWARD, and that one always used RIGHT 90 for the angle of turn. Her rule became: Use the same number for FORWARD as for RIGHT, a phenomenon observed frequently in Logo classes. Using this rule, she produced all kinds of interesting shapes, for example, she called the shape she got with RIGHT 99 FORWARD 99, a FLAG, but it turned out she had no idea why the picture had "come out like that." After a few RIGHT 20's and the like, she was in confusion and had to be taken back to the nested square project. Once back in the context in which she had started drawing squares, she was able to get her number choice sorted out.

That she had learnt something was evident from her subsequent progress (Valente, 1983). She was able, for example, to see a connection between the decreasing squares case and an almost similar situation. She was able to program decreasing sizes of circles to make her butterfly wings

(Figure 19.3). She was sufficiently in command of this limited analogy to use it as her model for another task. During a test session in which she was required to determine which of two numbers was greater, she explained that it was just the same as when FORWARD 70 made a smaller square than FORWARD 100 on the computer.

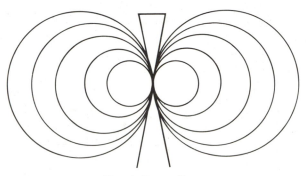

Figure 19.3   Kate's Butterfly

An explanation for context-dependent learning suggests itself as follows. Actions are carried out to achieve intentions. Suppose that during the process of building a tower out of blocks, a child learns about balancing one thing upon another. For a while, that knowledge will be stored in a specific place, namely, in the stored description of block-playing. That may be the only place in which any understanding of balancing is recorded, and access into that knowledge will be restricted to times when that particular intention is being served. Having learned something when she was carrying out intention A implies that it is recorded in a schema cluster labeled "intention A," and not under a schema cluster labeled "intention B."

I envisage the need for a subsequent *rerepresentation of this knowledge in a less detailed form*, for example in simple association lists, so that that knowledge can become more generally available. Only then can regularities be noticed and generalizations made. It seems to me that this is true for most learning by both children and adults -- that at an early stage of understanding some domain, knowledge is similarly encapsulated, and that knowledge becomes more generally accessible as expertize develops.

Moral: Owning knowledge implies that it has become attached to the learner's intentions, not someone else's. It is essential to provide learning environments that give scope for the intentions of all the participants to emerge and play a role in the learning that is going on: the intentions of the students doing the programming and the intentions of the teachers creating the learning situations. The informed perception of the more experienced person should not dominate over and obscure the intentions of the student. Logo learning environments are a beginning in this direction, in that they can support the emergence of shared intentions between teacher and student; the student's goals can be respected and even become ours, as we hope our goals will become hers. When that happens, fair assessment becomes possible.

Encouraging Conceptual Development

Principle: Computer-based interaction can encourage the maturation of concepts that usually emerge as children engage with their world.

In view of her poor spatial understanding, it was surprising that Kate could do Logo at all. We saw the development of a limited ability to generalize, to abstract, and to use her experiences as a model. The seriation task became a more systematic measure of progress. In seriation efforts before her Logo experience, not only was Kate unable to do the task in its real or graphic form, but she was *unable to recognize that her solution was wrong*. Her manipulation of the cursor was poor; it was disconcerting to watch her go off in the direction opposite to the one needed to achieve her stated purpose.

After one year of Logo she was retested. In the real seriation task, she had progressed to the point where she was able to order pairwise. In contrast to her lack of insight or debugging activity a year earlier, she could see that her solution was wrong. She made several attempts to correct the configuration she had produced but ended up with the same incorrect arrangement each time.

Her performance on the screen seriation task showed several interesting features. Her computer experience had lead to a noticeable improvement in her manipulation of the keys that controlled the cursor's movement. She made fewer incorrect key presses and was much more economical in traversing the screen than she had been at the first testing. Upon being shown the goal state (four sticks arranged in order) she noticed the decreasing size and *spontaneously described* it as: "the biggest, the second biggest, . . ." as she pointed in turn to the correct stick. She then successfully completed the task using the same *verbal* descriptions, picking the biggest stick still remaining in the pile each time, and placing it to the right of the growing "staircase." On her own initiative Kate had mobilized her linguistic skills to achieve the seriation goal. It is assumed that the prolonged period of navigation narratives, during which the usual mode of operation was to talk the turtle through its movements, provided a model and was responsible for the change.

Moral: Failing to supply access to a computer for handicapped persons amounts to educational neglect. Properly used, the computer becomes a tool for the provision of least restrictive environments for children with special needs, makes it feasible to bring many of them into the mainstream of education. Kate's ceiling of accomplishment remains for the future to determine. For her and for her caretakers, the important point is that she is making progress, however slowly. The Logo themes of user control and learning by doing are re-emphasized and exaggerated in handicapped individuals, exactly because this learning by doing has been so restricted. Little messing about happens in the life of a physically handicapped person. Computer-based activity can supply an opportunity to nurture the metacognitive potential for this kind of "play." The Logo theme, *learner as model builder*, takes on a poignant significance, since producing an effect on graphics objects can become a highly significant action for a severely handicapped person.

The notion that the computer can liberate intelligence has relevance beyond the issue of handicap. *Carefully designed computer-based activities can untrap the hidden intelligence of all students.* They can provide students with a way of experiencing concepts, and teachers with a way of monitoring progress.

Personal Agency

Principle: The positive affect associated with Logo is related to user control.

Academic performance is significantly affected by a *student's perception of her own ability, her self-image*. I am talking about an awareness of what she sees herself to be and of how this self-perception relates to a skill or piece of knowledge that she is asked to acquire. I find it useful to include in the concept of self-image a combination of physical self and interpersonal components, in addition to attitudes to one's own mental and physical traits and abilities. By the physical component, I mean the body schema, made up of sensorimotor schemas, together with complex collections of feelings and attitudes associated with actions. Interpersonal schemas contain descriptions of relations to other people, together with attitudes and characteristic response tendencies to interpersonal situations. Where does this self-image come from? To illustrate, I take as an example the origin of the active-passive distinction, *the difference between doing and being done-to*.

The development of action schemas is organized around achieving particular intentions. Sensorimotor skills such as hand-eye coordination depend on several kinds of information: visual, haptic, and kinesthetic, that is, position and movement information gained from the muscles and joints of moving body parts. I am proposing to extend this list to include "feeling" information that accompanies the action, as an essential ingredient of achieving a purpose (Chapter Ten). Each schema records what Piaget called "the internal history" of an experience. Suppose, for example, the storing of experiences as a primitive form of the schema begins while the fetus is in the uterus. At the stage where the fetus can move actively, there are two possible sensation patterns.

1. When the fetus is not actively moving, but is simply carried passively along by the mother's movement, the appreciation of passive movement only will be recorded; that is to say, kinesthetic sensation will be present as body parts are shifted around by the movements of the mother.
2. Active movement, on the other hand, is accompanied by both motor information and the sensation from the moving part.

This could be the beginning of the difference between *doing* and *being done to*, that, much later, could grow into the distinction in meaning between *active* and *passive*. At some point in this process, such an internal history could have added to it the feelings experienced as the being-carried or moving-oneself occurred, so generating emotionally toned experience of active versus passive behavior. Physical experience and interpersonal relationships are blended: one can be the agent or the object of an action, or the active or passive participant in a relationship.

Just how the balance between passive dependence and active control develops will decide the personality characteristics of the maturing individual, her self-image, and her potential for productive relationships. The teacher-student relation can be an important ingredient in this process. We met a manifestation of imbalance in the phenomenon of learned helplessness (Chapter Eight), where the child deliberately adopts a passive stance. For the physically handicapped individual, passivity is a way of life. She cannot believe in the potency of her actions, since it is so evidently true that she is dependent. Dependency on others for her every need has a devastating effect on her capacity for a positive self-image.

Moral: For me, the most profound aspect of Logo is the way it affects this active-passive balance. *Introducing turtle activity, with its strong sensorimotor flavor, attacks the problem of passivity at its roots.*

Emotional Factors in Learning

Principle: Access to knowledge structures is governed by emotional as well as by cognitive factors. Emotions can affect the mobilization of knowledge both positively and negatively. Assessment procedures that do not take this into account fail in their purpose.

It is a commonplace that emotional state can affect problem-solving performance, yet this everyday experience is often neglected in discussions of learning. Emotions play a vital role in organizing an individual's experience of the world. Feelings and attitudes can make a difference to cognitive processing and are central to successful cognitive activity, not merely an optional extra. The issues are complex and include motivation, self-image, and role perception.

It has been my experience that many children who are viewed as having a motivation problem become emotionally engaged by Logo. That this was the case among our Feltham students (Chapter Sixteen) was reflected in an intense competition for the use of machines. Students came in an hour before school began or skipped half the lunch break to work on the computer. Most importantly, there developed a frequency of animated discussion about various computer projects that represented a change in the behavior of these students. Some of this can be explained by the computer prestige effect and the novelty of it all. The nature of the activities, where one can get a large and dramatic effect on a graphics screen, can make one feel very important. When you have to find out something to achieve some goal you have set yourself, your motivation is high and you're likely to go after it.

I have proposed (Chapter Ten) that the emotional quality of an experience can decide whether particular pieces of stored knowledge will be accessed. Feeling components can combine with cognitive components to decide which schemas will be activated, can become the cues that trigger stored schemas containing matching feeling components. Conversely, the feeling component in a stored schema (i.e., the way one felt about an earlier situation) can be projected on to a new situation, turning an otherwise emotionally neutral situation into an emotionally charged one. This could make a routine take on the spirit of a much-loved activity or turn it into a dry-as-dust chore or a nightmare. On the positive side, projection can give emotions an attention-directing, knowledge-mobilizing role during problem-solving activity. On the negative side, the wrong emotions could inhibit knowledge-mobilization.

Certainly, the noticeable affective advantage in making the child's intention paramount, that is, in making the child the active agent, is often commented upon by Logo teachers. By taking the initiative and choosing what to do next, the child is in control, and this can have a powerful effect. Children feel good about themselves and they are motivated to learn. The Feltham experience showed how a poor self-perception can affect the level of performance, and how the Logo experience can influence that self-perception.

This was particularly true of Grace, a senior at the Feltham School. During the course of a year's Logo work, she moved from a totally dependent situation, where she made no move on her own and looked for reassurance after each command she typed, to one in which she worked on her own by choice, for long periods of time. Progress was slow, and the big change came during the third quarter of the year, as she worked on a HUT project. This generated the problem of using fractions, as she strove to find the relationship between the door and the windows to the overall size of the structure. Valente noticed that she had great difficulty with elementary arithmetic operations, like dividing by two. The research record described how this difficulty was burdensome in whatever she did in Logo. She "had a very bad image" about the problem, and whenever she had to carry out an operation, she said, "I am bad at that." Valente spent several sessions working with her on the idea of a variable, using concrete examples to start with. The exercise was to send the turtle forward a distance and then back half the distance. At first she had great difficulty with this. After much practice with specific numbers, she moved on to write a procedure for the general case, using X / 2 for the backward movement.

This exercise progressed to the use of X / 3 and other fractions and served to clear up her muddle about elementary fractions. It also improved her ability to work with variables. Most noticeable was what it did for her self-image. Valente's next entry recorded the fact that, for the first time ever, Grace had gone up to the computer room on her own three times since his last session with her and had worked by herself on the HUT project. From then on, she worked on her own, learned to ask questions when she was stuck, and in fact took control of her problem-solving.

It is difficult to sort out what "caused" what "improvement." There are many ways in which the Logo experience could have contributed to the change. It may have been the opportunity to approach the abstract notion of division via the manipulation of numbers in relation to relatively concrete screen objects; or the act of constructing a computer program that generalized the relation of half-as-far-as. Did she gain procedural control knowledge that made her learning more powerful, more readily recalled, more amenable to appropriate application? Or did it work the other way? Did her self-image improve as she confronted the "I'm bad at that" belief with successful doing, so that believing she would understand, taking control of her learning, made her able to remember what to do and when to do it, made the understanding "stick." Most likely all these features interacted and combined to produce an effect.

Moral: To reiterate yet again, a key aspect would have to be the fact that as a student works on her own, she begins to *own the ideas*; she takes control of her learning and develops the internal motivation that feeds her sense of self, her belief in her own power. ·

As the Logo enterprise proceeds, it provides increasing support for a set of ideas about the nature of learning and problem-solving that have been around for some time, but have failed to achieve respectability and acceptance, largely because they have resisted quantification. The answer is neither to dismiss the evidence as anecdotal and therefore unimportant nor to dismiss the problem.

Chapter Twenty

TEACHERS AND THE DEVELOPING LOGO CULTURE

Current classroom culture is based on a cluster of things that go together: a theory of learning, methods of educational practice, and methods for evaluating student progress. From the culture, the teacher takes a set of beliefs about her role, about what is deemed worth learning, and how it should be learned and taught. It is all too easy for the computer to be slotted into the existing classroom style of working, to be used as a means to deliver standard curriculum (Sheingold et al., 1983). My intention throughout this book has been to point to the possibilities for educational change brought by the computer, possibilities that challenge current teacher beliefs. In this closing chapter, I focus on some of the conditions necessary for the realization of these possibilities.

A Changing Classroom Culture

The decreasing cost of microcomputers has resulted in their widespread introduction into schools at every level. Logo implementations exist or are being developed for most of these machines. Does this mean we can sit back and wait for it all to happen? Not at all. Writer after writer has stressed the importance of the teacher in determining a successful outcome in the use of Logo (see, for example, Carmichael et al., 1985). What, then, is involved? A great deal of teacher training at present treats the problem as one of learning to program, and of course, this is important. But it is only the first step. How the computer is integrated into general classroom activity is what is going to matter. Back in 1978, the Brookline teachers wanted "a book to look it up in." There are plenty of books and a growing number of courses on Logo programming, but few of these have much to say about integrating Logo into the general curriculum. The most exciting part of the educational computing enterprise will be its effect on classroom culture: on attitudes and atmosphere, on patterns of intervention, and on location of control.

A teacher is concerned with the problem of how she can help her students achieve independent intellectual activity. Learning has been described as moving from understanding with the help of another to internalized, individual understanding; moving from being regulated by others to regulating oneself (Vygotsky, 1978). Finding the activity that leads into the next phase of understanding amounts to a *mapping of potential,* assessing the degree of competence a student can achieve *with aid* (Brown, 1984). Traditionally, the aid has come from the *teacher*. In future, it will also come from the *interactive nature of the computer*. Since a teacher can construct responsive materials that talk back to the students, a three-way interaction between child, teacher, and machine can develop. A third source of interaction is *peer interaction*. Not only is the active engagement of each participant an integral feature of computer learning environments, but there is a built-in expectation that groups of learners will interact and share activities and that peer instruction will occur. All this adds up to a substantial change in the flow of instruction, in the location of control in the classroom.

Peer Learning

In the Carmichael et al. study of the use of microcomputers in a sample of Canadian schools, teachers at every level reported enthusiastically on the high degree of social interaction among students (1985). When these children were offered the opportunity to learn together, most of them did so quite naturally. A frequent Logo experience for teachers has been the emergence of the student with a flair for programming, a student expert, who shoots far ahead of the rest of the class and of the teacher. A student who has mastered an area becomes the teacher of her peers, bypassing the teacher altogether.

In the Boston Headlight project (see page 37) sharing of know-how is spontaneous, extensive, and actively cultivated by the teaching staff. Students work daily at the machines and it is a commonplace to find second and third graders helping each other or seeking out an older student at a neighboring computer for more sophisticated guidance. A teacher new to Logo will arrange with a colleague to borrow a few students as peer tutors to help her get off the ground. In this situation, it is not just an occasional student who becomes the expert. Each class has a noticeable proportion of rapidly advancing students, including some who attend the resource room.

Changes in peer interrelationships have cognitive, affective, and social consequences. As a student alternates between tackling a problem and watching a neighbor solve a piece of a similar problem, the shifts in viewpoint that can help generate new understanding. This happened to Jesse during his first try at a Logo sailing program. The program allowed the student to experience the effect of changing the relation between the wind and the angle of the sail on the speed and direction of the boat. After Jesse had his turn, he sat watching other students try their hand at "sailing"; and as he watched, he figured out the principles. It was a kind of intuitive understanding, like grasping the moves in a basketball game. Soon Jesse had learned how to call up the program himself, and in no time at all he was helping his neighbors work out how to get the boat around the course. It was decided to put him in charge of the sailing disk and have him act as tutor for the rest of the class. A letter he wrote at the time in his language arts class describes his feelings:

Dear Peter,
I am working on the sailing program on my computer. I found the paper for the sailing program. I am working on looking for things to change to make it look like Pirate's Gold. I think I won't be in trouble next year. My teacher said I was much better. She said I was super smart.
TO BAD.
SO SAD.
BYE BYE
Sailor Jesse Smith

Aged 9, already on his way to a delinquent future, Jesse's natural intelligence had been receiving no recognition prior to his computer success. I think we are going to see more of this kind of thing, especially among *intelligent students who have had no incentive to achieve academically and, instead, have used their intelligence in socially deviant ways.*

As peer learning spreads, it brings with it a new currency among students: the sharing and ownership of programs. A special friend gets a copy of a program. It becomes a gift, dispensed or withheld, a source of power. I visited a school and watched the children program a Halloween pumpkin face. Many of the faces had a strong resemblance to one another, especially with respect to the asymmetric mouth. The reason, it seems, was that one child's program had been adopted by the rest of the class. Yet each child was engaged in using the program in her or his own way. The "other person's program" had become a good place to start, but at the time of my visit ownership had become blurred. One such program was demonstrated to us by a "borrower." The originator of the program sidled up to receive his share of the praise.

In such a classroom the transfer of know-how is happening sideways with respect to the traditional classroom hierarchy: child teaches child; the teacher is frequently an onlooker, often a learner. Along with this change in the flow of instruction comes a change in the location of control in the classroom. Different interpersonal dynamics will be a feature of the classroom of the future.

A Question of Control

In a traditional classroom control is located in the teacher who decides what will happen, who fixes the sequence of activities that the children in her class will be required to follow. This behavior corresponds to an implicit theory of instruction.

1. All children need to go through more or less the same learning path, the same sequence of activities.
2. There is a "logically obvious" explanation shared by expert and beginner, and that understanding is based on the internal logic of a clear presentation.
3. The ability to control the problem solving process is something that will be picked up automatically once the individual operations are understood.

A standard approach when teaching a beginning student is for the teacher to take control, to run the problem-solving process completely, so that the student does not have to worry about "which operation to choose and when" and can concentrate on learning the individual operations. This approach provides a temporary scaffolding and shelters the student from the need to supply her own metaknowledge. The teacher's role is to refine this scaffolding, to grade the steps the student can take alone, to sequence the activity so that the student's lack of sophisticated metaknowledge does not matter to start with. Providing a clear and logical explanation is what matters. If the child gets stuck, the teacher tracks back and comes forward again, step by step, reproducing her own stages of understanding, until the final denouement is reached.

All too frequently under the standard approach the student does not acquire skill in the control of the problem-solving process (see, for example, Lindquist et al., 1983). Often she uses clues like which chapter in the textbook the problem came from to decide which problem-solving method to try. But learning to recognize kinds of problems is a crucial part of problem-solving. At issue is the construction of complex structures of understanding in a student mind, not an initiation into the rote application of operations. If a student is to learn how to control the process of problem-solving, she requires experience in doing just that. An essential step is to mobilize existing procedural knowledge, acquired during previous experience. Making an appeal to existing knowledge is as important as clarity of presentation. The processes inside the head of the problem-solver are as important as the external task being presented.

The informal learning approach favors providing opportunities for seeing connections during extended interactions within a learning environment, rather than an explicit exposition of logical rules, especially in the initial stages of learning. An interactive computer environment provides the potential for self-directed exploration. *It allows the teacher to move in and out of the controlling role.* Ideally, we should aim at some sort of judicious mixture of traditional and informal methods. The traditional approach is well documented. What requires spelling out are the qualities of the extended interaction being advocated and the implications these have for teacher training, with an emphasis on how the new technology can make a difference. Since the only computer implementation of these ideas I know about is Logo, I will in effect be talking about Logo or Logo-like situations.

Ideals and Hurdles

1. *Need for structured freedom.* Optimum learning conditions should include the notion of structured messing about, during which pieces of ill-articulated intuitive knowledge can be mobilized. This means that the teacher needs to provide both structure and freedom.

The benefits of learning by exploration have been described by many authors (see, for example, Davis and McKnight, 1979; Skemp, 1979; and, in the case of Logo, Hoyles, 1984; Noss, 1985) and demonstrated quantitatively for Logo (Finlayson, 1984; Clements and Gullo, 1984). However, *the beginner student cannot herself provide the structure in which to do her exploring.* That framework has to be provided by the teacher. It is not interesting to place control of learning in the hands of the learner if all she has control over is working in an inadequate learning environment. There is an obvious similarity between Logo rhetoric and that of the open classroom visionaries. In some respects, Logo can be regarded as supplying the tools to achieve across the whole academic spectrum what open classroom pedagogy did for the kindergarten.

For this approach to be successful, a great deal has to be built into the environment, so that the student can actively engage with intellectual ideas.   Examples have been given in earlier chapters of the kind of environment envisaged in which the student directly manipulates the important concepts to be learned.   Open classroom settings have not always achieved this intellectual goal and have all too frequently become associated with a dropping of academic standards. But the choice need not be either happy children or academically well-trained children.   In the computer-rich open classroom, higher academic standards can and should go along with an increase in personal control and sense of fulfillment.

The important difference between precomputer informal learning and the present situation is that the *new technology allows exploratory messing about with technical ideas* in a way that previously was hard to achieve by all except the most gifted teachers. A priority goal of the Headlight project is to develop ways of using the computer to encourage this throughout the curriculum. The motion project, mentioned on page 114, makes a start in this direction. An exciting development that integrates computer activity with a traditional manipulable is Lego-Logo (Papert, 1985).

But how can we arrange for this to happen on a large scale? How can teachers who are just beginning to move into this complicated activity create the necessary computational environments?

2.   *Procedural control knowledge and reflective understanding.* Informal learning stresses the distinction between rote learning and "real" learning in terms of the difference between acquiring facts and acquiring know-how.

There is an emphasis on linking school work into the individual's own informal "goal-setting metaknowledge." If the student sets her own academic goals, she can tune into the system of procedural control she has acquired in connection with her non-academic activities. This is less likely to happen if the material is presented formally, in accordance with the teacher's goals.   A crucial part of learning is the development of self-awareness, the ability to reflect on what one is doing and thinking. In very particular ways, a teacher can use computer-based activities to facilitate this process.   A fruitful approach that provides an excellent learning experience for older students is to have them write programs to teach younger students some piece of subject matter. As they reflect on how to do this, the relationship between their goals and the methods they choose to achieve these goals becomes more explicit.

I have already referred to the unique character of a graphics object as halfway between an idea and a real object. In the example above, a discussion of how the program achieves a task can become a metaphor for thinking about the student's own processes. However, just when and how to invoke this comparison involves judgments on the part of the teacher, and the ability to make these judgments will require some kind of training, will require the provision of models.

3. *Individual working styles.* An important feature of the informal learning approach is its emphasis on allowing a student's own preferred style of working to surface. We can exploit the flexibility and power of the computer to construct learning environments that speak to the strengths of the individual learner.

The traditional classroom approach tends to favor one particular style of working, namely the serial thinker who likes to plan her work and can readily verbalize her thinking. Students with contrasting styles have to be especially talented in order to survive. We saw an example of this in the student Dennis described on page 133. Most students are pushed into the learning-disabled category. Especially sensitive to the restrictions of the average classroom are the individuals who parallel process in a relatively unconscious way without verbal mediation. At the extreme of this spectrum is the so-called hyperactive child (see Chapter Eleven). Interestingly enough, hyperactive children perceive an external locus of control, that is to say, they feel that events beyond their control happen to them (Margalit and Arieli, 1984). I am sure that at least part of the emotional lability they display is associated with the frustration of not being able to follow their own intentions, with the feeling they have of not being in control, engendered by the incompatibility of their working style with what is provided in a standard classroom.

When such children are given a chance to work in a computer-rich setting they shine. Often the result is a bright competent student for part of the day, and an alienated, non-cooperative "dullard" at other times. The discrepancy shows up particularly in the low scores such children achieve on conventional assessment tests.

4. *Assessment procedures.* The unexpected successes achieved by "poorer" students in their computer work challenges the prevailing educational paradigm that equates intellectual ability with performance on standard tests.

How much are the poor test outcomes a result of an inappropriate curriculum and how much are they a function of the unsuitability of standard testing procedures. In fact the two are deeply connected. Certainly, if the existing curriculum was being evaluated as part of a research project today, the poor academic results being achieved by many intelligent children would be enough to convince the authorities not to introduce the current curriculum into the schools at all. Methods of assessment are tied to a particular paradigm of learning and teaching.

> If you regard teaching as a transfer of factual knowledge, you will test your success in doing that by asking for a regurgitation of those facts.
> A teaching style that aims to influence students at a deeper level will employ more searching interview-type assessment techniques that more appropriately reflect what a student can do.
> If learning from feedback is built into the situation, activity that focuses on that aspect should feature in the assessment, including the use of computer-based activity as a window into the student's functioning.
> If teaching peers has become part of the tradition, then success at doing that could provide a useful measure of progress.
> If extended interaction with the microworld exhibiting the technical concepts is advocated, then assessment should not be undertaken too early in the experiment.

Just what constitutes "too early" and how to elicit early signs that the interaction is having an effect are issues being explored at the present time. One interesting suggestion is to grade the amount of help a student needs to perform some task, and use this as an index of progress (Brown, 1984). It is important to remember that, since we are in the early stages of the enterprise, *measuring outcomes tells us as much about our own ability as it does about the ability of our students.* We can learn about how successful *we* are being in blending freedom and structure as we use the new technology, about how well we are matching the needs of different work styles, and how well we are managing to incorporate concepts into the microworlds we are constructing.

     5.   *Control in the classroom.* The teacher will need to find a balance between maintaining general control of what goes on in her classroom, while locating control of any specific intellectual activity with the learner.

     The question is not whether there is a role for the teacher, but what that role should be. With respect to the subject matter she usually teaches, the teacher may be trapped in her own expertise; she may have lost freshness and innocence. In the process of becoming an expert, she learned how to decide what is important, what is relevant to the problem in hand, precisely what the novice cannot do. Indeed, the beginner cannot even formulate the questions she needs to ask in order to elicit help. When the teacher becomes a Logo learner, she finds herself in the position her students are usually in, and this can be a source of insight. She has to stop and think, and that is the beginning of self-awareness. She learns to say, "I don't know how to do that.   Why don't we sit down and figure it out together?"

Restoring control to the teacher could happen at many levels. There is a big difference between teachers who take the initiative to explore the possibilities of the computer and those who have it thrust upon them. Teachers need to reclaim control over the educational processes they and their students participate in, rather than act as passive consumers of educational software. They need to be able to suggest software they would like to have, to be able to modify any software they use, and, best of all, to be able to make their own software if they want to. They need to adjust to the presence of students who know more than they do, to find ways of using the expertise of their students productively.   This can present quite a challenge. Only when the teacher can do this comfortably will she really be in control.

6.   *Problems for the teacher.*   Being motivated to change is not enough. This is a time for experiment and flexibility, and the realities of the classroom do not readily lend themselves to that. There are problems in working in a setting where the teachers are under pressure to make improvements in the test performance of their students *now*. Mandates on curriculum by school districts limit teacher flexibility.

Equally important are the internal hurdles to be overcome. Many teachers are ambivalent about the whole computer enterprise. Change is threatening and difficult.   Just as individuals, influenced by their past history, show conservatism about changing their ways of thinking, so do the attitudes and beliefs of the social group, the cultural traditions, tend to linger.   It is naive to think that just by writing a few Logo programs, a teacher will be able to change, or even want to change the attitudes to teaching and learning that have guided her in the past.   These are too deeply entrenched in that they control the way she sees and does things. If that is her style of teaching, the teacher will use Logo in structured ways, laying down prescribed sequences of activities to be carried out by the students. Similarly, teachers use word processors in ways that conform to their usual teaching style (Morocco and Neuman, 1985). Some insist on compliance to standard spelling and grammar from the start while others delay any reference to these problems and concentrate on the creative process, helping the student to develop strategies for finding topics, generating and organizing their ideas, and revising their writing. In fact, once they have generated a piece of writing in which they are strongly invested, children will focus for extensive periods on editing for mechanics and spelling.

If teachers are to change, there is a need to provide time to work through conservative-assimilation phases.   Teachers need the kind of on-going interaction that provides direction and support for this change, extended interaction with . . . with what?   What will a microworld for teachers look like?

Fostering the Culture for Teachers

The Logo community has provided Logo implementations on a wide range of microcomputers (see page 14), and opportunities to learn how to program in Logo are becoming available to users all over the world. But, clearly, this is not enough.   Rather than taking short, single-shot programming courses, teachers need to belong to a community of teacher-learners, to become part of a wider "technologically aware" community of users.   Providing good models is more important than supplying prescriptive curricula. I have talked about allowing children to learn by messing about, by sharing with their peers, by teaching each other. Teachers are learners, too, and need messing about, safe places in which to try things out, and a community of learners and relationships they can trust.

One of the best examples of this is the St Paul's Community - School Collaborative in St. Paul, Minnesota.   Here Logo is part of a self-conscious effort to change learning environments in a whole city school system, in what director Geraldine Kosberg calls an "educational change process."   Established in 1982 as a K-12 microsystem of seven schools, the project now includes twenty schools. The scope of teacher training is continually expanding -- 200 teachers have been involved so far -- and extends far beyond an introductory course to include such things as monthly inservice days on site in each school, with the help of a Logo resource teacher; and regular training sessions with visiting experts, invited by the collaborative to provide help with more advanced programming topics.   A determined effort to integrate computer technology into the instructional program is evolving, initiated by Kosberg and a group of experienced teachers and community people.   Having realized that there were no prescriptions to follow, this ad hoc working group has initiated a series of self-help activities: sponsoring small research projects, forums for discussion, and the like.

Central to the St. Paul project is parental involvement.   Parents participate in Logo workshops, in implementing Logo in the schools, and in community-based Logo courses.   This involvement is taken even further in the idea of community access centers.   We will be launching one such center for special needs children and their families in the fall of 1986 in the Boston area.

Another kind of community that I have been interested in

promoting involves linking teachers into an electronic communications network via telephone lines. The idea is to counteract the effects of existing teacher isolation by providing a framework for shared discovery and continuing support, both through peer interaction and through access to expert advice. Indeed the network could enable a few consultants to serve a large number of teachers over a wide area. In addition to a machine network, I envisage a people network consisting of, for example, a teacher-developer working with a small number of core teachers, one at each participating school, who, in turn, would interact with their immediate colleagues. A diffusion of skills outward in ripples could follow, with the core teachers themselves becoming staff-developers. The expectation is that teachers will get into the habit of bursting into talk over the net about the latest wonderful thing that happened to them, of complaining about the latest piece of disappointing software, of shouting for help, and so on. By arranging to keep appropriate records, this kind of setting can yield the kind of data we need about teacher problems and teacher successes, about what works and what does not, about patterns of usage of the system. Most importantly, this could help form the substratum for the growth of a computer culture for teachers. Several realizations of this idea are being initiated in the Boston area.

Other structures to support the development of a classroom computer culture are springing up. Logo conferences proliferate, both here in the States and abroad. Computer journals and Logo newsletters, such as the *National Logo Exchange*, carry reports by teachers, based on their classroom observations. Much of what is happening in Logo classes has not been seen before, and the immediate research need is for a detailed descriptive approach, now, while the technology is new (Lepper, 1985): observing modes of teacher adoption of technology; recording student reactions to new curricula, such as spatial approaches to mathematics and language arts; exploring questions of gender differences in computer use and the role of the computer in fostering different styles of working. The possibilities are many and varied and are being pursued in many parts of the world.[1]

It is pleasing to see this piece of sophisticated technology become an instrument of humanitarian intervention, enlarging the choices for teacher and student. The combination of informed teacher and versatile technology generates entirely new educational possibilities. One always

---

1.   Current projects include those in Argentina, Australia, Brazil, Britain, Canada, France, Germany, Holland, and Israel.

will find some children and some teachers who like the computer more than others, some who will benefit more than others, and some who don't like it at all. A recent visitor described herself as "feeling like a sponge, ready to soak up all you can tell us. We're all getting these little machines, and we can see their potential, but we don't know quite what to do with them." We need to help her find out, and soon.

Bibliography

Abelson, H. (1982). *Apple Logo*. McGraw-Hill, New York.

Abelson, H., and A. diSessa (1981). *Turtle Geometry*. MIT Press, Cambridge, Mass.

Abercrombie, M. L. J., and M. C. Tyson (1966). Body Image and Draw-a-man Test in Cerebral Palsy. *Developmental Medicine and Child Neurology, 8*: 9-15.

Applebee, A. N. (1971). Research in Reading Retardation: Two Critical Problems. *Journal of Child Psychology and Psychiatry, 12*: 91-113.

Ary, T. (1986). Exploring Fractions with Logo. *The Computing Teacher, 13*: 47-50.

Bakker, D. J., and H. J. F. Schroots (1981). Temporal Order in Normal and Disturbed Reading. In *Dyslexia Research and Its Applications to Education*, ed. G. T. Pavlidis and T. R. Miles. Wiley, New York.

Bartlett, F. C. (1932). *Remembering*. Cambridge University Press, London.

Berger, J. (1972). *Ways of Seeing*. BBC and Penguin Books, Harmondsworth, England.

Birch, L. (1984). *Introducing Logo to Primary Children*. Houghton Mifflin, Boston.

Bishop, A. (1980). Spatial Abilities and Mathematical Education: A Review. *Educational Studies in Mathematics, 11*: 257-269.

Blake, W. (1803). Auguries of Innocence, *Complete Writings*, ed. G. Keynes. Oxford University Press, Oxford.

Boden, M. (1977). *Artificial Intelligence and Natural Man*. Harvester Press, Hassocks.

Boder, E. (1971). Developmental Dyslexia: Prevailing Diagnostic Concepts and a New Diagnostic Approach. In *Progress in Learning Disabilities*, vol. 2, ed. H. R. Myklebust. Grune and Stratton, New York.

Bortner, M. and H. G. Birch (1962). Perceptual and Perceptual Motor Dissociation in Cerebral Palsied Children. *Journal of Nervous and Mental Diseases, 134*(2): 103-108.

Bower, T. G. R. (1979). *Development in Infancy*. Freeman, San Francisco.

Brown, A. (1984). Metacognition, Executive Control, Self-regulation and Other Even More Mysterious Mechanisms. In *Metacognition, Motivation and Learning*, ed. F. E. Weinert and R. W. Kluwe, Kuhlhammer, W. Germany.

Bruner, J. (1957). *Beyond the Information Given*. Norton, New York.

Brunswick, E. (1947). *Systematic and Representative Design of Psychological Experiments*. University of California Press, Berkeley.

Bull, G., and P. Cochran (1985). *Logo Tools for Communication Disorders*. Curry School of Education, University of Virginia, Charlottesville.

Carmichael, H. W., J. D. Burnett, W. C. Higginson, B. G. Moore, and P. J. Pollard (1985). *Computers, Children and Classrooms: A Multisite Evaluation of the Creative Use of Microcomputers by Elementary School Children*. Toronto, Ontario Ministry of Education.

Chall, J. (1967). *Learning to Read: The Great Debate*. McGraw-Hill, New York.

Chomsky, C. (1971). Invented Spelling in the Open Classroom. *Word, 27*: 499-518.

Churchill, D. (1972). The Relation of Infantile Autism and Early Childhood Schizophrenia to Developmental Language Disorders of Childhood. *Journal of Autism and Childhood Schizophrenia, 2*: 182-197.

Churchill, D. (1978). Language: The Problem Beyond Conditioning. In *Autism: A Reappraisal of Concepts and Treatment*, ed. M. Rutter and E. Schopler. Plenum, New York.

Clements, D. H., and D. F. Gullo (1984). Effects of Computer Programming on Young Children's Cognition. *Journal of Educational Psychology, 76*: 1051-1058.

Clowes, M. (1973). Man the Creative Machine: A Perspective from Artificial Intelligence Research. In *The Limits of Human Nature*, ed. J. Benthall. Allen Lane, London.

Colby, K. M., and D. C. Smith (1971). Computer in the Treatment of Non-speaking Autistic Children. In *Current Psychiatric Therapies*, vol. 2, ed. J. Masserman. Grune & Stratton, New York.

Cole, M. (1982). A Model System for the Study of Learning Difficulties. *The Quarterly Newsletter of the Laboratory of Comparative Human Cognition, 4* (3): 39-66.

Conners, C. K. (1973). Rating Scale for Use in Drug Studies With Children. *Psychopharmacology Bulletin, 9*: 24-29.

Critchley, M. (1981). Dyslexia: An Overview. In *Dyslexia Research and Its Applications to Education*, ed. G. T. Pavlidis and T. R. Miles. Wiley, New York.

Critchley, M., and E. A. Critchley (1978). *Dyslexia Defined*. Heinemann, London.

Cronbach, L. J., and R. E. Snow (1977). *Aptitudes and Instructional Methods: A Handbook for Research on Interactions*. Irvington, New York.

Davis, R. B., and C. McKnight (1979). Modeling the Processes of Mathematical Thinking. *The Journal of Children's Mathematical Behavior, 2*(2): 89-113.

Décarie, T. G. (1968). A Study of the Mental and Emotional Development of the Thalidomide Child. In *Determinants of Infant Behaviour*, vol. 4, ed. B. M. Foss. Methuen, London.

Denckla, M. B., R. G. Rudel, and M. Broman (1980). The Development of a Spatial Orientation Skill in Normal, Learning Disabled, and Neurologically Impaired Children. In *Biological Studies of Mental Processes*, ed. D. Caplan. MIT Press, Cambridge, Mass.

de Sousa, R. (1980). The Rationality of Emotions. In *Explaining Emotions*, ed. A. Rorty. University of California Press, Berkeley.

Dewey, J. (1938). *Experience and Education*. Dover, New York.

Dillard, J. L. (1972). *Black English: Its History and Usage in the United States*. Random House, New York.

diSessa, A. (1980). Computation as a Physical and Intellectual Environment for Learning Physics. *Computers and Education, 4*: 67-75.

diSessa, A. (1982). Unlearning Aristotelian Physics: A Study of Knowledge-Based Learning. *Cognitive Science, 6*: 37-75.

diSessa, A. (1983). Phenomenology and the Evolution of Intuition. In *Mental Models*, ed. D. Gentner and A. Stevens. Erlbaum, Hillsdale, N. J.

Dixon, N. F. (1981). *Preconscious Processing*. Wiley, New York.

Donaldson, M. (1978). *Children's Minds*. Fontana, London.

duBoulay, B., and R. Emanuel (1975). *Logo Without Tears*. DAI Working Paper no. 11. Department of Artificial Intelligence, University of Edinburgh. Edinburgh.

Duffy, F. (1980). Dyslexia: Regional Differences in Brain Electrical Activity by Topographical Mapping. *Annals of Neurology, 7*(5): 412-420.

Dweck, C., and J. Bempechat (1980). Children's Theories of Intelligence: Consequences for Learning. In *Learning and Motivation in the Classroom*, ed. S. Paris, G. Olson, and H. Stevenson. Erlbaum, Hillside, N. J.

Dyson, F. (1979). *Disturbing the Universe*. Harper & Row, New York.

Falbel, A. (1986). *Language Microworlds*. Logo Memo 106. MIT, Cambridge, Mass.

Finlayson, H. (1984). *What Do Children Learn Through Using Logo.* **Paper** presented at the Annual Conference of the British Logo Users Group. University of Technology, Loughborough, England.

Fodor, J. (1983). *Modularity of Mind.* MIT Press, Cambridge, Mass.

Foulds, G. A. (1965). *Personality and Personal Illness.* Tavistock Publications, London.

Friere, P. (1972). *Cultural Action for Freedom.* Seabury Press, New York.

Gagnon, D. (1985). Videogames and Spatial Skills: An Exploratory Study. *Educational Communication and Technology Journal, 33*(4): 263-275.

Geschwind, N. (1983). Biological Associations of Left-Handedness. *Annals of Dyslexia, 33*: 29-39.

Geschwind, N. (1984). The Biology of Cerebral Dominance: Implications for Cognition. *Cognition, 17*: 193-208.

Ginsburg, H. (1977). *Children's Arithmetic: the Learning Process.* Van Nostrand, New York.

Ginsburg, H. (1981). The Clinical Interview in Psychological Research on Mathematical Thinking: Aims, Rationales, Techniques. *For the Learning of Mathematics, 1*(3): 4-11.

Goldenberg, E.P. (1979). *Special Technology for Special Children: Computers to Serve Communication and Autonomy in the Education of Handicapped Children.* University Park Press, Baltimore, Md.

Goldenberg, E. P., S. J. Russell, and C. J. Carter (1984). *Computers, Education and Special Needs.* Addison-Wesley, Reading, Mass.

Graves, D. H. (1983). *Writing: Teachers and Children at Work.* Heinemann, London.

Greenfield, P. (1983). Video Games and Human Development: A Research Agenda for the '80s. *Papers and Proceeding of a Symposium held at the Harvard Graduate School of Education.* Monroe Gutman Library, Cambridge, Mass.

Gregory, R. L. (1966). *Eye and Brain: The Psychology of Seeing.* McGraw-Hill, New York.

Gregory, R. L. (1970). *The Intelligent Eye.* Weidenfeld and Nicolson, London.

Hadamard, J. (1945). *The Psychology of Invention in the Mathematical Field.* Dover, New York.

Harvey, B. (1984). Why Logo? In *New Horizons in Educational Computing*, ed. M. Yazdani. Ellis Horwood, Chichester, England.

Harvey, B. (1985). *Computer Science Logo Style: Intermediate Programming.* MIT Press, Cambridge, Mass.

Hawkins, D. (1974). *The Informed Vision.* Agathon, New York.

Heider, F., and M. Simmel (1944). An Experimental Study of Apparent Behavior. *American Journal of Psychology, 57*: 243-259.

Hermelin, B. (1976). Coding and the Sense Modalities. In *Early Childhood Autism*, ed. L. Wing. Pergamon Press, Elmsford, N. Y.

Hermelin, B. (1978). Images and Language. In *Autism: A Reappraisal of Concepts and Treatment*, ed. M. Rutter and E. Schopler. Plenum, New York.

Hermelin, B., and N. O'Conner (1970). *Psychological Experiments with Autistic Children.* Pergamon Press, Elmsford, N. Y.

Hillel, J. (1984). *Mathematical and Programming Concepts Acquired by Children, aged 8-9, in a Restricted Logo Environment.* Research Report no. 1. Concordia University, Montreal.

Howe, J. A. M. and T. O'Shea (1978). Computational Metaphors for Children. In *Human and Artificial Intelligence*, ed. F. Klix. Deutsche Verlag, Berlin,

Hoyles, C. (1985). Developing a Context for Logo in School Mathematics. *Logo '85 Theoretical Papers*, no. 1: 23-42.

Hoyles, C., R. Sutherland, and J. Evans (1984). *The Logo Mathematics Project, Interim Report*. University of London Institute of Education, London.

Johansson, G. (1971). *Visual Perception of Biological Motion and a Model for its Analysis*. Report 100. Department of Psychology, University of Uppsala, Sweden.

Itard, J. M. G. (1801). *The Wild Boy of Aveyron*, trans. 1932. Appleton-Century-Crofts, N. Y., 1962.

Kahn, K. (1979). Creation of Computer Animation from Story Descriptions. Unpublished doctoral dissertation, MIT, Cambridge, Mass.

Kanner, L. (1943). Autistic Disturbances of Affective Contact. *Nervous Child, 2*: 217-250.

Kanner, L. (1946). Irrelevant and Metaphorical Language in Early Infantile Autism. *American Journal of Psychiatry, 103*: 242-245.

Kanner, L. (1973). *Child Psychosis: Initial Studies and New Insights*. Winston, Washington.

Kellison, P. (1983). Two Kinds of Measurements: The Way Children Think About Angles and Lines. Unpublished manuscript.

Kinsbourne, K., and E. K. Warrington (1963). The Developmental Gerstmann Syndrome. *Archives of Neurology and Psychiatry, 8*: 490-502.

Kozloff, M. A. (1974). *Educating Children with Learning and Behavior Problems*. Wiley, New York.

Krutetski, V.A. (1968). *Psychology of Math Abilities in Schoolchildren*, trans. 1976. University of Chicago Press, Chicago.

Kuhn, T. (1962). *The Structure of Scientific Revolutions*. University of Chicago Press, Chicago.

Laurendeau, M., and A. Pinard (1970). *The Development of the Concept of Space in the Child*. International University Press, New York.

Lepper, M. (1985). Microcomputers in Education: Motivational and Social Issues. *American Psychologist, 40*(1): 1-18.

Leron, U. (1985). Logo Today: Vision and Reality. *The Computing Teacher, 12*(5):

Levy, J. (1969). Possible Basis for the Evolution of Lateral Specialization of the Human Brain. *Nature, 224*: 614-615.

Lindquist, M. M., T. P. Carpenter, E. A. Silver, and W. Matthews (1983). The Third National Mathematics Assessment: Results and Implications for Elementary and Middle Schools. *Arithmetic Teacher, 31*: 14-19.

MacLeod, C. M., E. B. Hunt, and N. N. Matthews (1978). Individual Differences in the Verification of Sentence-Picture Relationships. *Journal of Verbal Learning and Verbal Behavior 17*: 493-508.

Margalit, M., and N. Arieli (1984). Emotional and Behavioral Aspects of Hyperactivity. *Journal of Learning Disabilities, 17*(6): 374-376.

Marmor, G. S. (1975). Development of Kinetic Images: When Does the Child First Represent Movement in Mental Images? *Cognitive Psychology 7*(4): 548-559.

Martin, F. H., and A. Friedberg (1987). *Writing to Read.* Warner Books, New York.

Mattis, S. (1981). Dyslexia Syndromes in Children: Toward the Development of Syndrome-Specific Treatment Programs. In *Neuropsychological and Cognitive Processes in Reading*, ed. F. J. Pirozzola and M. C. Wittrock. Academic Press, New York.

McCulloch, W. (1965). *Embodiments of Mind.* MIT Press, Cambridge, Mass.

Meehl, P. E. (1954). *Clinical vs Statistical Prediction.* University of Minnesota Press, Minneapolis.

Menyuk, P. (1978). Language: What's Wrong and Why. In *Autism: A Reappraisal of Concepts and Treatment*, ed. M. Rutter and E. Schopler, Plenum, New York.

Michotte, A. (1950). The Emotional Significance of Movement. In *Feelings and Emotions*, ed. M. L. Reymert. McGraw-Hill, New York.

Michotte, A. (1963). *Perception of Causality*. Methuen, London.

Miles, T. R., and N. C. Ellis (1981). A Lexical Encoding Deficiency II: Clinical Observations. In *Dyslexia Research and Its Applications to Education*, ed. G. T. Pavlidis and T. R. Miles. Wiley, New York.

Minsky, M. (1968). *Semantic Information Processing*. MIT Press, Cambridge, Mass.

Minsky, M. (1975). A Framework for Representing Knowledge. In *The Psychology of Computer Vision*, ed. P. Winston. McGraw-Hill, New York.

Minsky, M., and S. Papert (1971). *Research at the Laboratory in Vision, Language and Other Problems of Intelligence*. Artificial Intelligence Memo 252. MIT, Cambridge, Mass.

Montessori, M. (1912). *The Montessori Method*. Repr. 1964. Schocken Books, New York.

Morocco, C. C., and S. B. Neuman (1985). *Teaching Children to Write with Computers: Three Approaches*. The Writing Project, Education Development Center, Inc., Newton, Mass.

Nelson, H. (1982). Logo: Not Just for Kids. *Microcomputing*, March, pp. 96-107.

New York Times Education Fall Survey, November 11, 1984, pp 45-48.

Noss, R. (1985). *Creating a Mathematical Environment Through Programming: A Study of Young Children Learning Logo*. University of London, Institute of Education, London.

Oatley, K. (1975). New Metaphors for Mind. *New Behavior*, May, pp. 68-71.

Oatley, K. (1981). Representing Ourselves: Mental Schemata, Computational Metaphors, and the Nature of Consciousness. In *Aspects of Consciousness*, ed. G. Underwood and S. Stevens. Academic Press, London.

Ornitz, E. M. (1978). Neurophysiologic Studies. In *Autism: A Reappraisal of Concepts and Treatment*, ed. M. Rutter and E. Schopler. Plenum, New York.

Orton, S. T. (1925), "Word-blindness" in School Children. *Archives of Neurology and Psychiatry, 14*: 581-615.

O'Shea, T., and J. Self (1983). *Learning and Teaching with Computers.* Harvester, Hassocks.

Owen, F. W., P. A. Adams, T. Forrest, L. M. Stolz, and S. Fisher (1971). Learning Disorders in Children: Sibling Study. *Monograph of the Society for Research in Child Development, 36*(4).

Papert, S. (1980). *Mindstorms.* Basic Books, New York.

Papert, S. (1985). Computer Criticism vs. Technocentric Thinking. In *Logo '85 Theoretical Papers*, no. 1: 53-67.

Papert, S., H. Abelson, J. Bamberger, J., A. diSessa, S. Dunning, G. Hein, D. Watt, and S. Weir (1978). *Interim Report of the Logo Project in the Brookline Public Schools.* Logo Memo 49. MIT, Cambridge, Mass.

Papert, S., and S. Weir (1978). *Information Prosthetics for the Handicapped.* Artificial Intelligence Memo 496; Logo Memo 51. MIT, Cambridge, Mass.

Papert, S., D. Watt, A. diSessa, and S. Weir (1979). *Final Report of the Brookline Logo Project.* Logo Memos 53 and 54. MIT, Cambridge, Mass.

Park, C. (1967). *The Siege: the Battle for Communication with an Autistic Child.* Pelican, Harmondsworth, England.

Pea, R. and M. Kurland (1984). *Logo Programming and the Development of Planning Skills.* Technical Report no. 16. Center for Children and Technology, Bank Street College of Education, New York.

Perlman, R. (1974). *Tortis: A Toddler's Own Recursive Turtle Interpreter System.* Logo Memo 9. MIT, Cambridge, Mass.

Piaget, J. (1936). *The Origins Of Intelligence in Children*, trans. 1952. International Universities Press, New York.

Piaget, J. (1937). *The Construction of Reality in the Child*, trans. 1954. Basic Books, New York.

Piaget, J. (1941). *The Child's Conception of Number*, trans. 1952. Routledge & Kegan Paul, London.

Quine, W. V. (1969). *Word and Object*. MIT Press, Cambridge, Mass.

Richer, J., and B. Richards (1975). Reacting to Autistic Children: the Danger of Trying Too Hard. *British Journal of Psychiatry, 127*: 526-529.

Rimland, B. (1964). *Infantile Autism*. Appleton-Century-Crofts, New York.

Rosenthal, R., and L. Jacobson (1968). *Pygmalion in the Classroom*. Holt, Rinehart and Winston, New York.

Rubin, A. (1980). Making Stories, Making Sense. *Language Arts, 57*(3): 285-293.

Rudel, R. G. (1980). Learning Disabilities: Diagnosis by Exclusion and Discrepancy. *Journal of the American Academy of Child Psychiatry, 19*(4): 547-569.

Rudel, R. G., H-L. Teuber, and T. E. Twitchell (1974). Levels of Impairment of Sensori-motor Functions in Children with Early Brain Damage. *Neuropsychologia, 12*: 95-108.

Rumelhart, D. E. (1977). Toward an Interactive Model of Reading. In *Attention and Performance*, Erlbaum, Hillside, N. J.

Rutter, M., and E. Schopler (1978). *Autism: a Reappraisal of Concepts and Treatment*. Plenum, New York.

Schank, R., and R. P. Abelson (1977). *Scripts, Plans, Goals and Understanding: An Inquiry into Human Knowledge Structures*. Erlbaum, Hillsdale, N.J.

Scheerer, M., E. Rothmann, and K. Goldstein (1945). A Case of *Idiot Savant*: an Experimental Study of Personality Organization. *Psychological Monographs*, no. 58.

Schoenfeld, A. (1982). *Beyond the Purely Cognitive: Metacognition and Social Cognition as Driving Forces in Intellectual Performance*, Paper given at the Annual American Research Association meeting, New York.

Science July, 1984, 225: 296.

Segalowitz, S. J. (1983). *Two Sides of the Brain: Brain Lateralization Explored*. Prentice-Hall, Englewood Cliffs, N. J.

Semmes, J., S. Weinstein, L. Ghent, and H-L. Teuber (1955). Spatial Orientation in Man After Cerebral Injury: Analysis of Locus of Lesion. *Journal of Psychology, 39*: 226-244.

Shapiro, D. (1965). *Neurotic Styles*. Basic Books, New York.

Sheingold, K., J. Kane, and M. Endreweit (1983). Microcomputer Use in Schools: Developing a Research Agenda. *Harvard Educational Review, 53*(4):412-432.

Skemp R. (1979). Goals of Learning and Qualities of Understanding. *Mathematics Teaching, 88*: 44-49.

Sklar, B., J. Hanley, and W. W. Simmons (1972). An EEG Experiment Aimed Toward Identifying Dyslexic Children. *Nature, 240*: 414-416.

Sloman, A. (1978). *The Computer Revolution in Philosophy*. Harvester, Hassocks.

Snow, C. (1975). The Development of Conversation Between Mothers and Babies. *Pragmatics Microfiche*, vol. 1, fiche 6.

Spelke, E. (1985). Perception of Unity, Persistence, and Identity: Thoughts on Infants' Conceptions of Objects. In *Neonate Cognition*, ed. J. Mehler and R. Fox. Erlbaum, Hillsdale, N. J.

Springer, S. P., and G. Deutsch (1981). *Left Brain, Right Brain*, Freeman, San Francisco.

Sylla, S. F. (1985). *Computers and Literacy in Senegal.* Master's thesis, MIT, Cambridge, Mass.

Symmes, J. S., and J. L. Rappaport (1972). Unexpected Reading Failure. *American Journal of Orthopsychiatry, 42*: 82-91.

Taylor, R. P. (1980). *Computer in the School: Tutor, Tool, Tutee.* Teachers College Press, New York.

Teachers College Record (1984). The Computer in Education in Critical Perspective. *85*(4): 539-639.

Technology and Handicapped People, May, 1982, pp. 20-23. Office of Technology Assessment, Washington, D. C.

Turkle, S. (1984). *The Second Self: Computers and the Human Spirit.* Simon and Schuster, New York.

Ullman, S. (1980). Against Direct Perception. *Brain and Behavioral Sciences, 3*: 373-415.

Valente, A. (1983). Learning from Your Mistakes. In *Computers and the Handicapped: Expository Materials.* Final Report, Grant no. G008101272, MIT Logo group, Cambridge, Mass.

Valente, J. (1983). Creating a Computer-Based Learning Environment for Physically Handicapped Children. Unpublished doctoral dissertation, Department of Mechanical Engineering, MIT, Cambridge, Mass.

Vygotsky, L. S. (1934). *Thought and Language*, trans. 1962. MIT Press, Cambridge, Mass.

Vygotsky, L. S. (1978). *Mind in Society: The Development of Higher Psychological Processes.* Harvard University Press, Cambridge, Mass.

Waber, D. P. (1980). Maturation: Thoughts on Renewing an Old Acquaintanceship. In *Biological Studies of Mental Processes*, ed. D. Caplan. MIT Press, Cambridge, Mass.

Waber, D. P. and J. Holmes (1985). Assessing Children's Copy Productions of the Rey-Osterrieth Complex Figure. *Journal of Clinical and Experimental Neuropsychology, 7*(3): 264-280.

Watt, D. (1983). *Learning with Logo*. McGraw-Hill, New York.

Wedell, K., C. V. Newman, P. Reid, and I. R. Bradbury (1972). An Exploratory Study of the Relationship Between Size Constancy and Experience of Mobility in Cerebral Palsied Children. *Developmental Medicine and Child Neurology, 14*: 615-620.

Weir, S. (1975). The Perception of Motion: Actions, Motives, and Feelings. In *Progress in Perception*, DAI Report no. 13. Department of Artificial Intelligence, University of Edinburgh, Edinburgh.

Weir, S. (1978). The Perception of Motion: Michotte Revisited. *Perception, 7*: 247-260.

Weir, S. (1981a). Logo and the Exceptional Child. *Microcomputing*, September, pp. 76-83.

Weir, S. (1981b). *Logo as an Information Prosthetic for the Handicapped*. Working Paper no. 9. Division for Study and Research in Education, MIT, Cambridge, Mass.

Weir, S., and R. Emanuel (1976). *Using Logo to Catalyse Communication in an Autistic Child*. DAI Research Report no. 15. Department of Artificial Intelligence, University of Edinburgh, Edinburgh.

Weir, S., S. J. Russell, and J. A. Valente (1982). Logo: An Approach to Educating Disabled Children. *Byte*, September, pp. 342-360.

Weir, S., and D. Watt (1981). Logo: A Computer Environment for Learning-Disabled Students. *The Computer Teacher, 8*(5): 11-17.

Weizenbaum, J. (1984). Another View from MIT. *Byte, 9*(6): 225.

Wertheimer, M. (1959). *Productive Thinking*. Harper & Row, New York.

White, B. (1981). *Designing Computer Games to Facilitate Learning*. Unpublished doctoral dissertation, Artificial Intelligence Laboratory, MIT, Cambridge, Mass.

Wing, J. K. (1976). Kanner's Syndrome: A Historical Introduction. In *Early Childhood Autism*, ed. L. Wing. Pergamon Press, Elmsford, N. Y.

Wing, J. K. (1976). Kanner's Syndrome: A Historical Introduction. In *Early Childhood Autism*, ed. L. Wing. Pergamon Press, Elmsford, N. Y.

Witkin, H. A., R. B. Dyk, H. F. Faterson, D. R. Goodenough, and S. A. Karp (1962). *Psychological Differentiation*. Wiley, New York.

Wood, K. (1984). Probable Passages: A Writing Strategy. *The Reading Teacher*, February, pp. 496-499.

Zaidel, D. and R. W. Sperry (1973). Performance on the Raven's Colored Progressive Matrices Test by Subjects with Cerebral Commisurotomy. *Cortex, 9:* 34-39.

Zangwill, O. L. (1981). Foreword to *Dyslexia Research and Its Applications to Education*, ed. G. T. Pavlidis and T. R. Miles. Wiley, New York.

Zeitschel, K. A., R. A. Kalish, and R. Colarrusso (1979). Visual Perception Tests Used with Physically Handicapped Children. *Academic Therapies, 14:* 565-576.

Index

250